Quick Start Drawing

ANIMALS

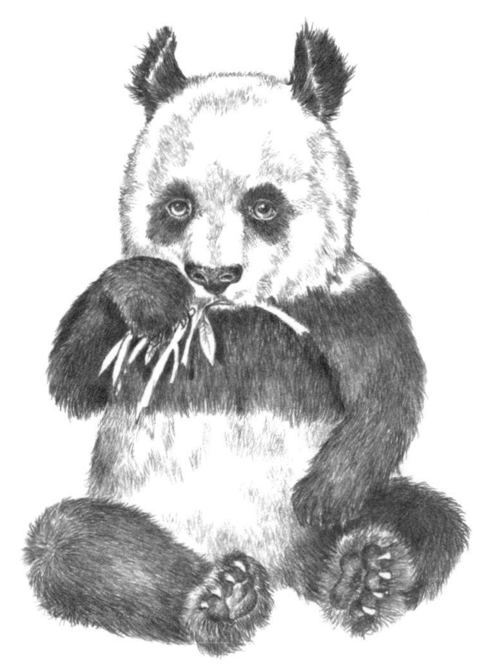

Walter Foster

About This Book

Welcome to *Quick Start Drawing Animals.* Packed with dozens of drawing prompts, helpful techniques, step-by-step lessons, and easy tracing exercises, this drawing pad is ideal for beginning and aspiring artists who enjoy learning by doing. As such, you will build basic art knowledge and drawing skills in a short time, while learning to create your own unique artwork along the way.

After learning more about the tools of the trade, you will discover basic skills, including how to hold the pencil and how to draw basic strokes. From there, you'll learn to draw basic shapes and develop them with shading, and then you'll learn to hone your skills through dozens of drawing tutorials focused on a variety of popular animals, including dogs, cats, birds, safari animals, and other creatures of the wild. The art in this drawing pad is designed to be enhanced by you, so we've also included unfinished drawings printed in light gray to use as a foundation on which to build your skills. It's the perfect starting point for beginners. High-quality paper means you can draw inside without worrying about the pages underneath, so be brave and experiment! We recommend keeping a sketchbook or sketch pad in addition to this drawing pad so that you can continue to practice the featured lessons.

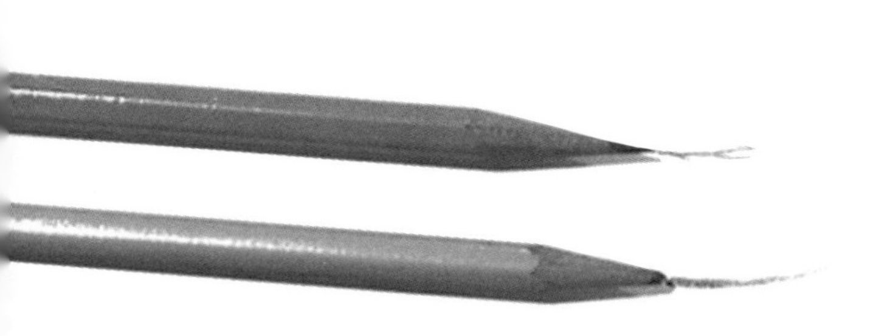

Getting Started

Drawing doesn't require a lot of materials. A good HB pencil and this drawing pad are perfect for getting started. The next few pages go over the fundamentals of drawing, including some basic tools, how to hold and sharpen a pencil, and how to create a variety of basic strokes. A good drawing features an interplay between light and dark, so you will learn a bit about shading techniques and creating a value scale. Throughout this pad, look for step-by-step projects to help guide you through the drawing process. Let's get started!

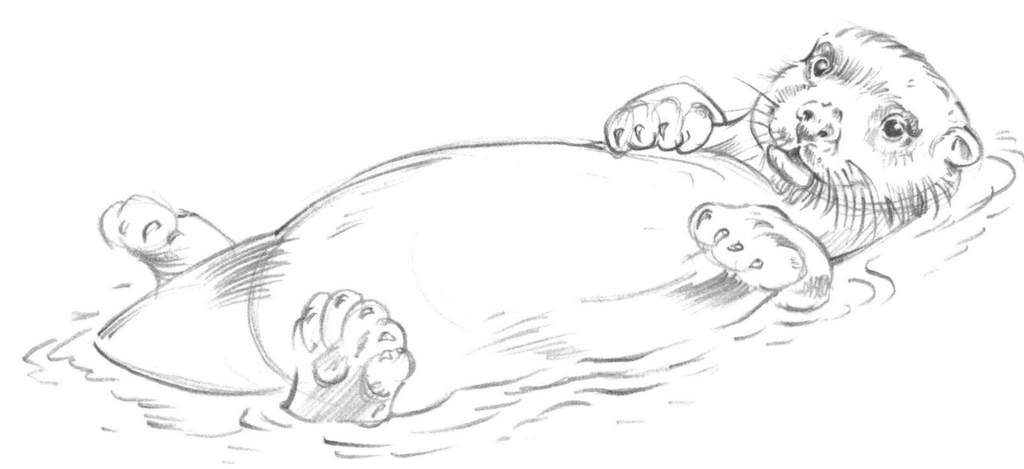

Tools and Materials

Pencils are classified according to the hardness of the lead. H leads are hard and perfect for light sketchy strokes. B leads are soft and better for darker lines. HB leads are in between H and B; these pencils are incredibly versatile. Start with an H pencil and an HB pencil. Make sure you have a standard pencil sharpener on hand, as well as an artist's knife for more precise sharpening. You will also need erasers and extra drawing paper for practicing. As your skills improve, you can expand your artist's tool kit.

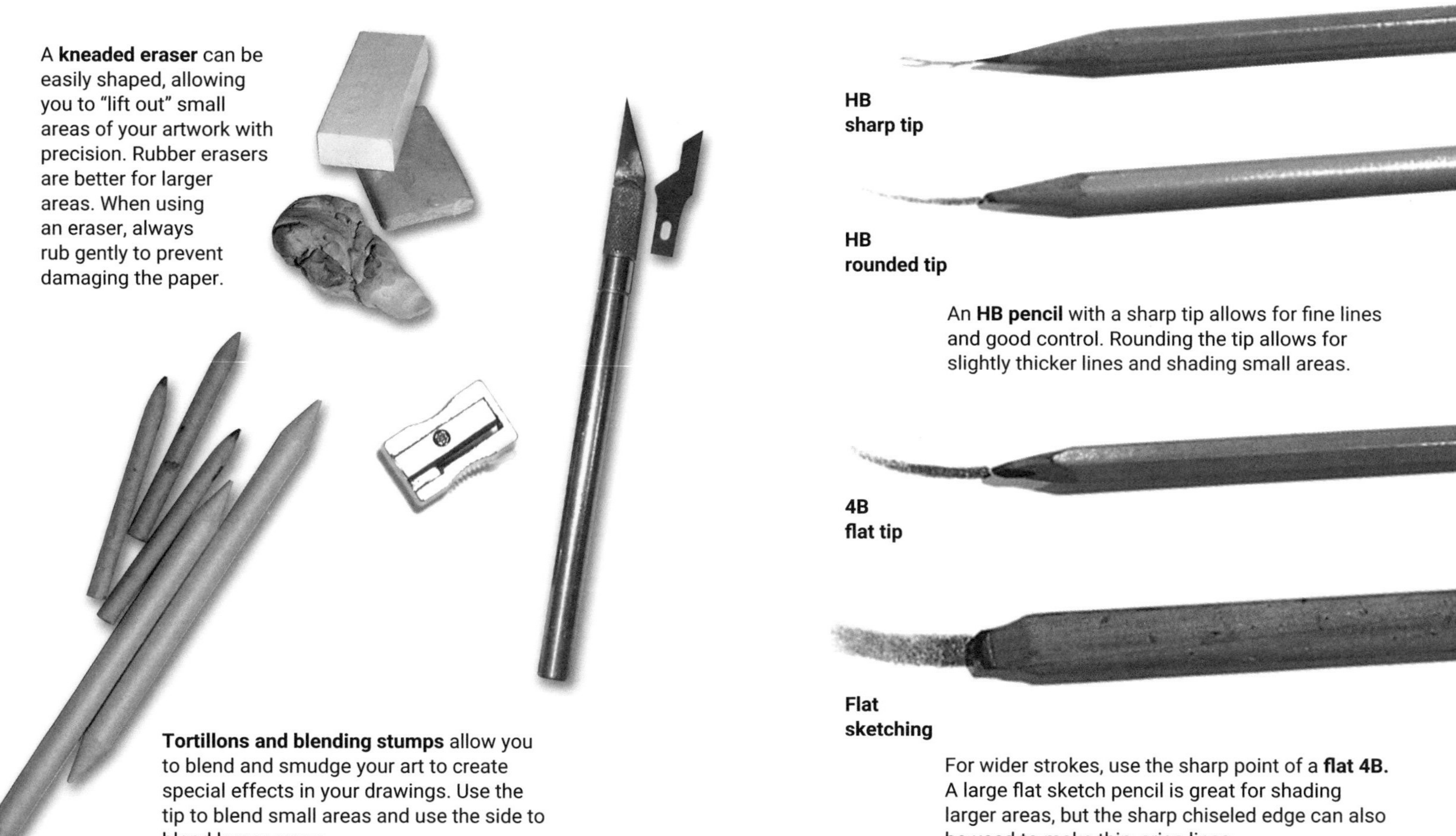

A **kneaded eraser** can be easily shaped, allowing you to "lift out" small areas of your artwork with precision. Rubber erasers are better for larger areas. When using an eraser, always rub gently to prevent damaging the paper.

Tortillons and blending stumps allow you to blend and smudge your art to create special effects in your drawings. Use the tip to blend small areas and use the side to blend larger areas.

An **HB pencil** with a sharp tip allows for fine lines and good control. Rounding the tip allows for slightly thicker lines and shading small areas.

For wider strokes, use the sharp point of a **flat 4B.** A large flat sketch pencil is great for shading larger areas, but the sharp chiseled edge can also be used to make thin, crisp lines.

Sharpening Pencils

There are many ways to sharpen your drawing pencils outside of using a standard handheld sharpener. Try each of the methods below to see which one you prefer.

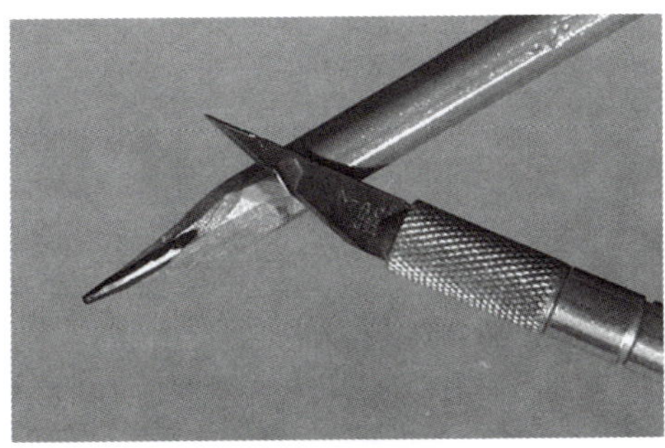

Artist knives are ideal for shaping pencils in specific ways to give them a chisel-shaped, blunt, or flat tip. Hold the knife at an angle to the pencil and carve away from the body. Always cut only a small amount of the lead and wood.

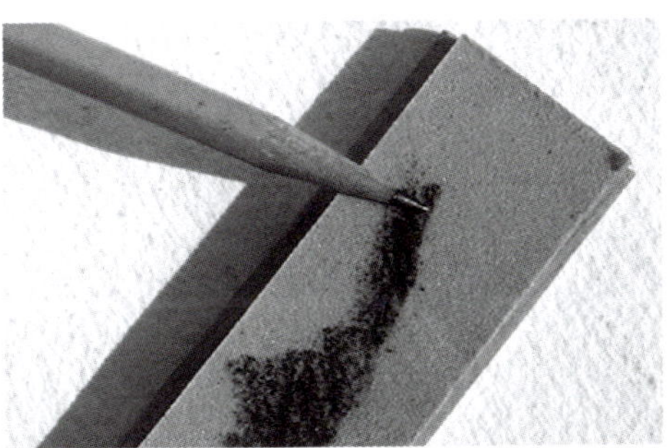

Use a **sandpaper block** to quickly shape a lead. Sandpaper also removes some of the wood coating. The finer the grit, the better you can control the result. You'll need to roll the pencil in your hand while sharpening to ensure the lead sharpens evenly.

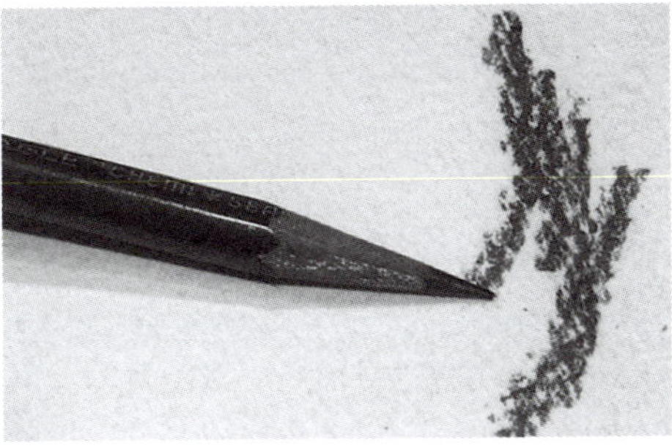

Rough paper is ideal for smoothing a lead that you've sharpened with sandpaper. This is a great way to create a fine point for tiny details. Gently rotate the pencil to sharpen the lead evenly.

Holding the Pencil

There are different ways to hold a pencil, each of which has its own purpose. When drawing, use the strength and dexterity of your entire arm to prevent your wrist and fingers from cramping or getting too tight. Try to maintain a relaxed position and hold the pencil lightly.

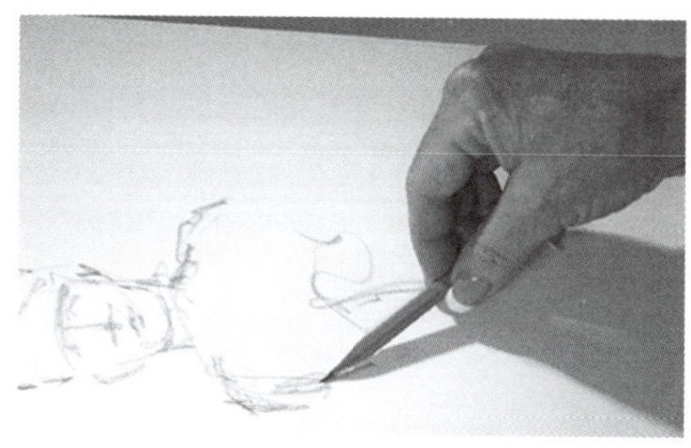

Basic Underhand This technique allows your arm and wrist to move freely, which results in fresh, lively sketches. Drawing in this position makes it easy to use both the point and the side of the pencil lead.

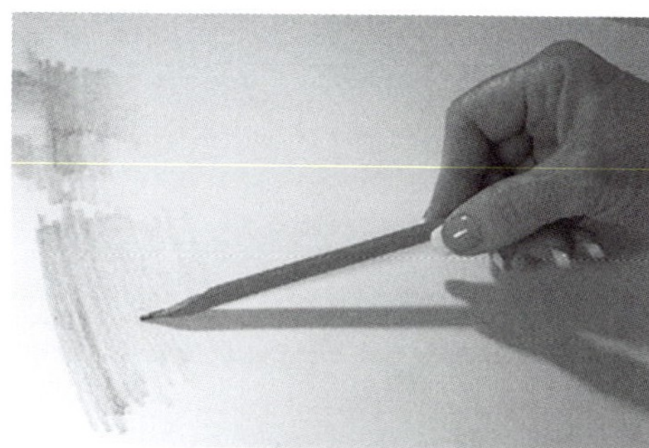

Underhand Variation Holding the pencil at its end enables you to make long and short light strokes. It also gives you control over lights, darks, and textures. It can help to place a protective sheet of paper under your hand so you don't smudge your drawing.

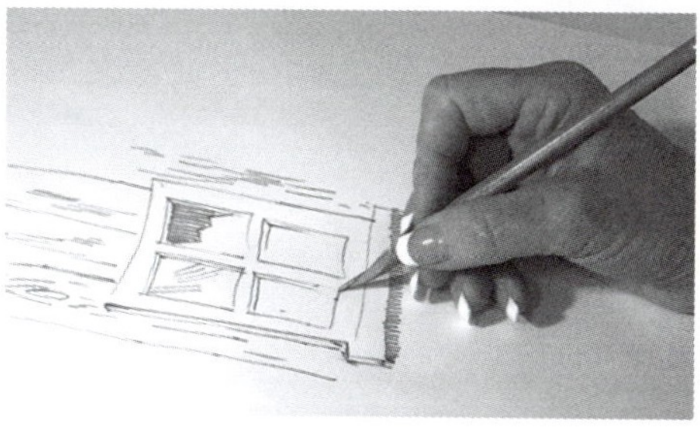

Writing The writing position is the most common, and it provides the most control for precise lines and fine details. Be careful not to press on your drawing too hard or grip the pencil too tightly.

Draw a few lines and squiggles using the three different pencil-holding techniques. How does each grip change your art?

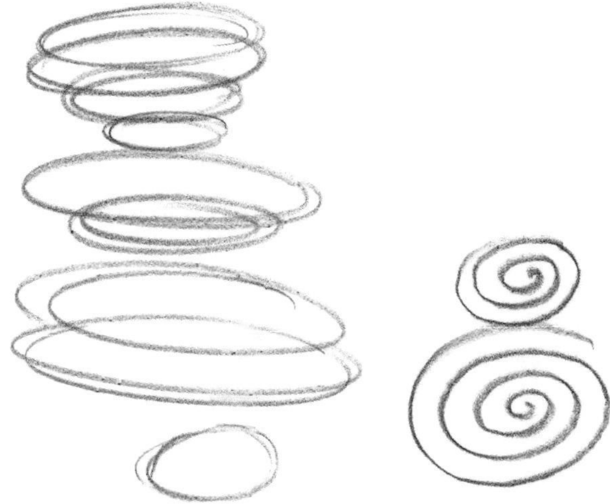

Basic Techniques

When learning to draw, it's helpful to try out a variety of drawing pencils to observe how the lines you draw change with each pencil. Finely detailed drawings are best rendered with a sharpened pencil, held in the writing position. Larger areas of a drawing are easier to shade with the flat side of a pencil held from your wrist. Be curious and try each hand position with different pencils. You'll be excited by the different results!

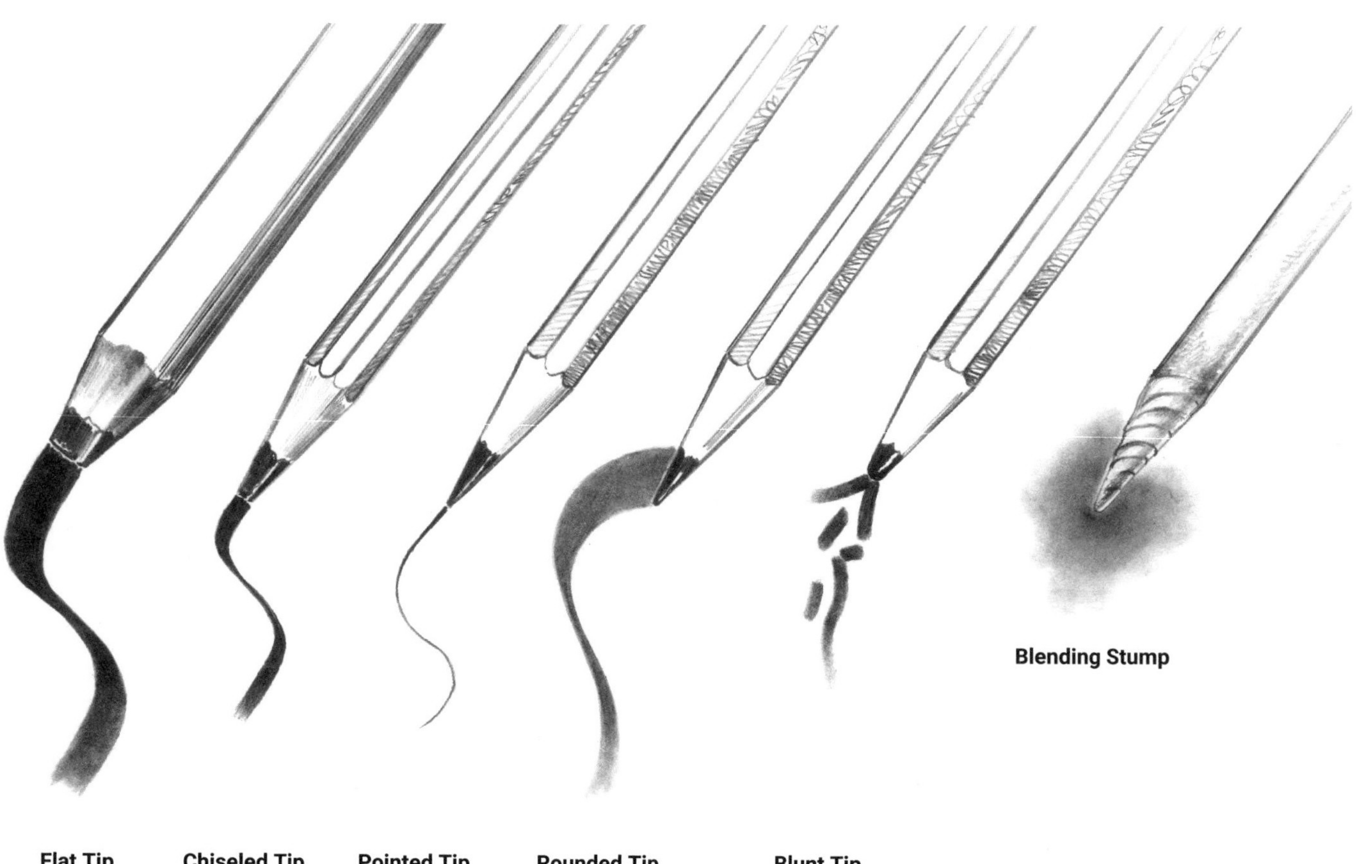

Practicing basic techniques will help you understand how to manipulate the pencil to achieve a variety of effects. Practice the techniques shown below in the areas provided.

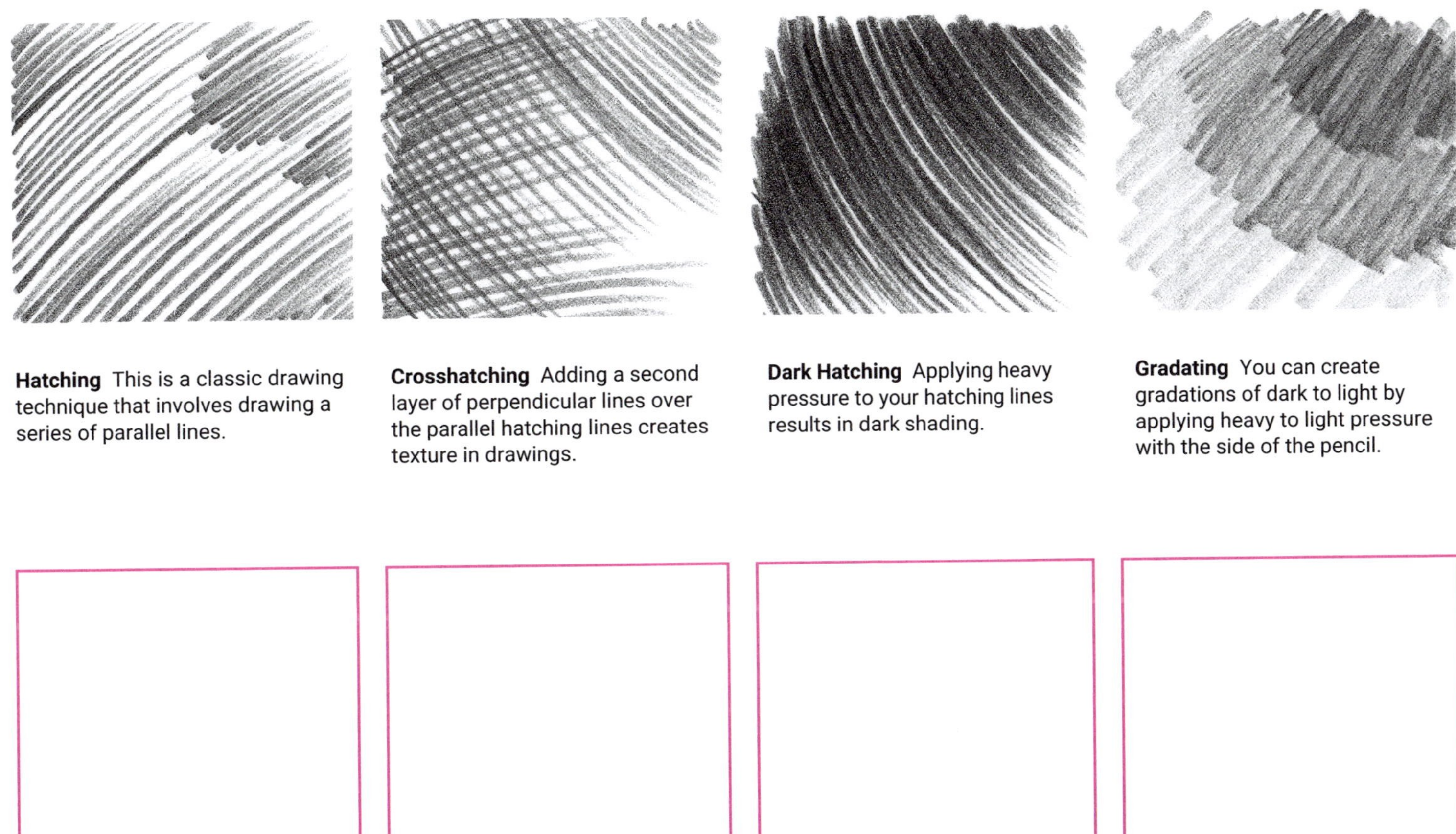

Hatching This is a classic drawing technique that involves drawing a series of parallel lines.

Crosshatching Adding a second layer of perpendicular lines over the parallel hatching lines creates texture in drawings.

Dark Hatching Applying heavy pressure to your hatching lines results in dark shading.

Gradating You can create gradations of dark to light by applying heavy to light pressure with the side of the pencil.

Seeing Values

Value is the basic term used to describe the relative lightness or darkness of a color. In pencil drawing, the values range from white to grays to black, and it's the variation among lights and darks (made with shading) and the range of values in shadows and highlights that give a two-dimensional drawing a three-dimensional look. This value scale shows the gradation from black, the darkest value, through various shades of gray and ending with the lightest value.

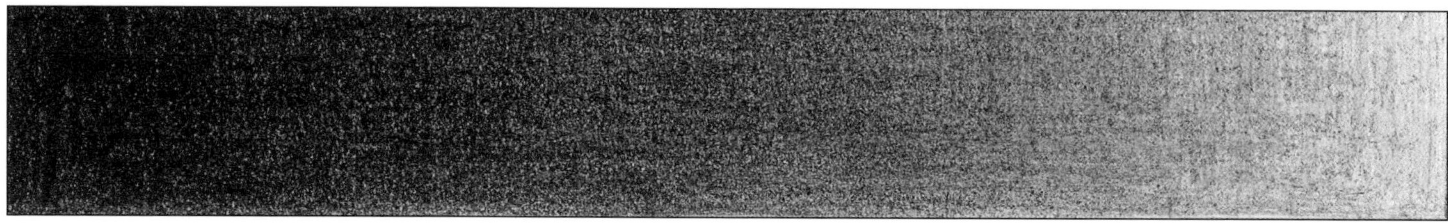

Create your own value scales in the areas below. Use an HB pencil to create one value scale. Then use pencils of varying hardness (2B, HB, and H) to create another value scale. Compare how the different pencils create different effects.

Basic Shapes

Anyone can draw just about anything by simply breaking down the subject into a few basic shapes: circles, rectangles, squares, and triangles. By drawing an outline around the basic shapes of your subject, you have drawn its shape. But your subject also has depth and dimension, or form. The corresponding forms of the basic shapes are spheres, cylinders, cubes, and cones. Sketching the shapes and developing their forms is the first step of every drawing. After that, it's essentially just connecting and refining the lines and adding details.

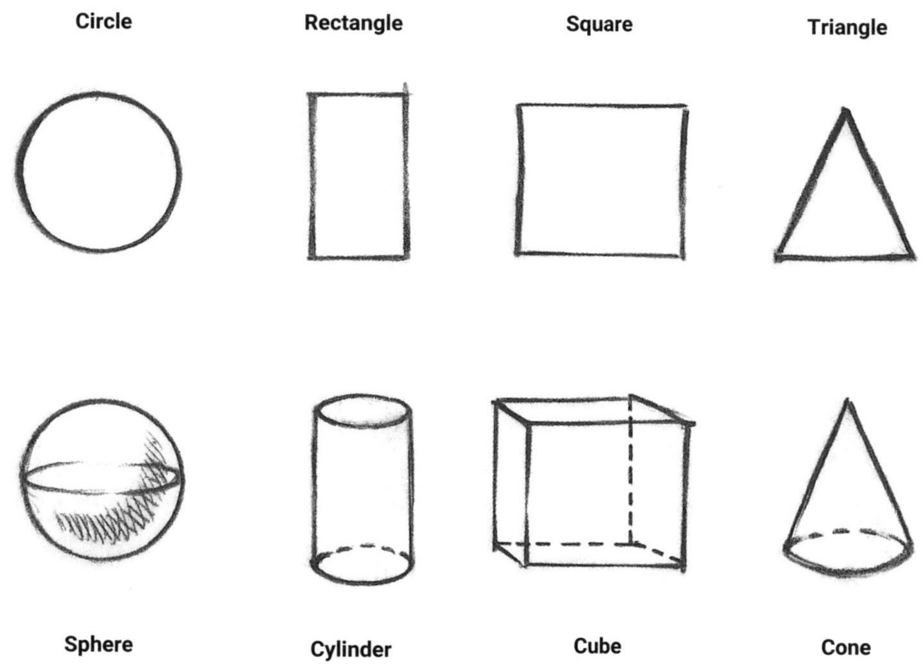

These diagrams show to how to draw the forms of these four basic shapes. The ellipses show the backs of the circle, cylinder, and cone, and the cube is drawn by connecting two squares with parallel lines.

Seeing Basic Shapes

For beginners, drawing animals is often challenging. First attempts may result in frustration because you may be trying to capture how the animal *should* look instead of drawing it as it actually looks. Remember to start by breaking the subject down into shapes: circles, ovals, squares, and triangles. As you layer shapes and lines on top of each other, you will see the body structure and proportions emerge. Sometimes it helps to draw live subjects. The goal is to take quick "snapshots" in pencil, filling your pages with views from different angles. Don't get bogged down in details at this stage. Simply develop a sense of the animal.

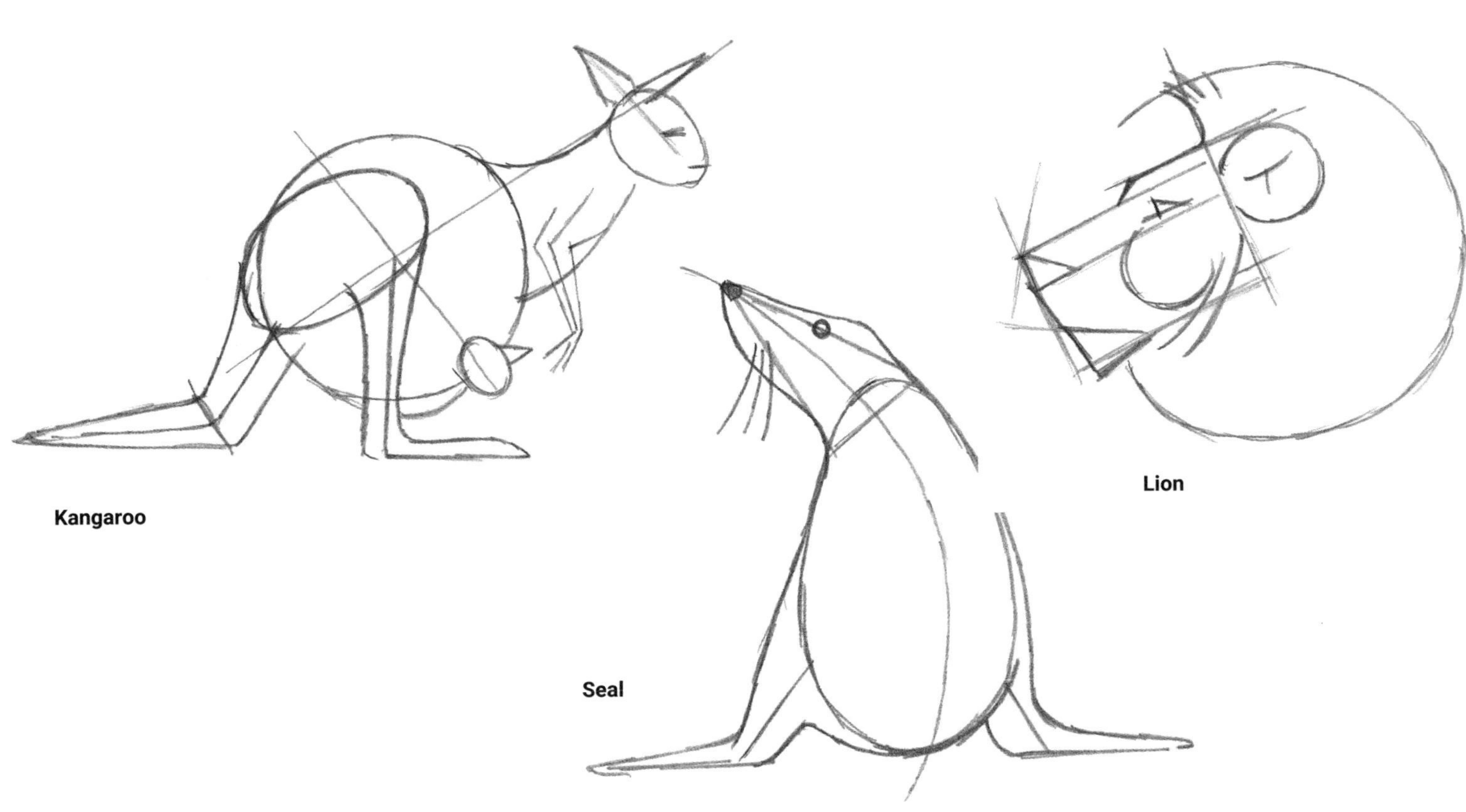

Drawing from Basic Shapes

Once you've learned to break down a subject into its basic shape, you can draw anything. All subjects begin with circles, ovals, rectangles, squares, and triangles. From there, build out the form of the subject using simple lines.

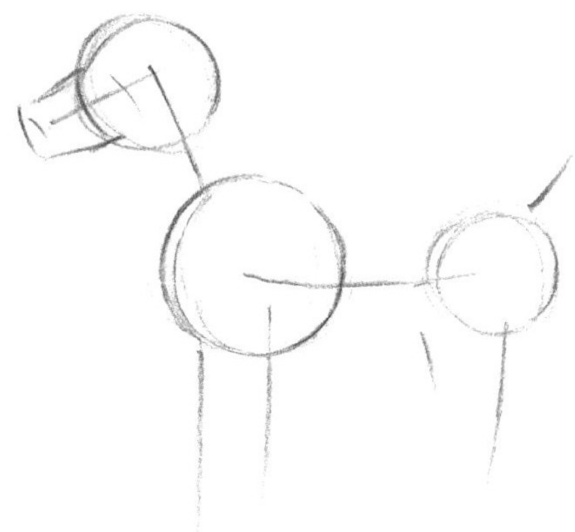

Basic Shape Start with the basic shapes and sketch lines until you have an outline of the subject.

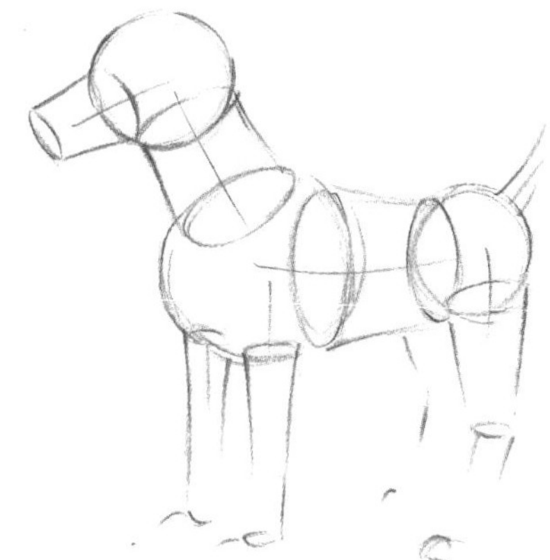

Body Once the outlines are in place, develop the circles and triangles into spheres and cones to create depth and dimension.

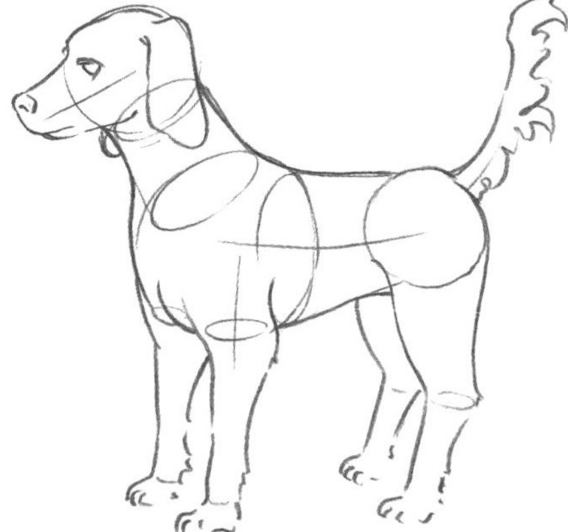

Tracing Connect the shapes with construction lines, and watch as the subject emerges in all its physicality.

Trace the basic shapes and guidelines of the monkey, and then draw it freehand.

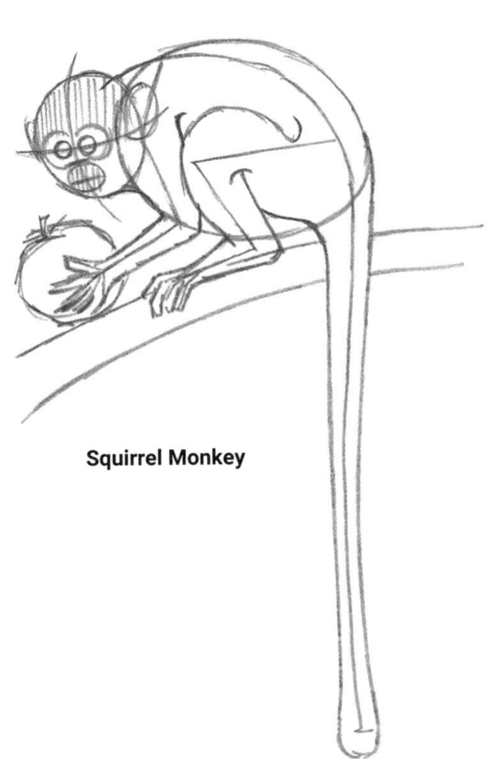

Squirrel Monkey

Building Form

Once you've established the general shape and form of the subject using basic shapes, refine your drawing by applying value through hatching, crosshatching, and gradating. Gather some objects from around your home or continue to practice using basic shapes.

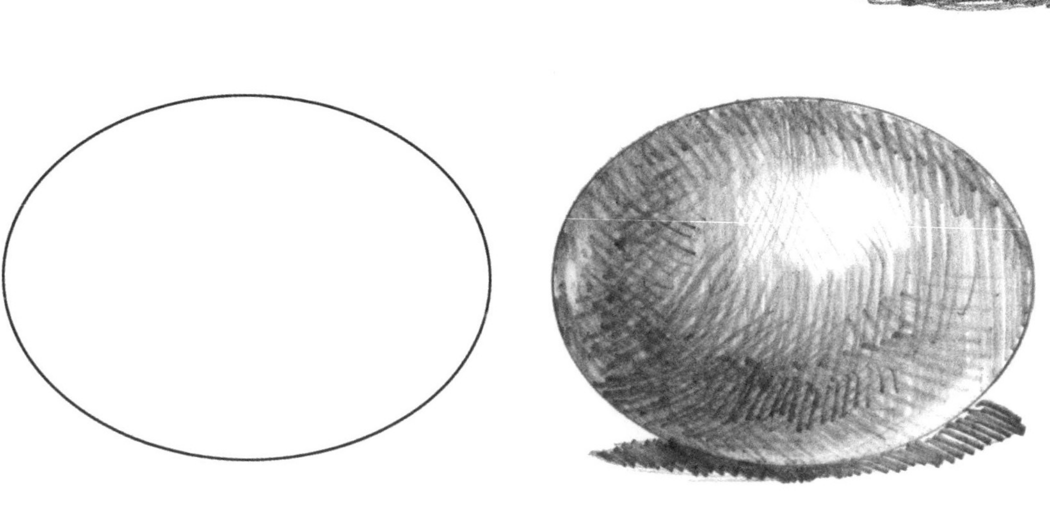

Outline

with Depth

The secret to transforming an outline into a form is proper shading. Use less pressure for lighter areas and more pressure for darker areas. When hatching, consider where the light is coming from. Where it falls directly onto the object, a light reflection is created, creating the brightest area. Also consider the cast shadow, which is the shadow cast by your object. Directly above the darkest part of the cast shadow, the object is very light—like the egg shown here.

Develop some forms and their shadows. Use different types of pencils, and experiment with pressure to get a feel for them.

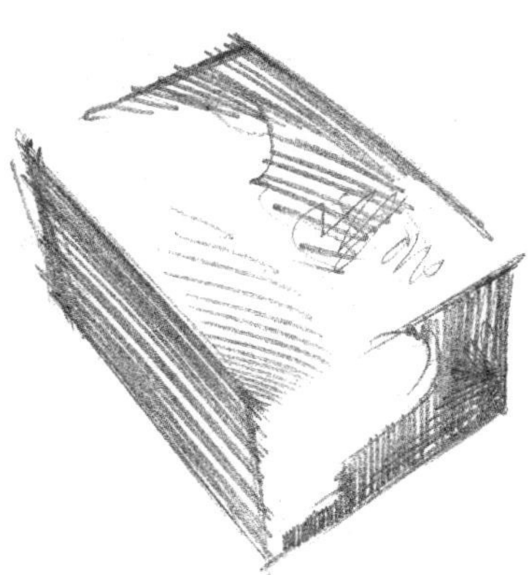

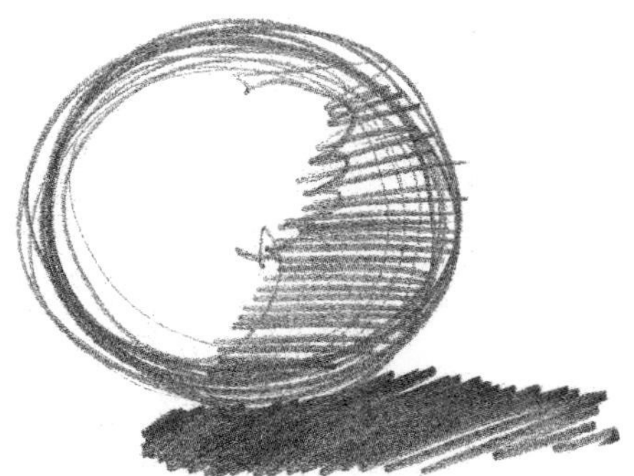

Shading Techniques

The following shading techniques can be used for a range of animals. One of the most important rules is to draw in the direction of hair growth to ensure your sketches and drawings look more realistic.

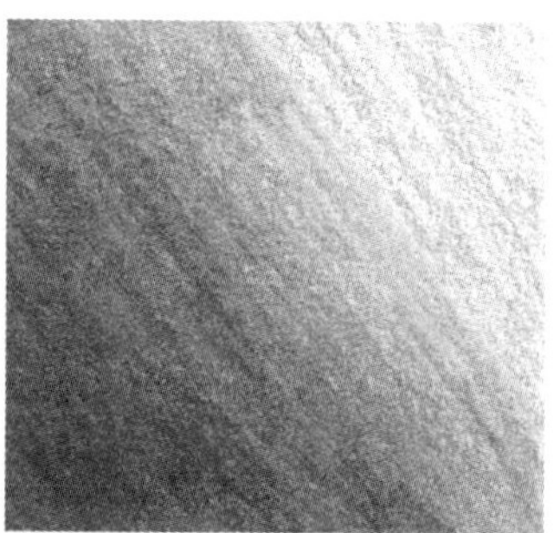

Gradation Start with the side of a soft pencil, such as a 6B. With medium pressure, lay in the darkest value, gradually lessening pressure as you move.

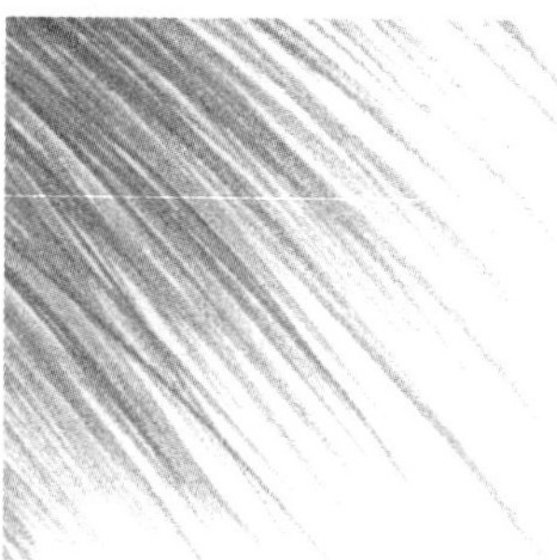

Drawing Hair Using a sharp graphite pencil and sweeping strokes, quickly move your hand in an arc, lifting the pencil from the paper at the end of the stroke. It's best to lift the pencil at the end of the hair (from the darkest to lightest), but experiment to find out what works for you. With a little practice, you will master the art of drawing hair.

Blended Gradation These examples show gradated values that were blended and softened with a tortillon. This technique works well for moving tones into a lighter area.

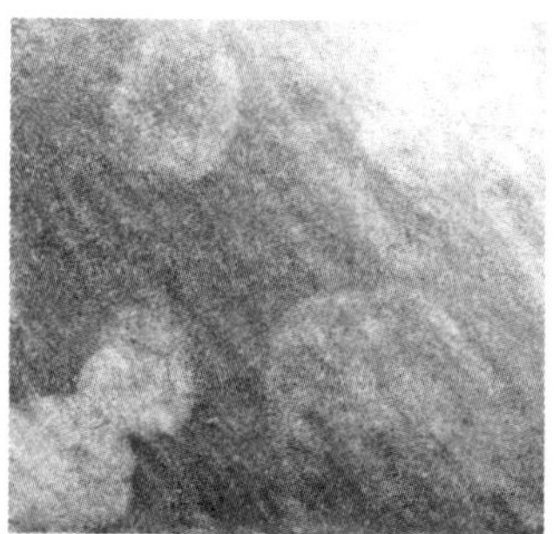

Erasing These examples show how tone can be lifted from the page using a kneaded eraser (such as for creating highlights). Because a kneaded eraser can be molded to fit small areas or flattened out for larger areas, it's a versatile and useful tool for this purpose.

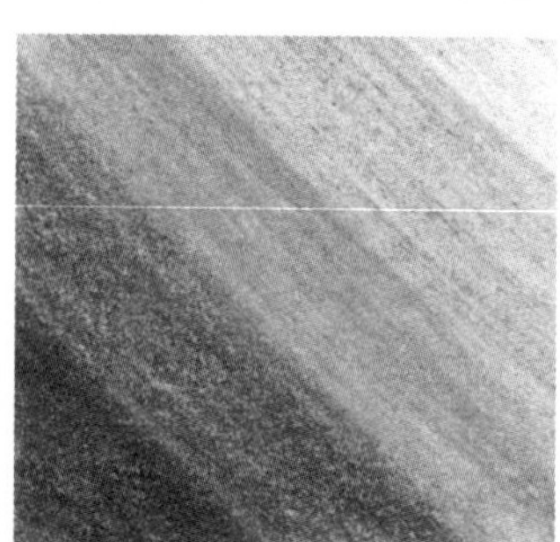

Pencils and Pressure Harder pencils create lighter values, so you may opt to switch pencils when shading to achieve different results. The banding at left indicates where a harder pencil was used to shade. By varying the amount of pressure, you can achieve a wide range of values in your drawings.

Crosshatching This illustrates the way that layering in different directions creates texture and adds interest. Crosshatching works especially well for preliminary drawings.

Use the spaces below to practice the shading techniques shown.

Drawing from Life

Drawing animals from life is exciting because every detail, movement, and pose is unique and original. Don't expect to render a complete likeness on the spot. Instead, make several sketches and record the details you'll need to complete the drawing later on in your studio.

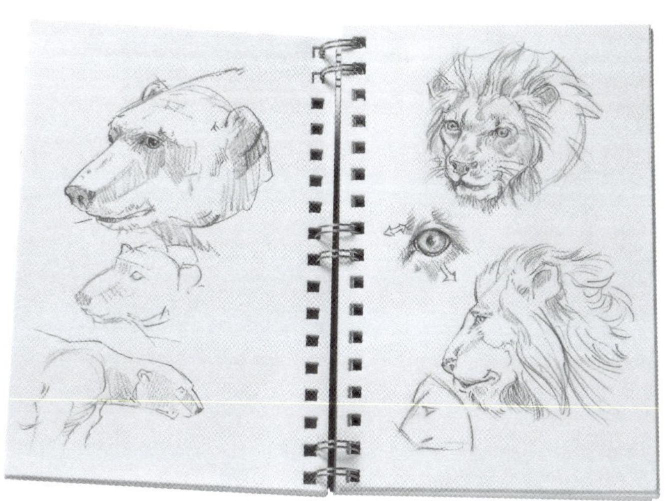

Using a Sketchbook Whether you're sketching animals in the wild or at a zoo, make sure you note down everything about the lighting, the time of day, and anything else you think will help you create a realistic drawing. If you're particularly interested in a detail, such as the eyes or a facial expression, make several sketches from different angles.

Basic Shapes Your sketches don't have to be as accurate as those shown at left. In fact, it's better to break down the subject into its basic shapes and then transfer the sketch to a clean sheet of paper.

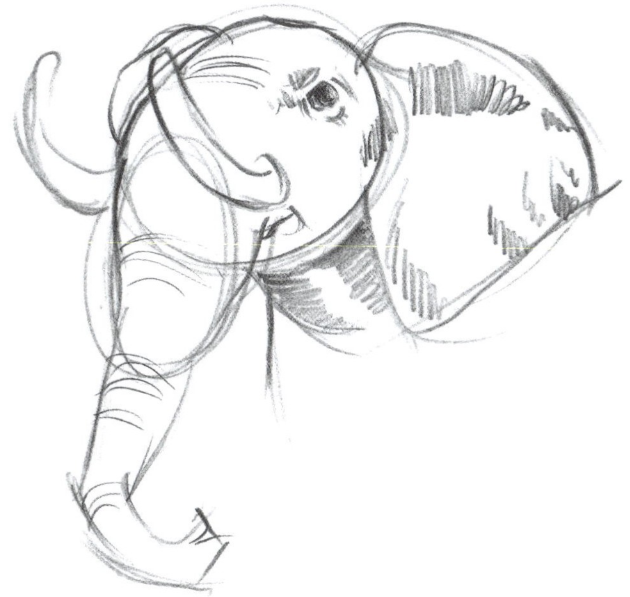

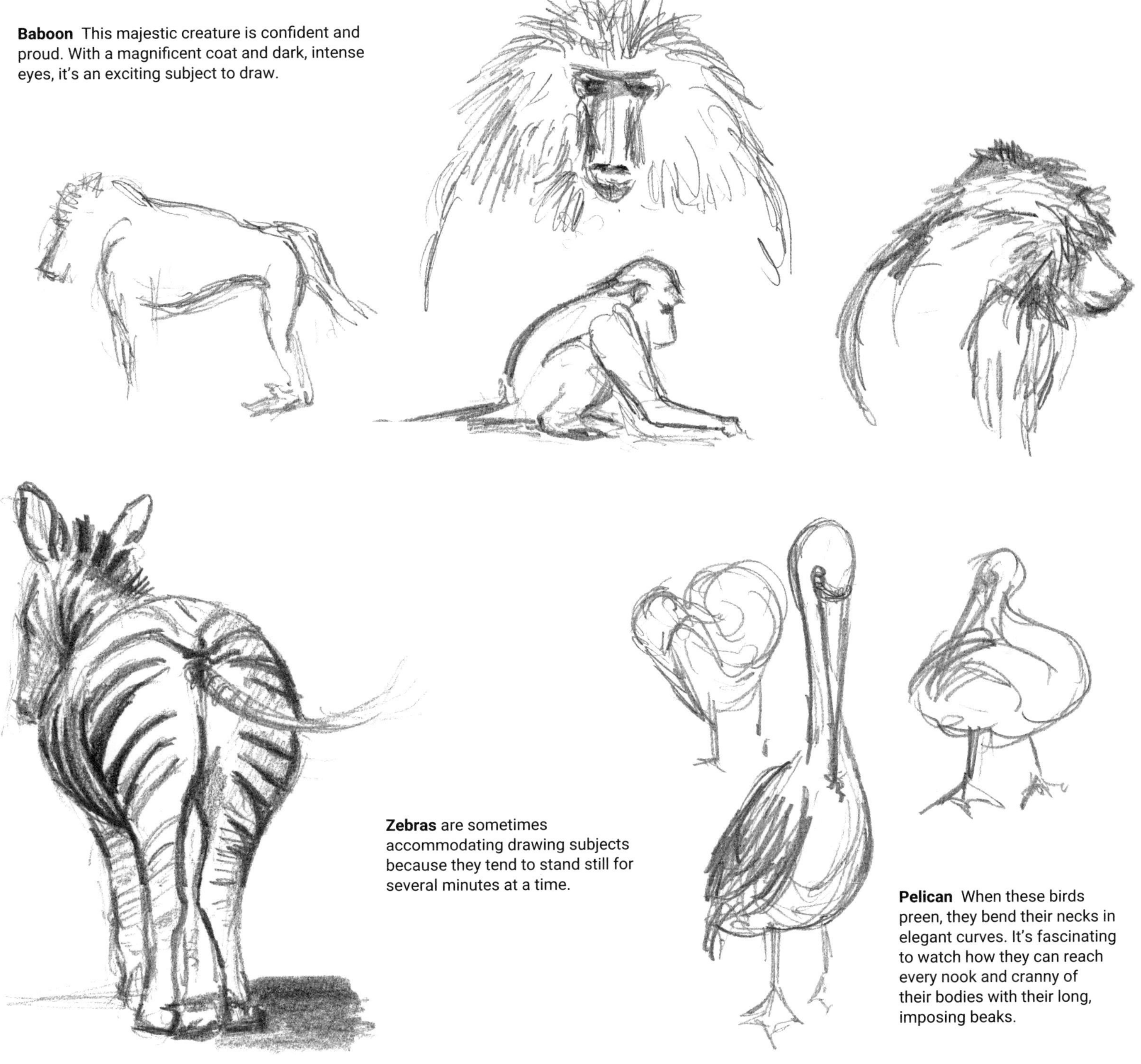

Baboon This majestic creature is confident and proud. With a magnificent coat and dark, intense eyes, it's an exciting subject to draw.

Zebras are sometimes accommodating drawing subjects because they tend to stand still for several minutes at a time.

Pelican When these birds preen, they bend their necks in elegant curves. It's fascinating to watch how they can reach every nook and cranny of their bodies with their long, imposing beaks.

Animals in Motion

Drawing animals in motion is ideal for learning to master body shapes, sizes, and attributes. You have to be quick, observe closely, and capture as much information as possible in a short time. Otters are lively animals that are almost always in motion when they're awake. Draw these little creatures with quick, flowing lines—a few strokes are enough to suggest shadows and surroundings.

Otter Sketch the otter's head and body shape with loose circles or ovals. Then, place the arms, legs, and tail. Once the animal's outline is complete, you can easily add details, such as ears, eyes, and paws.

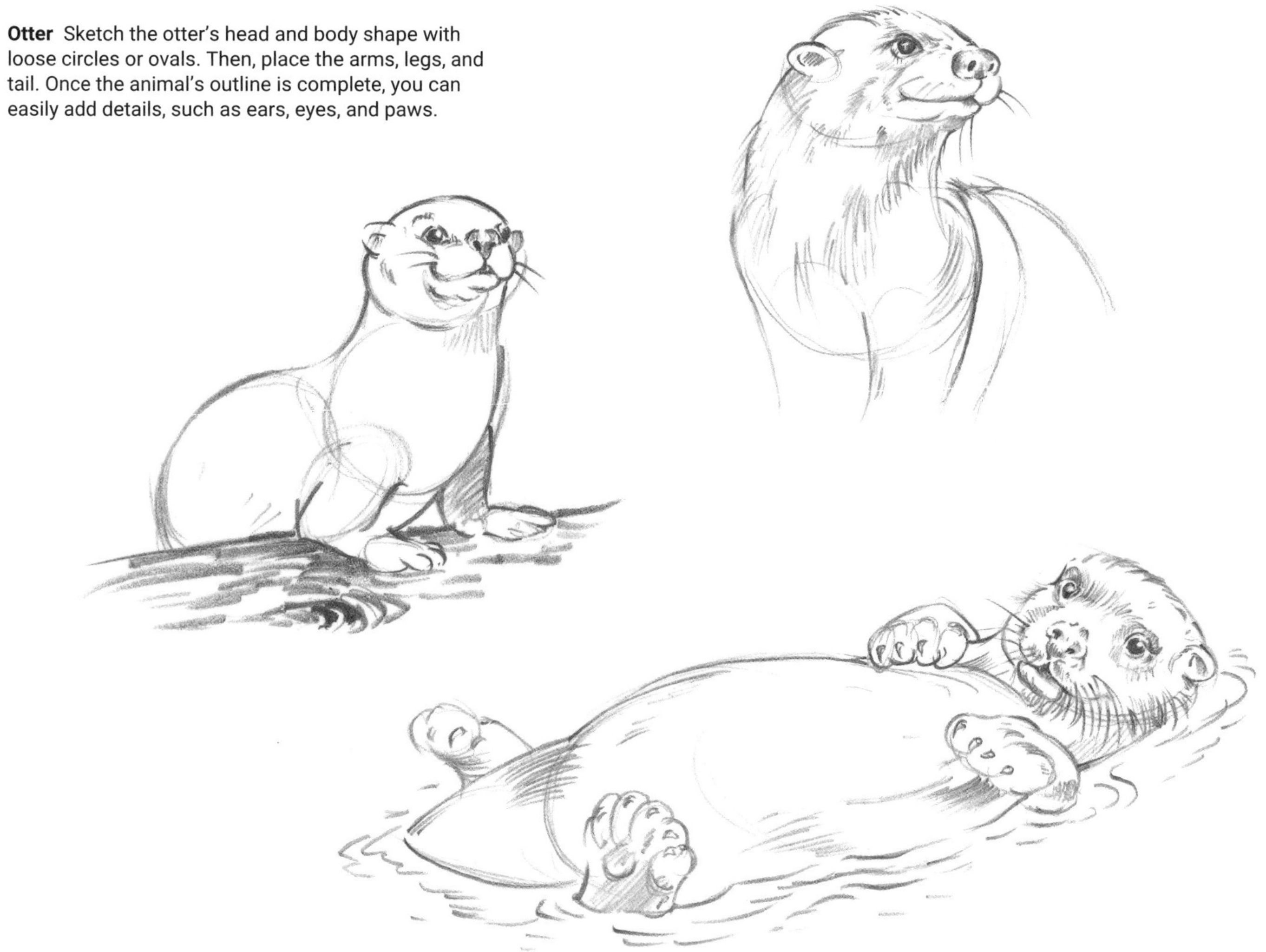

Draw the otter in the poses shown above, or try drawing the otter in different poses. Feel free to use references, if needed.

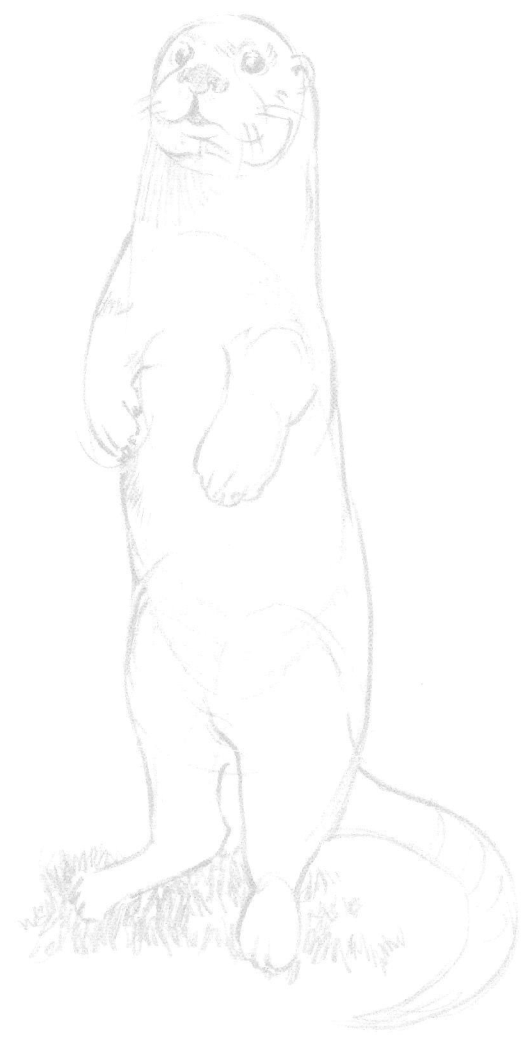

Lion

With its muscular frame, massive paws, and huge head, it's no surprise that the lion is at the top of the food chain. This forward–facing subject is at a slight angle. Notice how its right front paw appears larger than the others due to foreshortening.

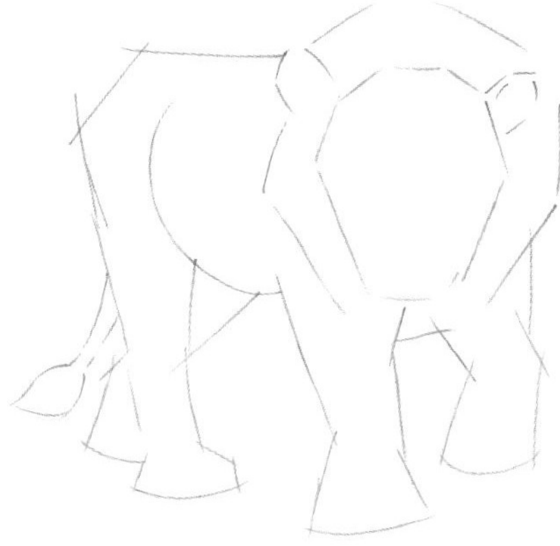

1 Block in the basic shape with a series of short, rough lines. Use an HB pencil so that the markings are light enough to erase thoroughly. Adjust the proportions as needed before moving on.

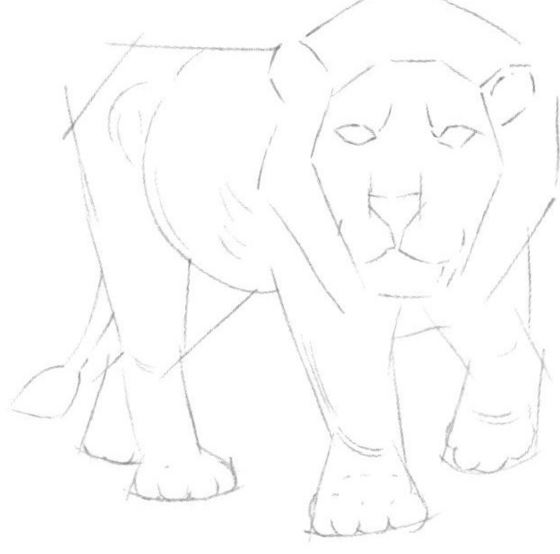

2 Block in the eyes, nose, and mouth. Note that the top of the nose is about halfway down the face, and the eyes are about one-third of the way down. Begin to indicate the lion's form with a few lines near the leg joints and its side; these marks will later serve as guides for shading.

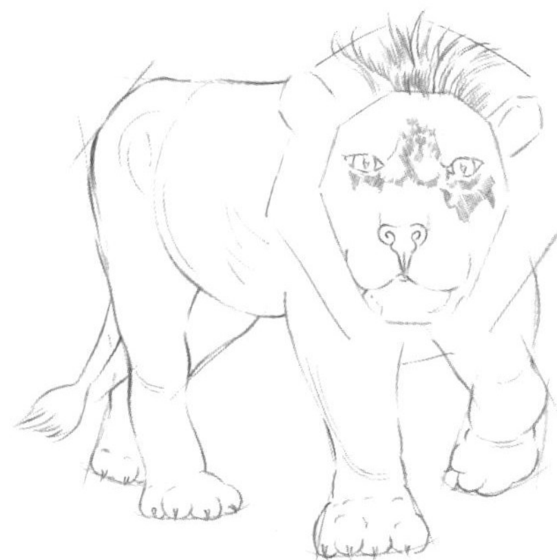

3 Start refining the outlines by rounding out the sharp corners. For the mane, begin adding the hair with curved lines, stroking from the edge of the lion's face outward. Next, begin to shade the face, applying small patches of parallel strokes.

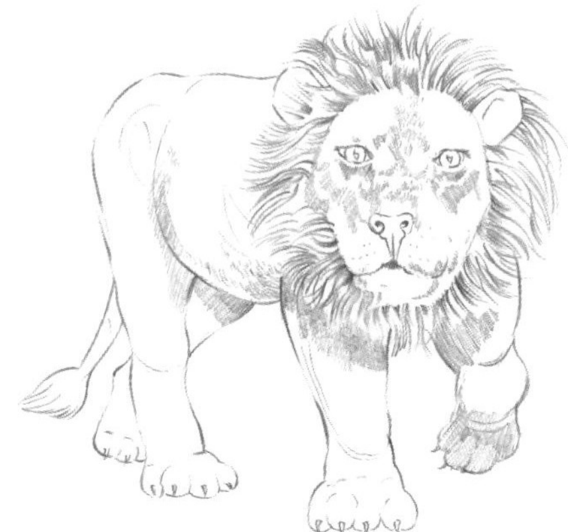

4 Continue to develop the lion's mane, placing the strokes close together and changing the values by altering the pressure on the pencil. Erase any initial sketch marks and begin to shade other areas of the body.

Trace over the outline below.
Focus on shading the lion's mane, face, and body.

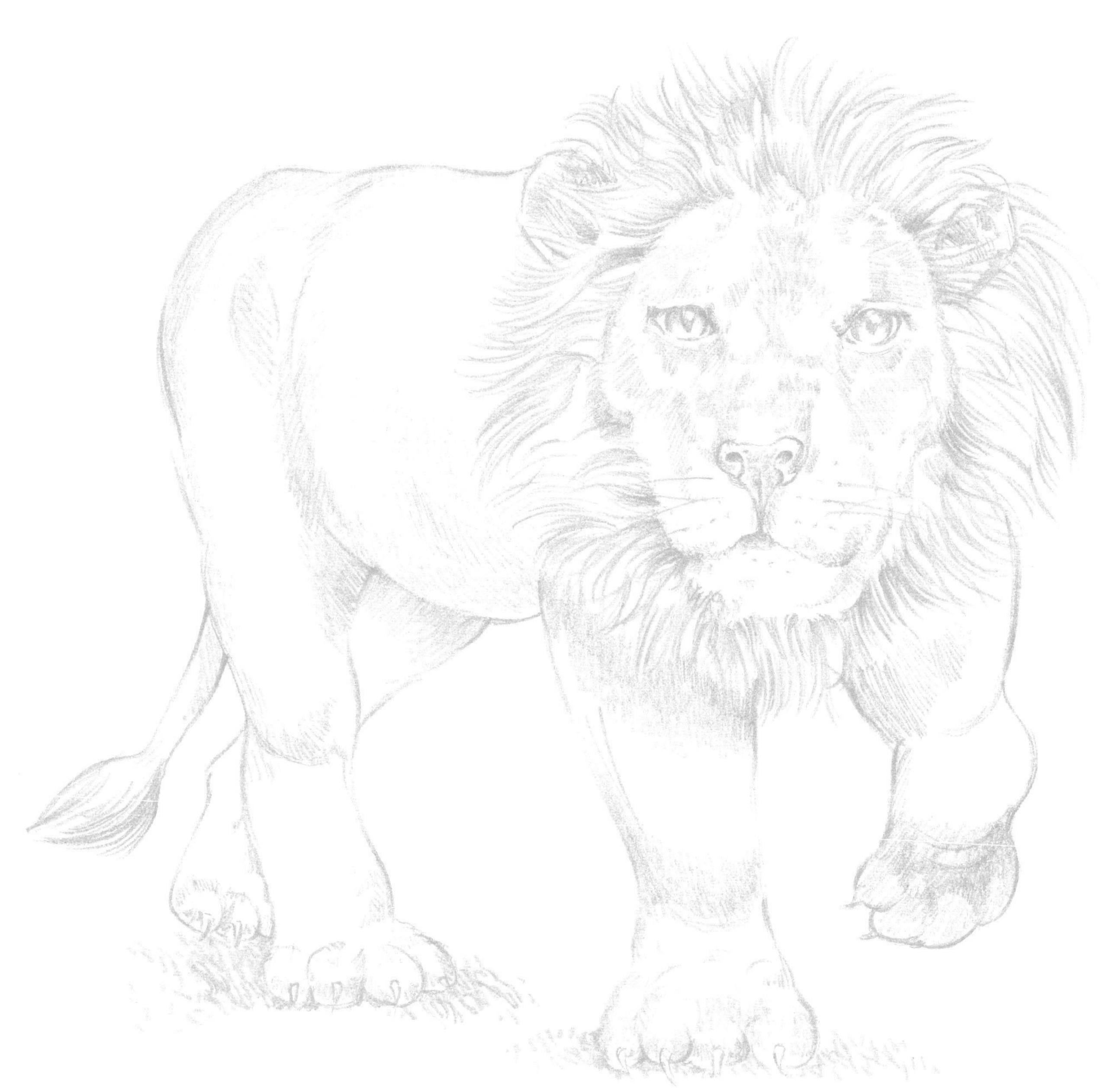

Male and Female Lions

When drawing animals, it's helpful to observe the differences between males and females within the species. Capturing these subtle differences will make your drawings more realistic.

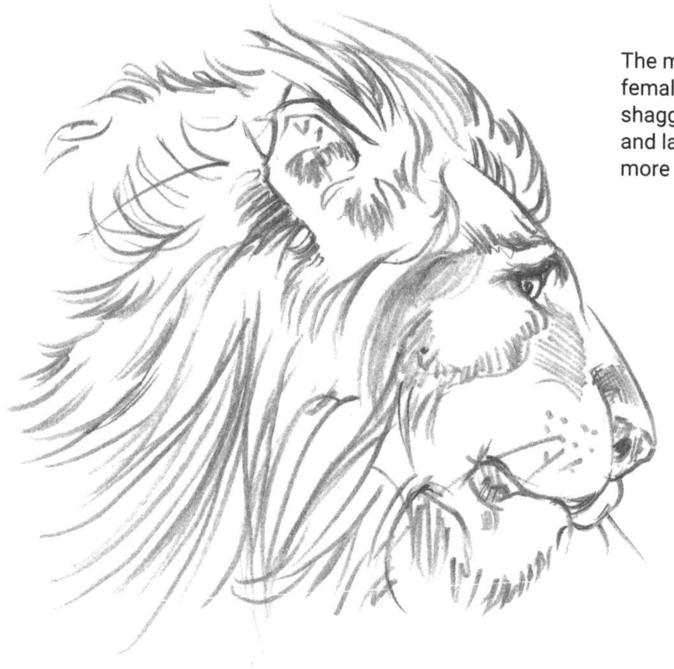

The male lion has a larger head than the female, accentuated by the presence of a shaggy mane. The male also has a broad face and large jaw, making him appear bigger and more threatening than the female.

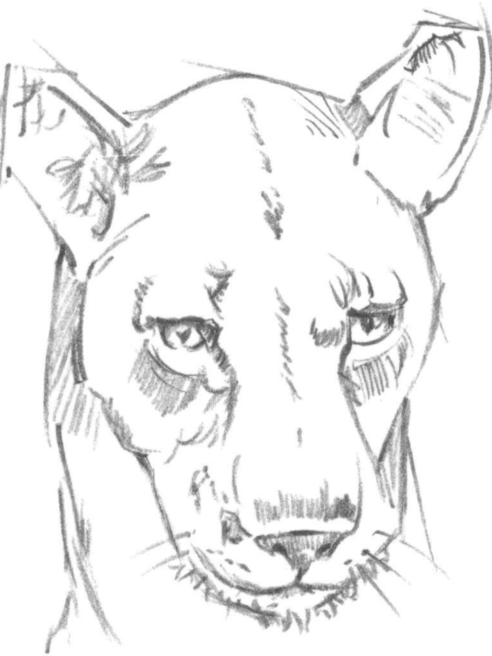

The female lion lacks a mane, making her easy to distinguish from a male. Her head appears slimmer with a sleeker look.

Practice drawing a male and female lion in the boxes below, focusing on the qualities that make them different.

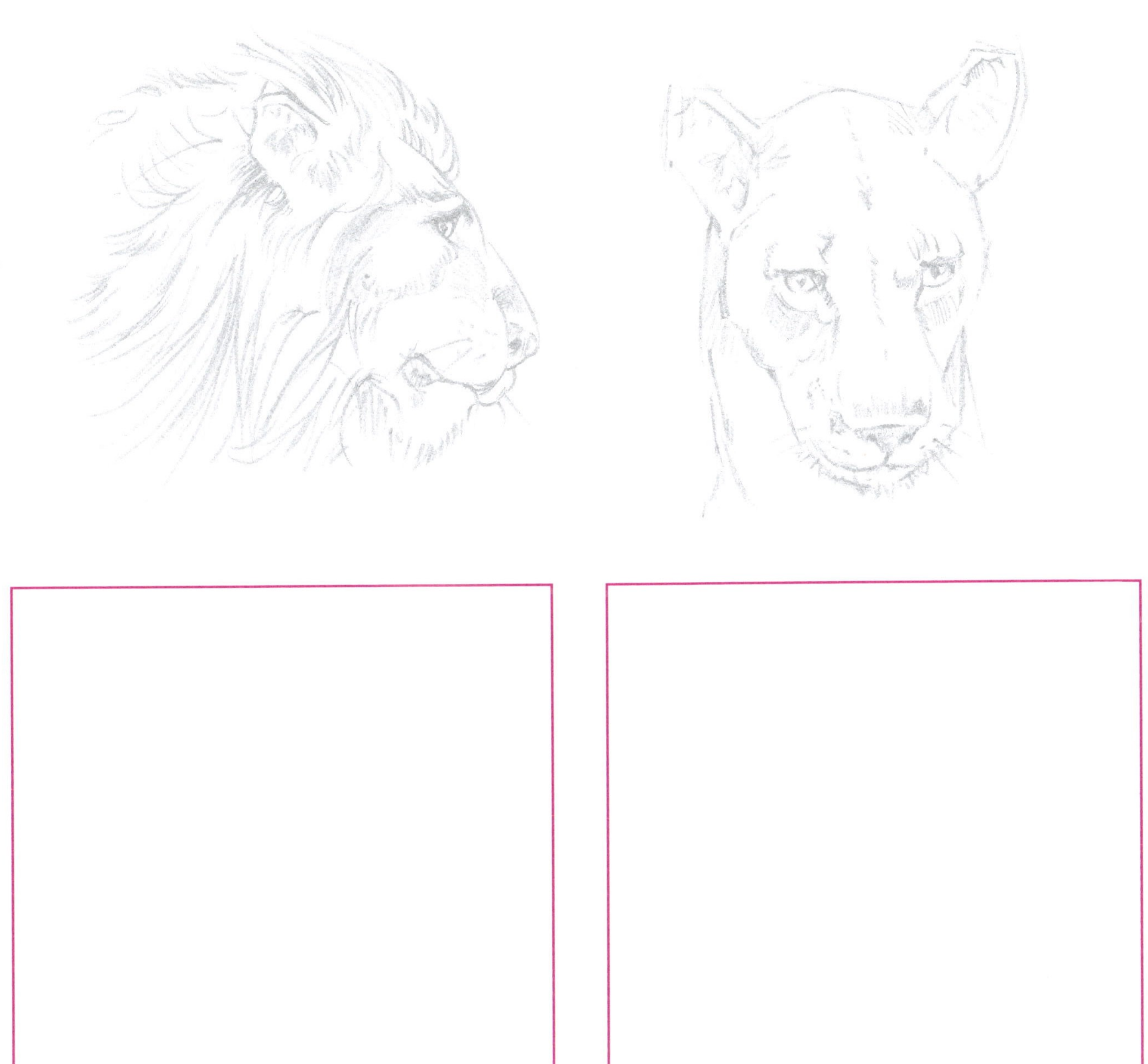

Drawing Accurately

Animals only appear realistic when they are drawn accurately. In more impressionistic drawings, accuracy is less important, but even then, a certain degree of realism must be maintained to make the image seem credible to the viewer. Here's a method for drawing a lioness in profile.

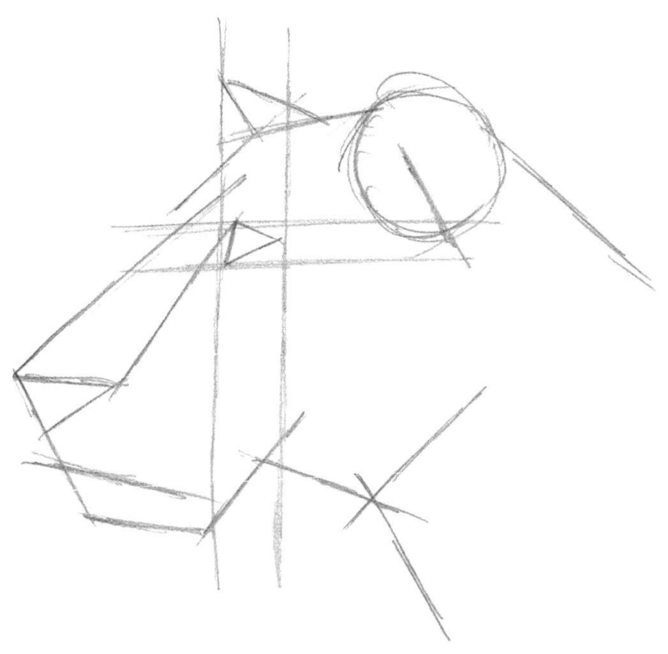

1 Break the profile down into a combination of simple lines and shapes, including triangles, wedges, and circles.

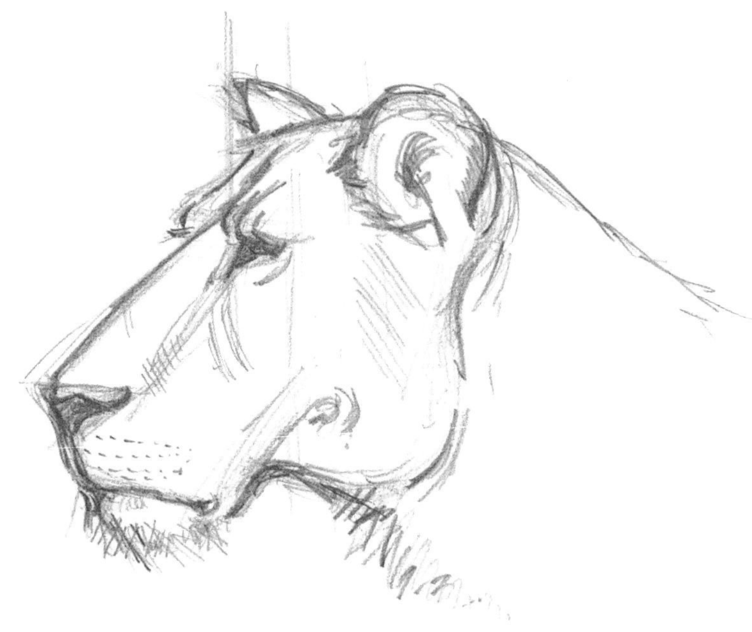

2 Use bold strokes to give the head shape clearer contours. Don't erase all the construction lines right away; you can use them as a base if you're looking for better proportions.

Trace over the outline below, building up the details as you work. Focus on the proportions of the angular face.

Drawing Fur

Bears are characterized by a large head, a ponderous body, massive hips, and short but powerful legs. Their long, sharp claws are perfect tools for digging and hunting. But one of its most distinguishing features is its thick, heavy fur, which can be easily rendered using simple lines and squiggles.

Using a variety of simple lines and squiggles is ideal for creating realistic fur on nearly any animal.

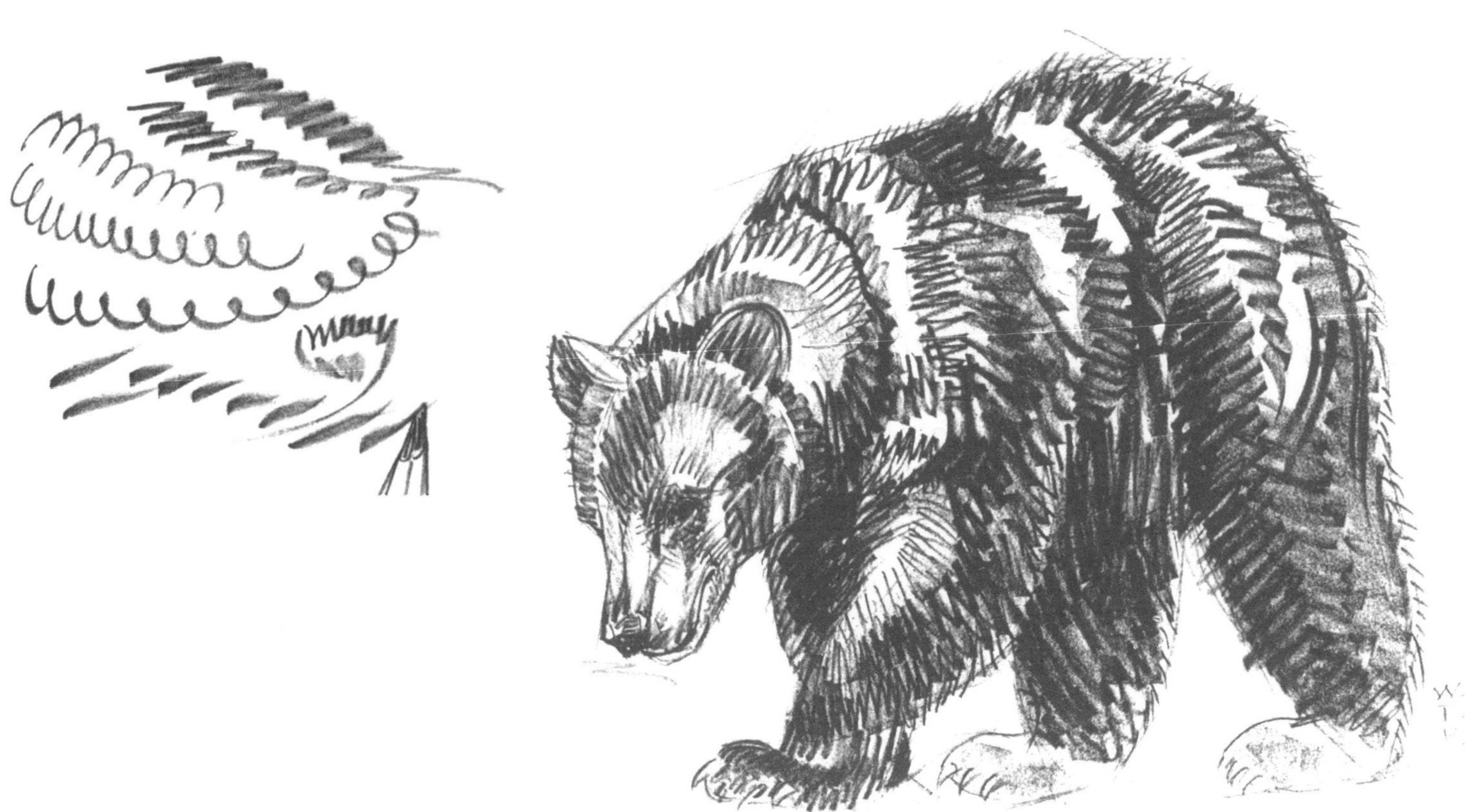

Continue drawing the different fur types, following the grayed-out patterns in the boxes below.

Short Fur Draw short, shimmering fur using small strokes and the broad side of your pencil. Body folds can be rendered with a few horizontal bands that are lighter than the rest of the fur.

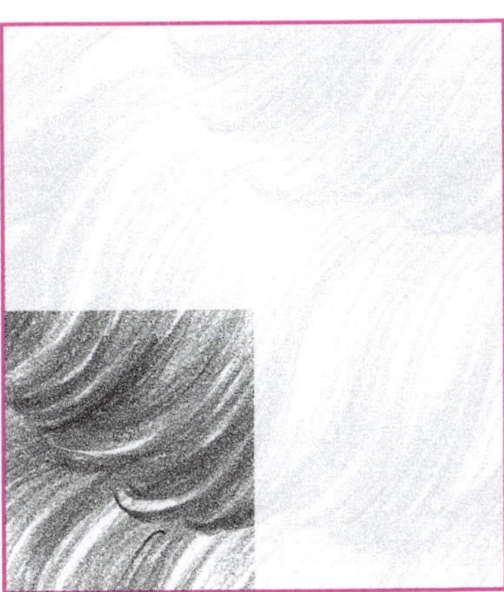

Curly Fur Draw layers of curly, soft fur with S-shaped strokes that end in a small curve. Add deeper pressure to enhance shading, while leaving some areas white to emphasize highlights.

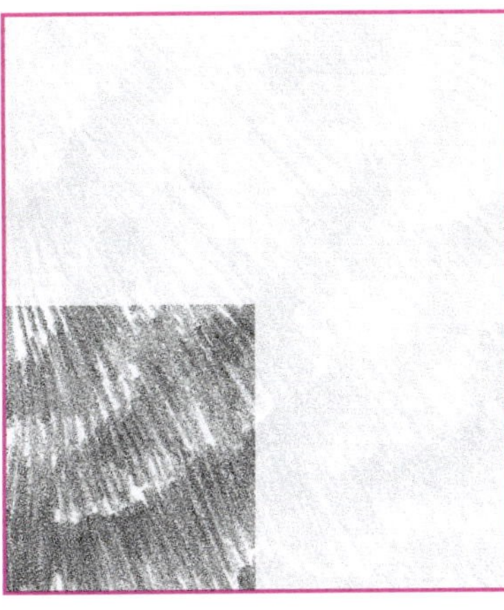

Striped Fur To depict striped fur, draw short strokes in the direction of hair growth. Then, add irregular darker lines for texture. Lift out highlights with an eraser or leave some areas white.

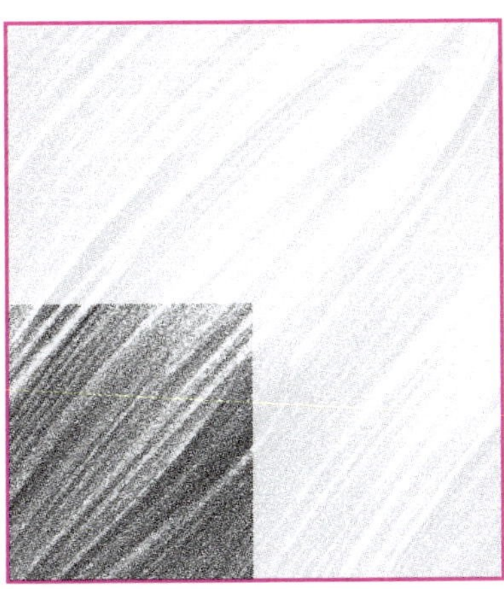

Soft Fur Draw hatching lines to create the impression of soft, silky fur. Alternate using the tip and the broad side of your pencil. Lift out highlights to create depth.

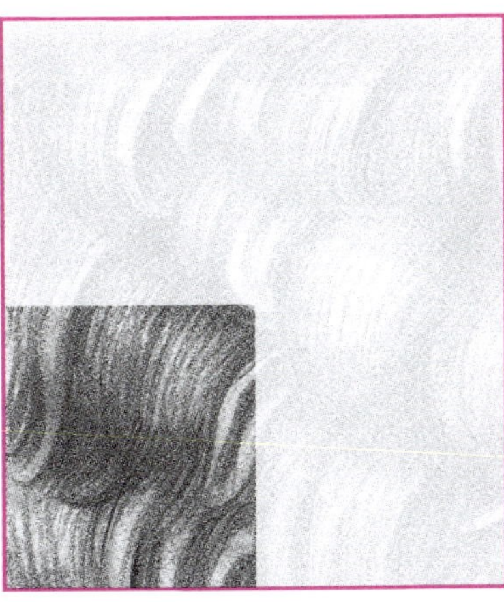

Wavy Fur Draw thick, wavy hair with lines that blend into one another and vary in size. To make the fur appear natural and soft, lift out bright highlights where the curls bend.

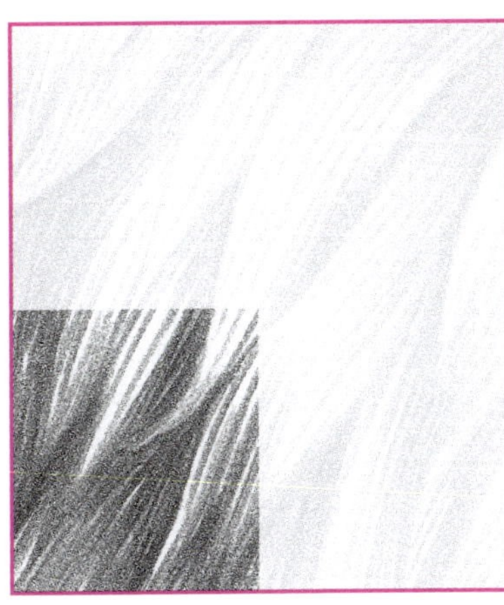

Long Hair Draw tails, manes, and longer hair using long, tapered lines with soft curves.

Fur Step by Step

Follow the steps below to practice drawing short fur and long fur. Leave white space to indicate reflections of light, or use a kneaded eraser to lift out highlights. The more texture you can achieve in rendering fur, the more realistic the results will be.

Short Fur

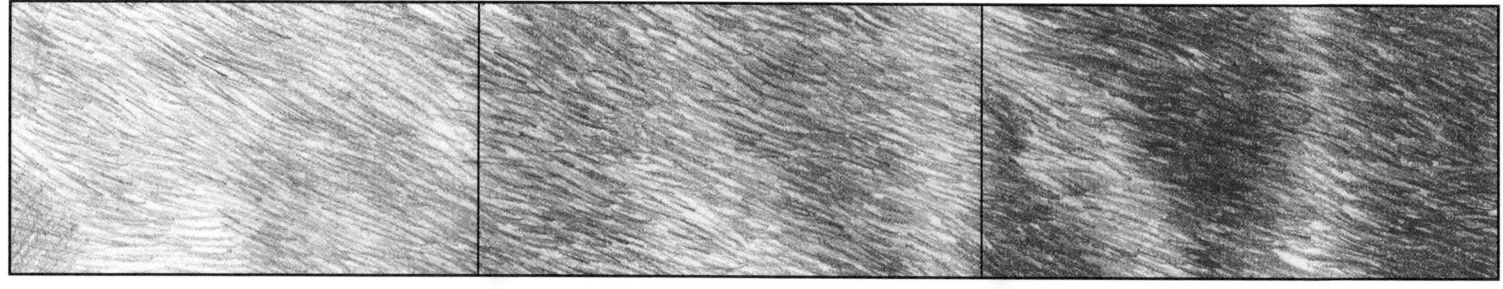

1 Using a blunt pencil, add light, even tone to the area. Then, using a 2H pencil, add individual hairs. In some places, place the strokes closely together to indicate dark areas of fur.

2 With the HB pencil, continue to draw short, quick strokes, following the direction of growth. For darker areas, draw strokes close together. For lighter areas, leave strokes spaced farther apart. For highlights, leave some white areas.

3 Go over the dark areas with a sharp 2B pencil, varying the pressure. Darken the light areas slightly with a sharp HB pencil.

Long Fur

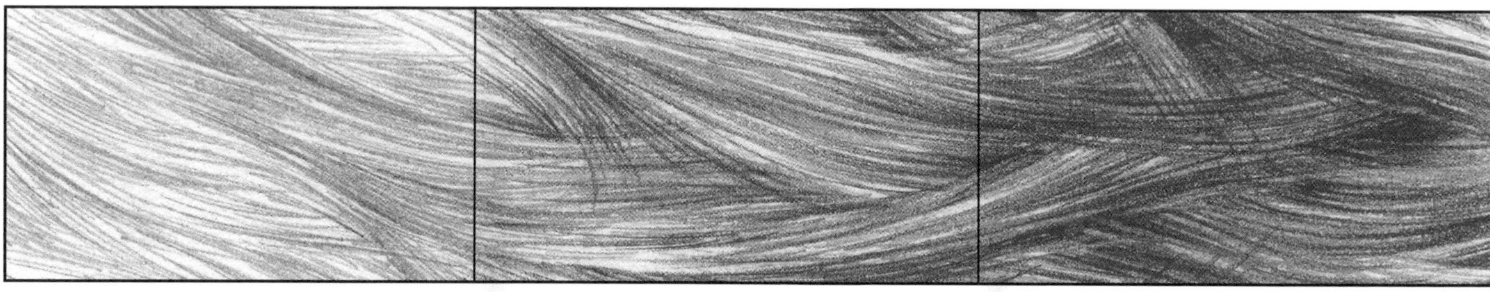

1 Using a sharp pencil, draw long curved strands of hair. Allow some strands to overlap for a more natural look.

2 As with the short fur, continue working with a sharp HB pencil. Draw these strokes more unevenly and allow the white of the paper to show through between them.

3 Using a 2B pencil, darken areas to indicate shadow and depth. The contrast creates the impression of natural fur with highlights.

Use 2H, HB, and 2B pencils and a kneaded eraser to create some different fur types in the boxes below.

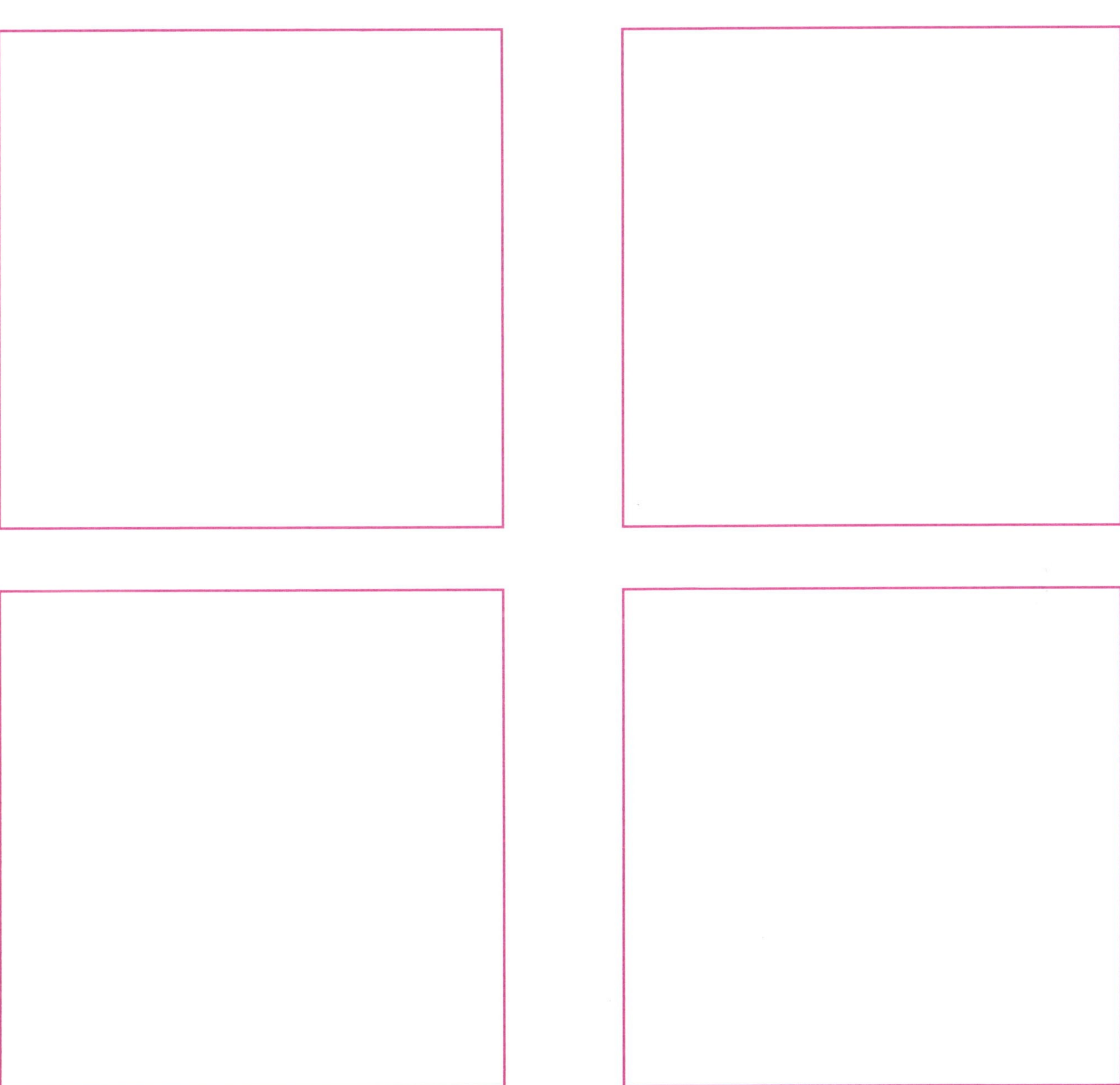

Skin Step by Step

Not all animals have fur. Snakes and elephants, for example, have very distinctive skin textures that display wrinkles, folds, or patterns.

Rough, Wrinkled Skin

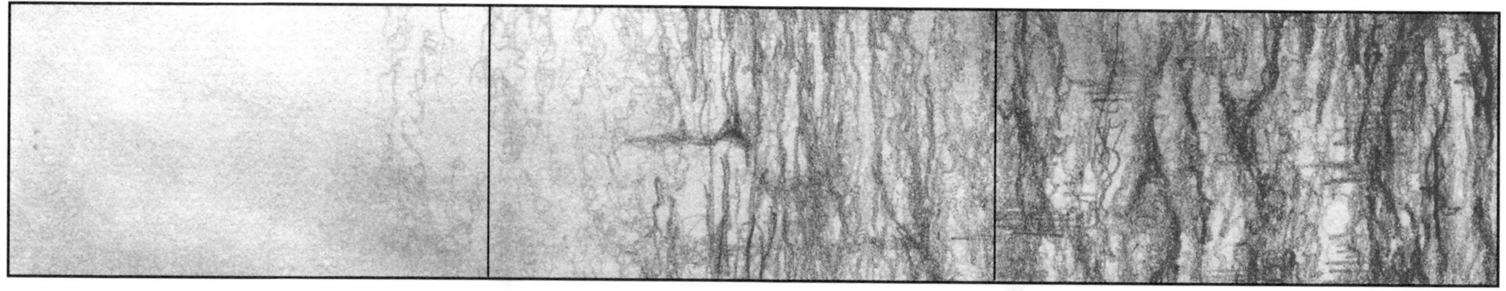

1 Lightly shade the paper with a blunt F pencil. Then blend the lines with a clean blending stump to create tone. To prevent the surface from appearing completely solid, add a bit of shading in some areas.

2 Depict wrinkles by drawing irregular, wavy lines over the shading with a sharp 2H, without lifting your pencil. Let the lead "wander" around to indicate a bumpy surface. Then, using an HB pencil, add slightly darker, vertical lines of varying lengths. These are the deeper wrinkles.

3 Alternating between HB and 2B pencils, cover the area again with more irregular scribbles. This technique is well-suited for the skin of elephants, rhinos, and similar animals. It can also be used for leathery noses and paws.

Reptile Skin

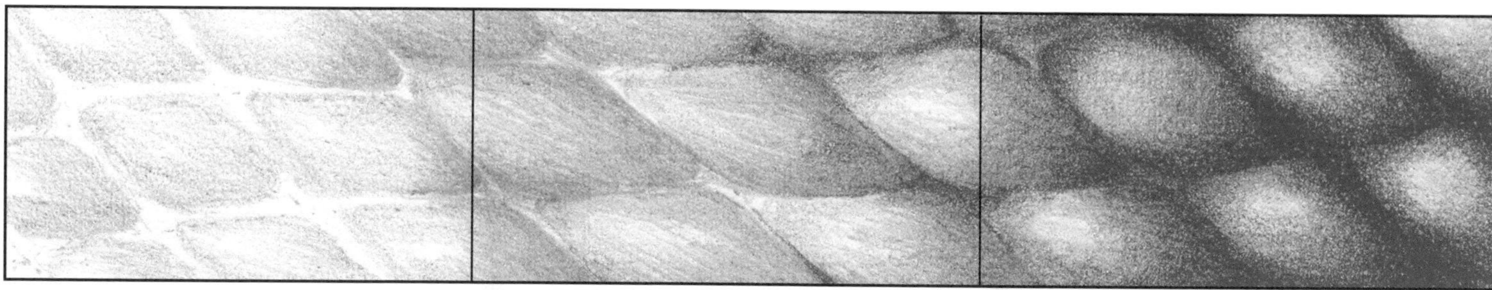

1 Use a 2H pencil to create a diamond pattern. Then fill in each diamond shape using short, tight strokes and a blunt F pencil. Leave some areas of white between each diamond shape.

2 Continue to add shading, defining each diamond with heavier strokes. Darken the outlines of the diamonds with an HB pencil to indicate shadows between the scales.

3 Use a 2B pencil to fill in the darkest shadows between each diamond. Then, use an HB pencil to smooth out the lines and even out the gray tone inside each scale.

Gather F, 2H, HB, and 2B pencils, a blending stump, and a kneaded eraser. In the boxes below practice drawing wrinkled skin and reptile skin, focusing on light and dark areas.

Feathers

Drawing animals is exciting because nature has graced them with a variety of interesting textures and characteristics. Learning to master any animal's fine details, such as the unique plumage of a peacock, will help your art appear more lively and realistic.

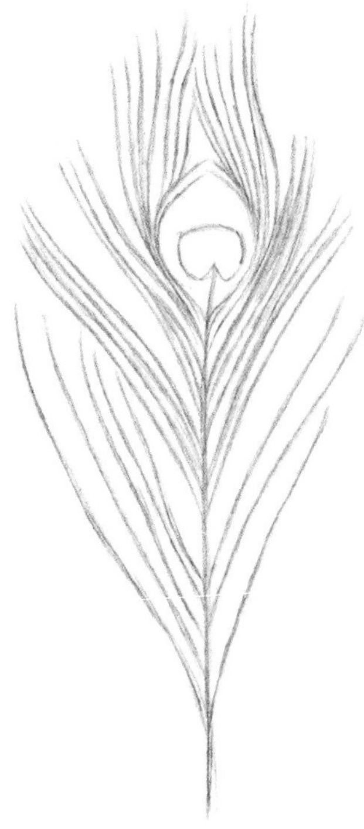

1 Start with lines drawn in the direction of the feather's growth that extend from a vertical line. For the feather's eye, draw a circle toward the top and draw lines that sweep past the eye and curve around it.

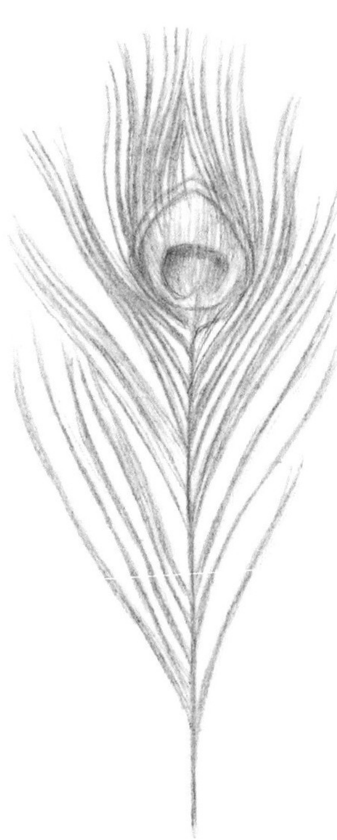

2 Next, follow the pattern of the feather and darken the center of the eye. Some of the feather fibers should remain light and wispy.

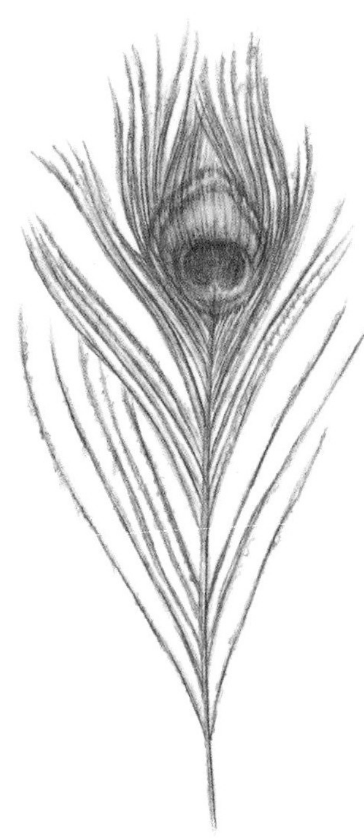

3 Once all the dark areas have been drawn, use an eraser to lift out highlights in the eye.

Drawing with an Eraser

You can use your kneaded eraser as a drawing tool. In the example at right, a feather has been "drawn" using an eraser to lift out highlights from a toned background, followed by the application of darker shading inside the curved feathers with an HB pencil.

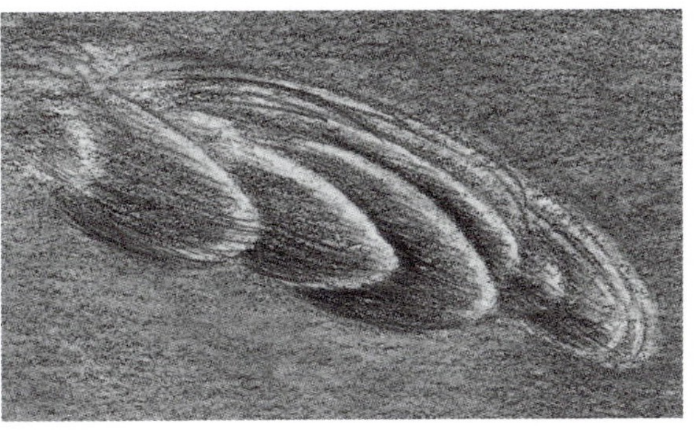

Look for different types of feathers and draw them below using a toned background and a kneaded eraser.

Drawing Dogs

Dogs are an extremely popular subject in art. Even people who don't own dogs enjoy drawing and painting them because they are so lively and approachable. Plus, they come in so many different sizes and shapes that you'll always find a new subject.

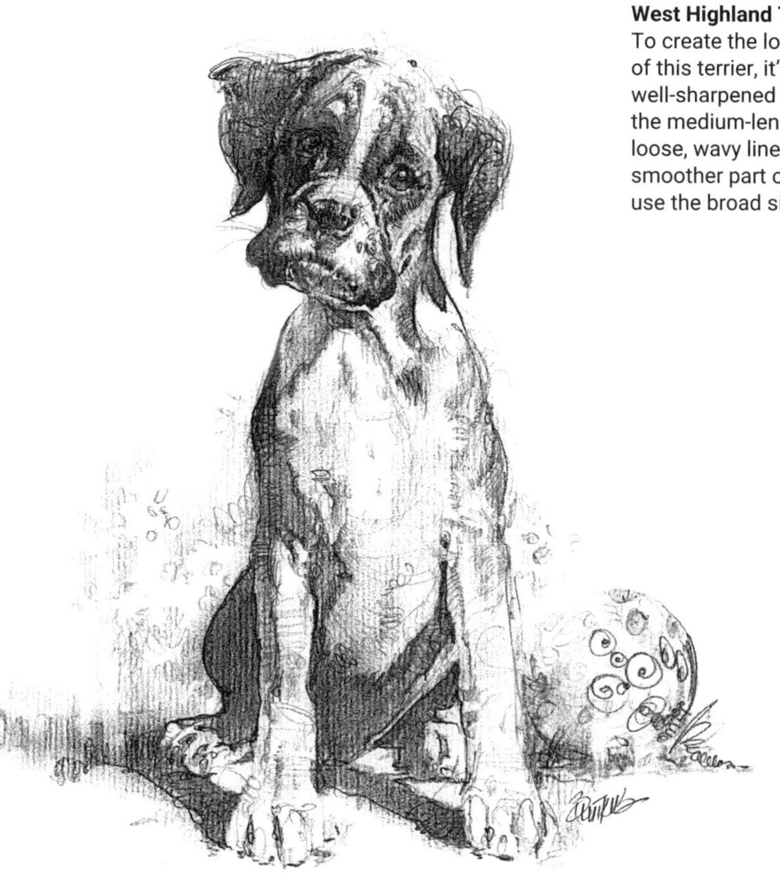

West Highland Terrier
To create the long, curly hair of this terrier, it's best to take a well-sharpened pencil and draw the medium-length coat with loose, wavy lines. For the softer, smoother part of the topcoat, use the broad side of the pencil.

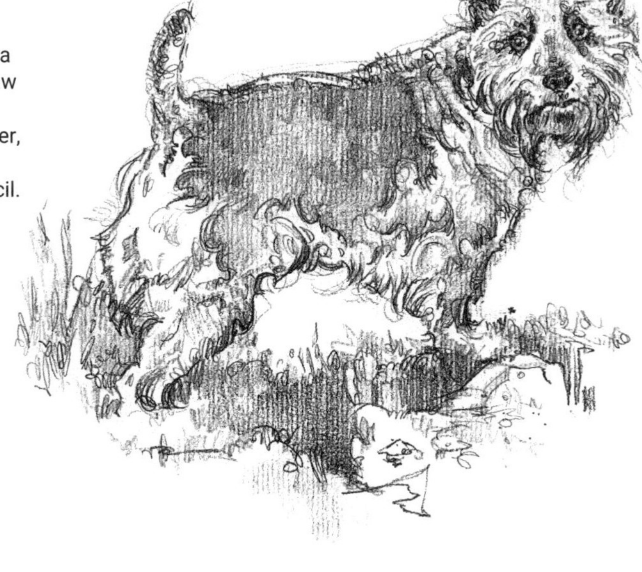

Golden Retriever
This breed has such long, thick fur that you can't see the actual shape of its body underneath. Therefore, it's best to use an HB pencil and use loose strokes to draw its shaggy coat.

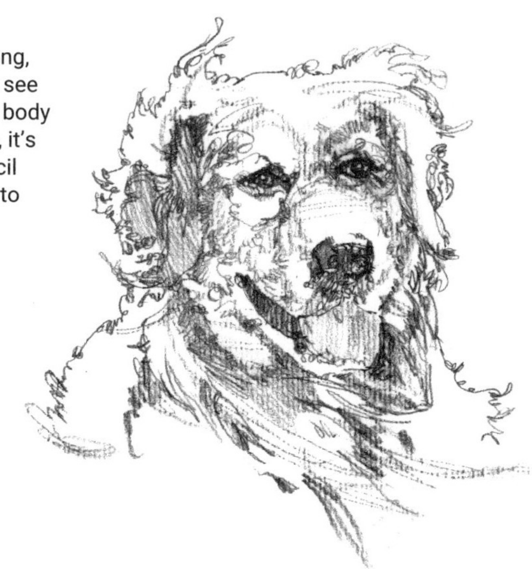

Boxer This dog is still a puppy, which is apparent from its oversized paws and narrow chest. When drawing, pay attention to the specific characteristics, such as the square muzzle, flat face, and prominent cheeks.

Practice drawing some dogs of your choice below. Use different pencils to work out the fur. Don't forget to add shadows and shading.

Dog Fur

Most dog fur is easily rendered using a variety of hatching lines. To create depth and volume, darken the areas of shadow, such as near the opening of the ear, under the muzzle, and around the eyes.

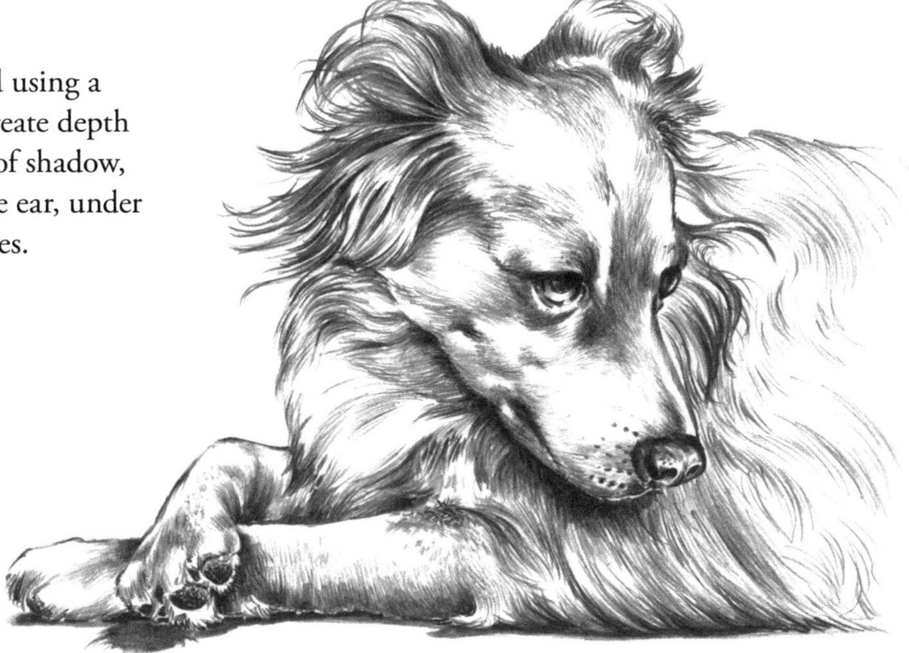

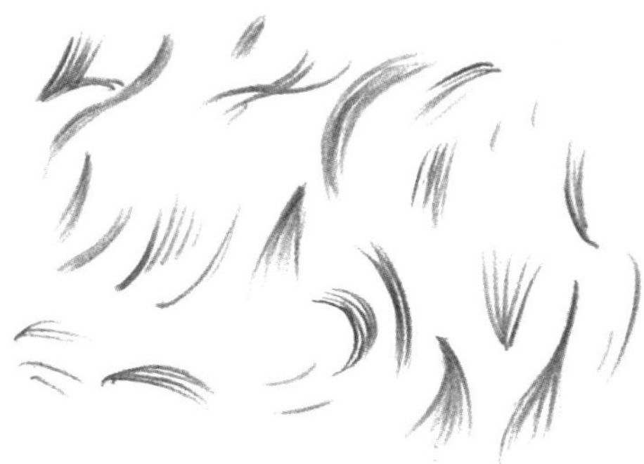

1 Draw some irregular hatching lines curving in different directions.

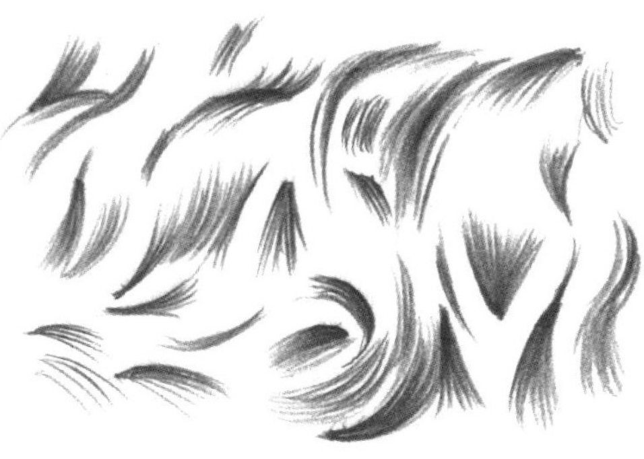

2 Next, add shading using denser, darker strokes, creating the appearance of curls or strands.

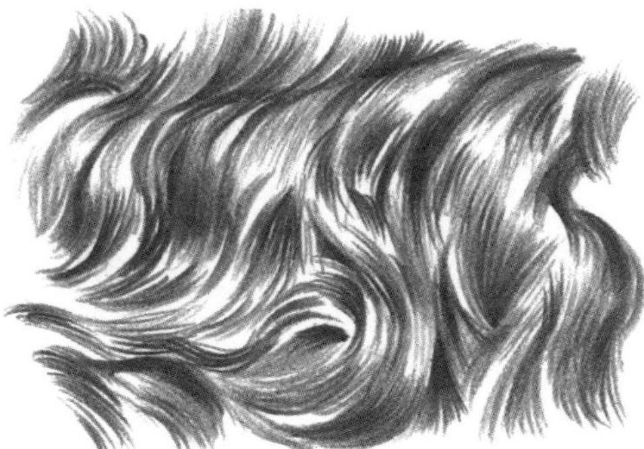

3 If you want to portray the dog up close, you'll need to work slowly and take your time with the fur so it doesn't appear unfinished or "muddy."

Familiarize yourself with the different strokes and lines you can draw using different materials. Then draw the sections of fur shown in the boxes below.

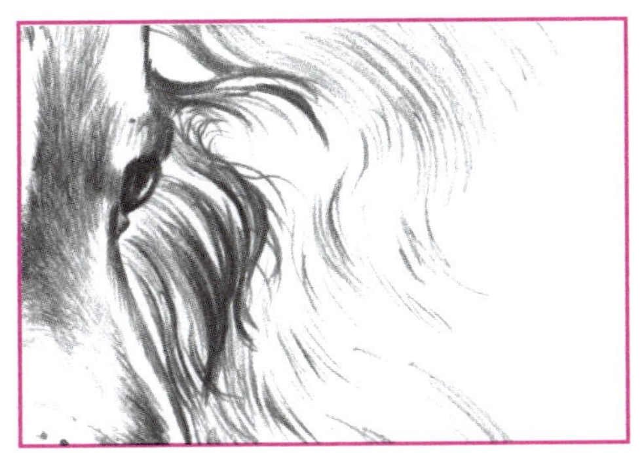

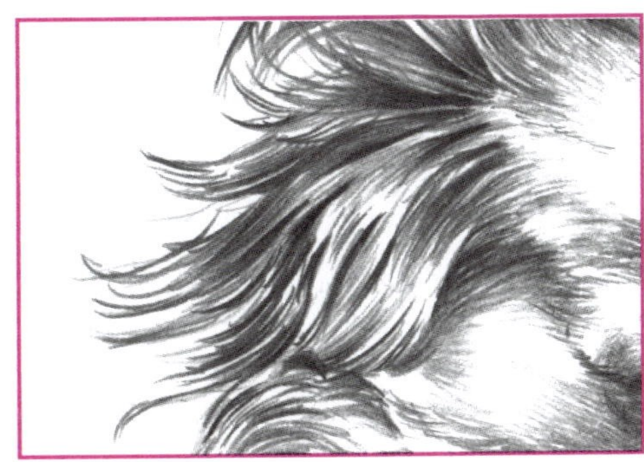

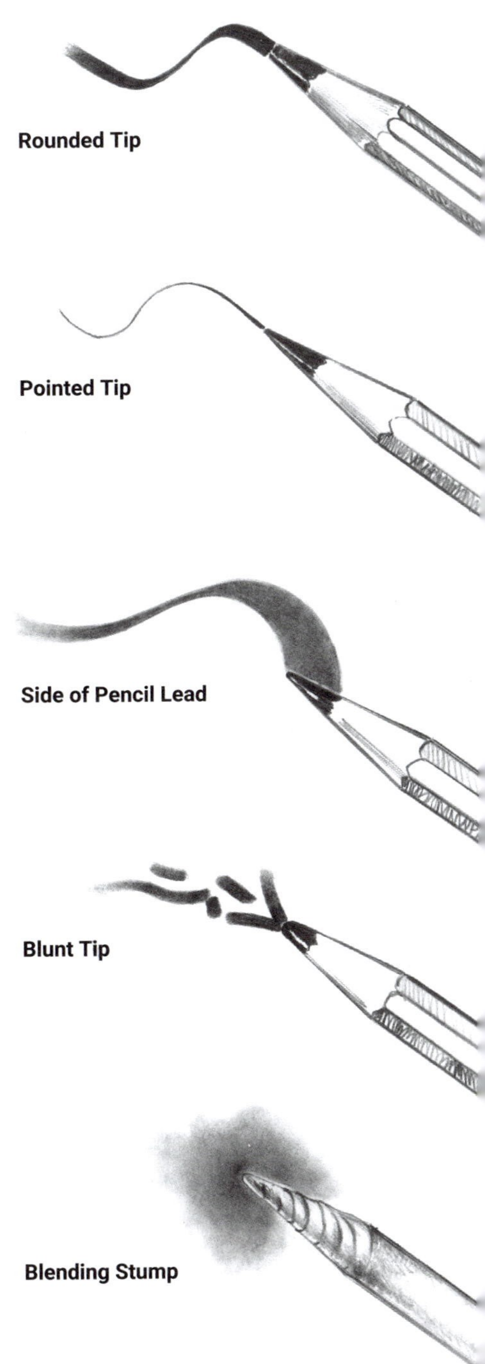

Proportion and Anatomy

To accurately render various dog breeds, it's necessary to draw the body parts in the proper proportion. Proportion is the relationship between the different aspects of your drawing. An effective method for establishing proportion is to use one body part as a unit of measurement for determining the size of the other parts. For instance, you can use the dog's head to determine the length and height of the dog's body; the dog to the right is about 4 heads long and 3½ heads high. Make certain the proportions are accurate before working on any details.

Knowledge of basic anatomy will also help you accurately draw your subject. The diagram below illustrates the various parts of the dog. As you study different dogs, notice how these parts differ according to breed.

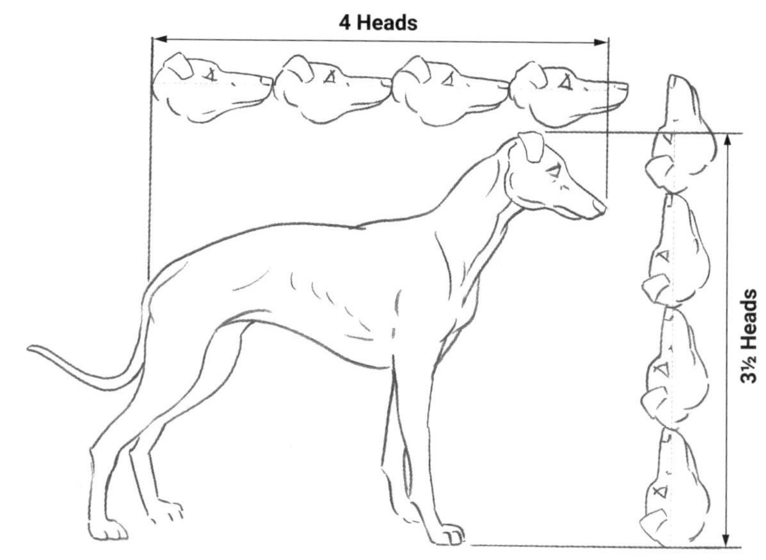

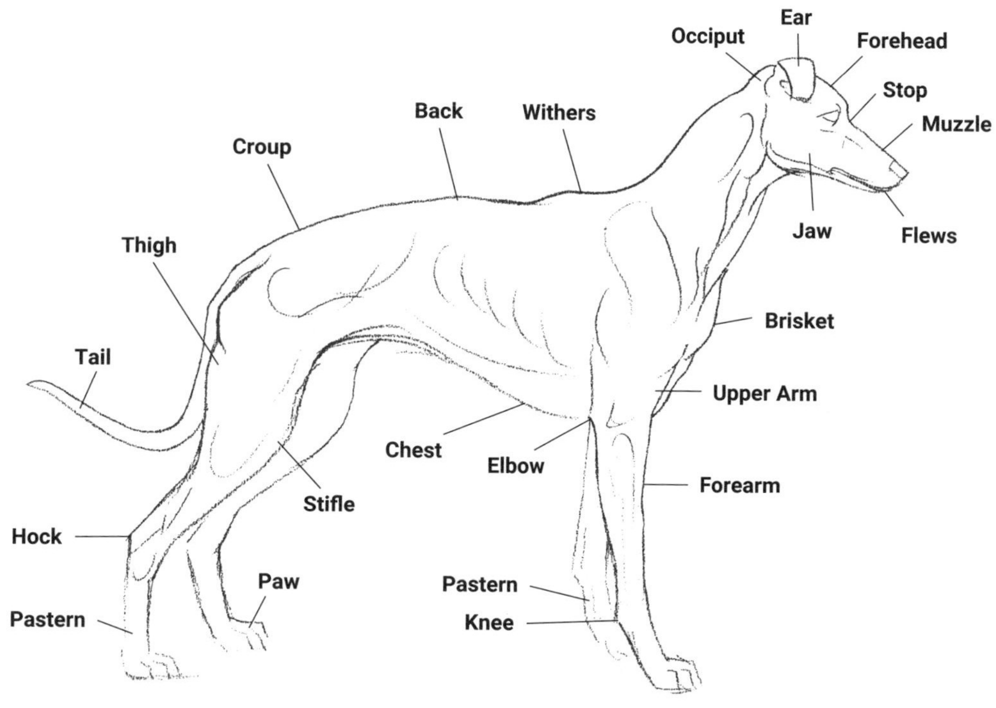

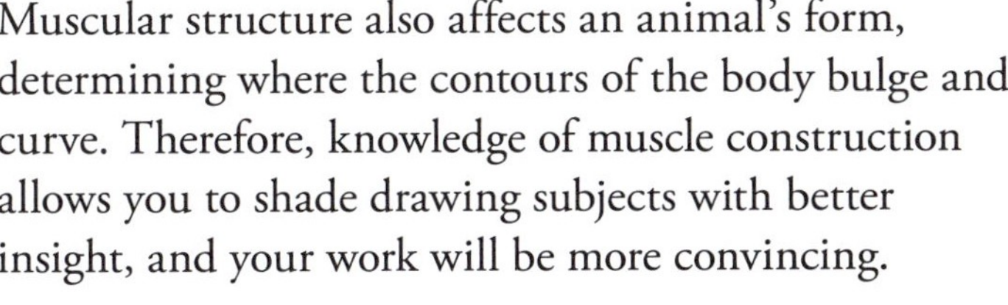

Muscular structure also affects an animal's form, determining where the contours of the body bulge and curve. Therefore, knowledge of muscle construction allows you to shade drawing subjects with better insight, and your work will be more convincing.

The diagrams on this page illustrate the dog's basic muscular structure. Study the muscles closely, and keep them in mind as you draw. As you observe your subject or model, consider how the location of the muscles might affect your shading.

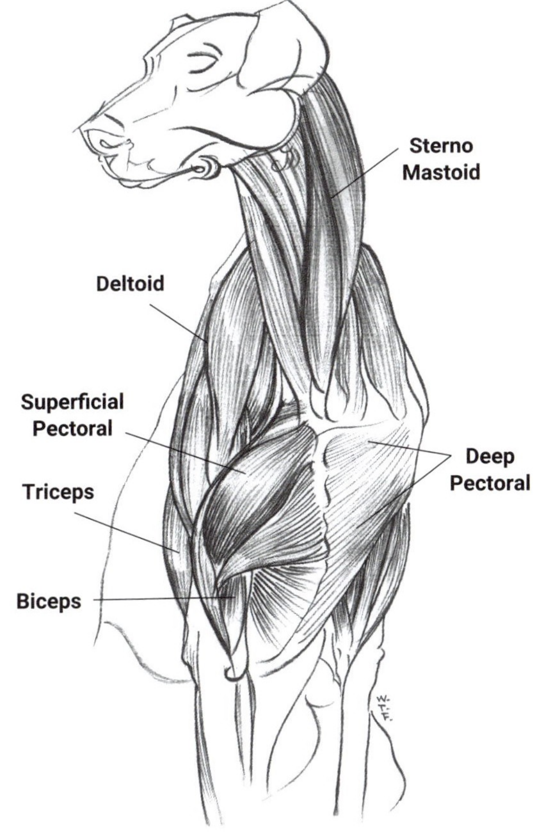

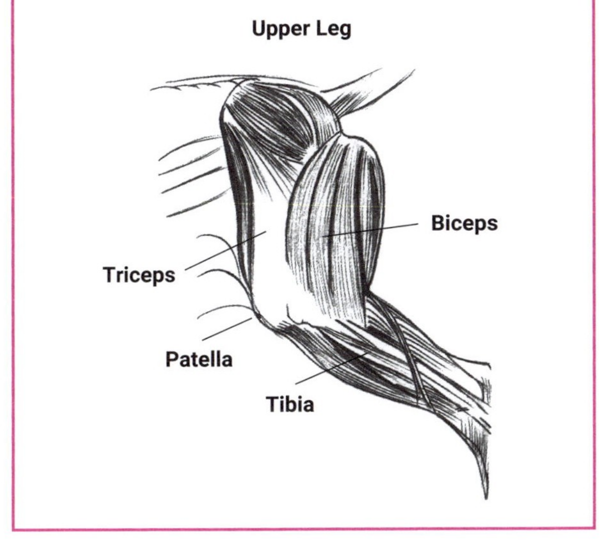

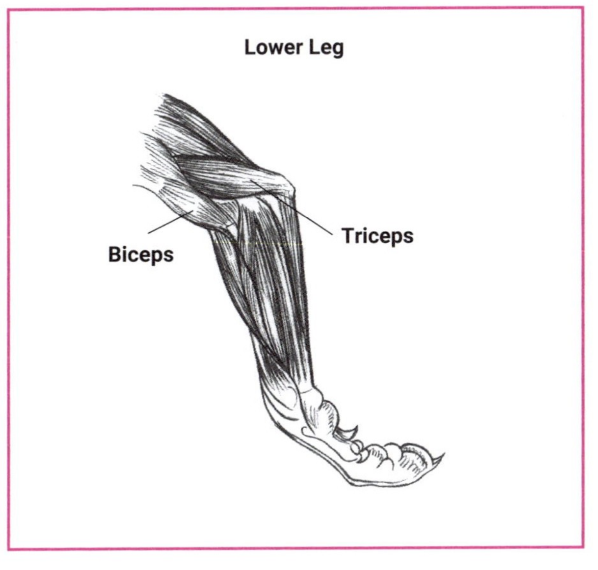

Dog Features

Once the basic drawing is correct, you can begin to develop the details. The illustrations below demonstrate how to render a dog's eye and paw. Begin with simple lines, and slowly refine the shapes. Use a sharp pencil for bringing out the fine details in the eye and for rendering the fur along the paw. Follow the steps closely to achieve a good likeness.

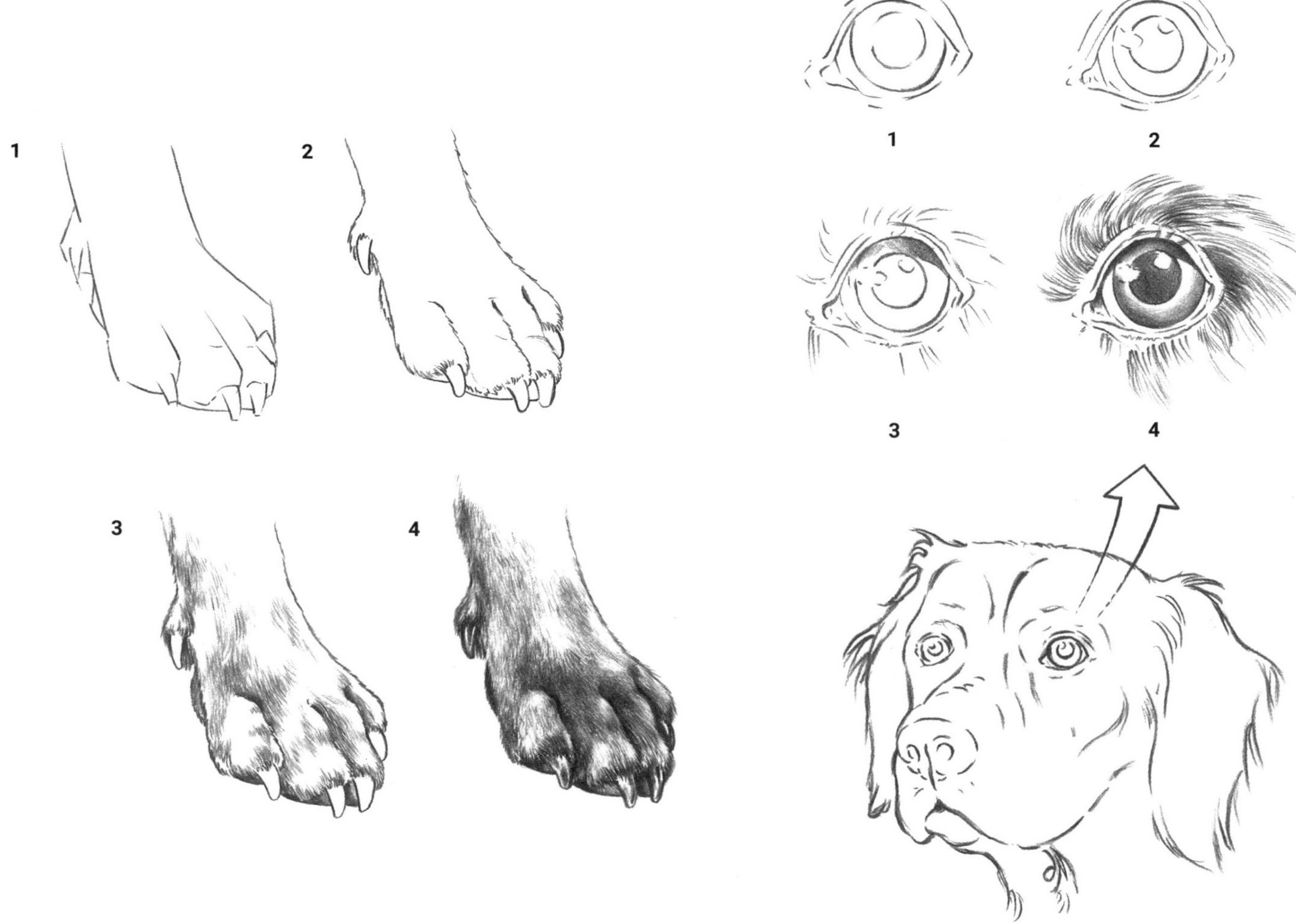

Use the space below to practice drawing the dog's eyes or any other features you'd like to master.

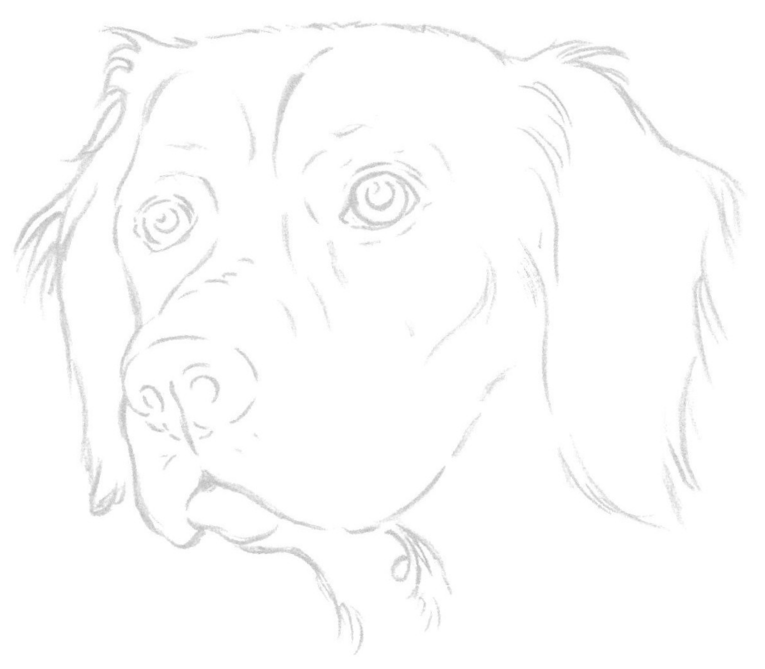

Dog Muzzle

Every dog breed has a typical muzzle shape. Take a look at the muzzles on this page. Some are long and narrow, others are short and wide. The more accurately your eye perceives these shapes, the better your drawing will turn out, so observe your model closely.

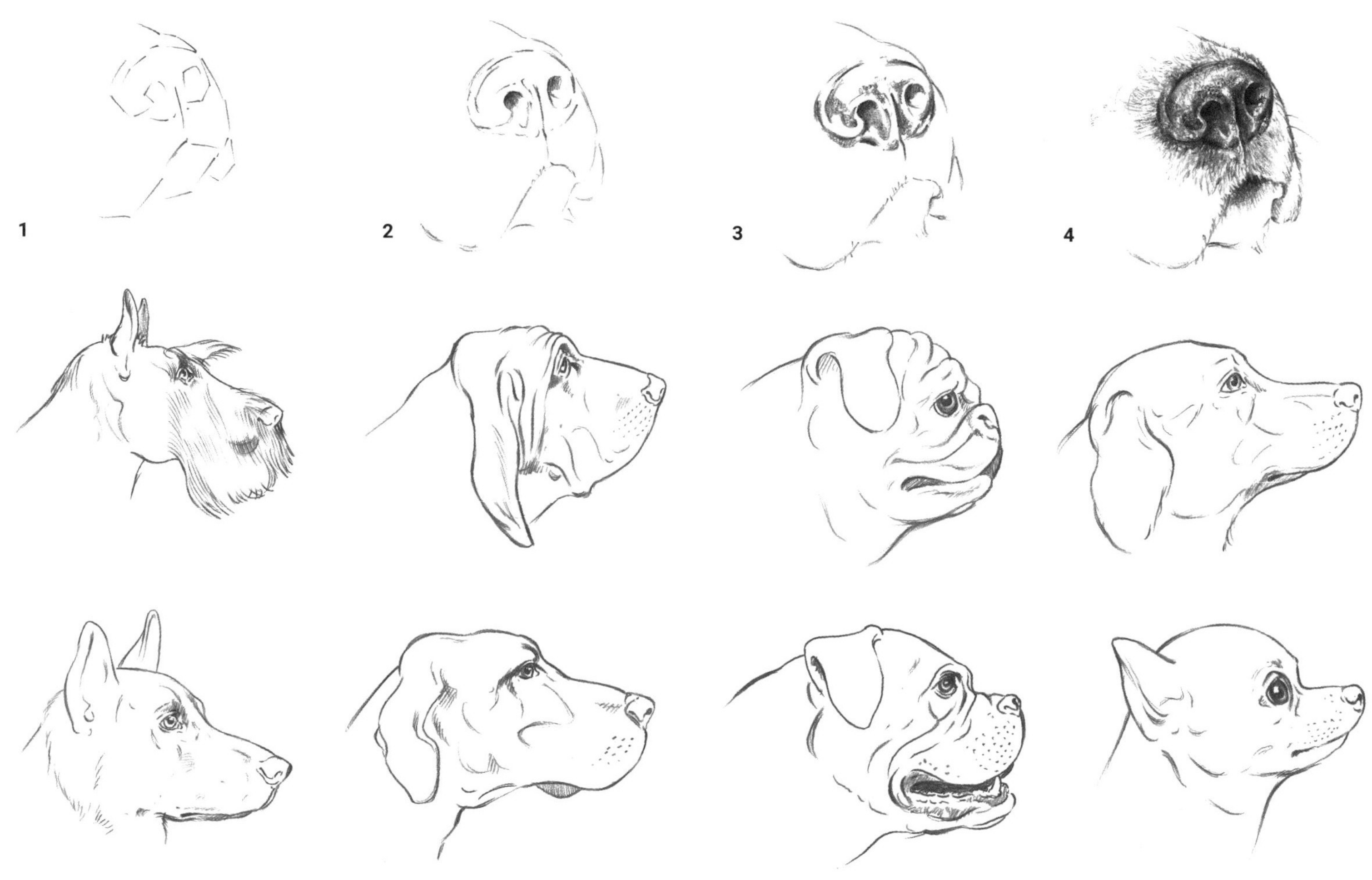

Once the basic shape of the snout is complete, move on to the nose. First, sketch the rough outlines (step 1). Then, shade the dark areas in the nostrils with a sharp pencil. The darkest areas are where the curve of the nostril tapers inward (step 2). Continue shading the nose, paying attention to how the shape develops (step 3). Refine the shading and hairs around the muzzle, and lift out highlights with an eraser (step 4).

Look closely at the dogs and their snouts. How do these dog breeds differ? Are the snouts pointed, elongated, or rounded? Do the ears stick up or droop? Draw these dogs in profile in the space below.

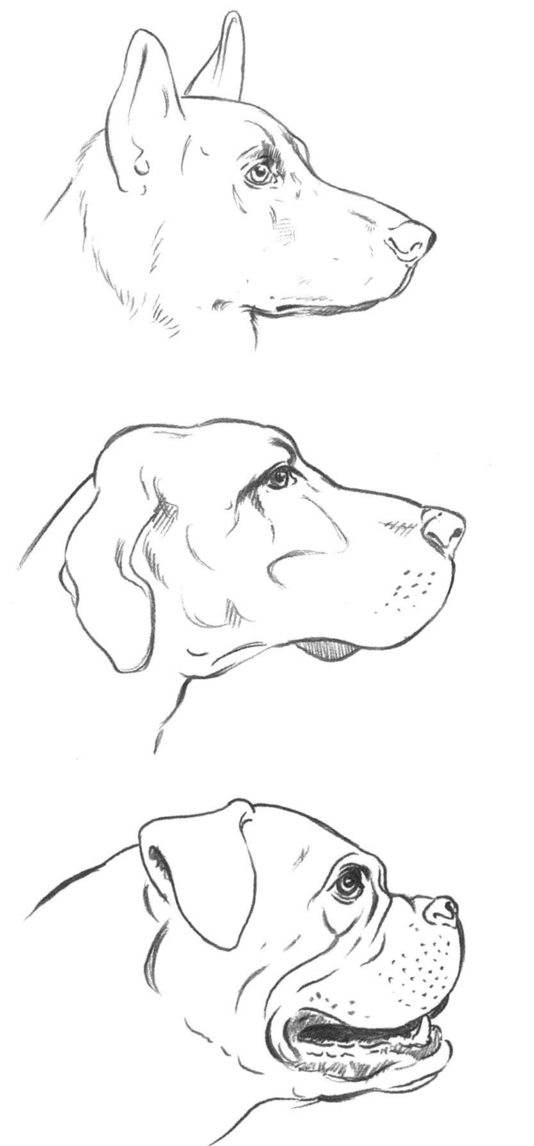

Dog Proportions

Study the dog carefully before drawing, and make an effort to accurately capture its distinctive features. Is its muzzle pointed or rounded? Is its hair long and soft or short and smooth? Don't forget to start your drawing using basic shapes.

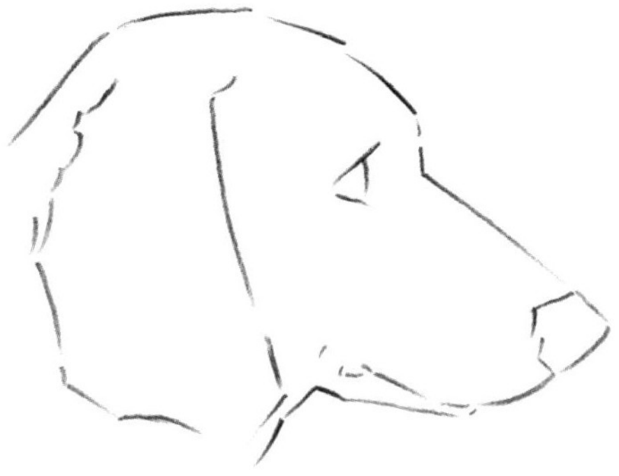

1 Lightly sketch the basic outline and structure of the head. Use the side of an HB pencil to draw the corners.

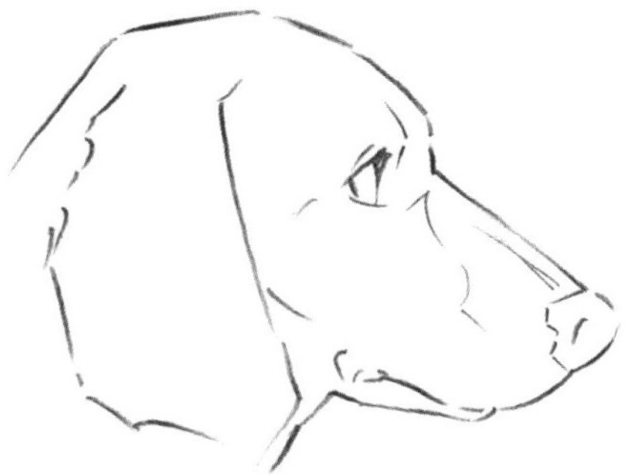

2 Indicate the details of the face and the nose with a few basic lines.

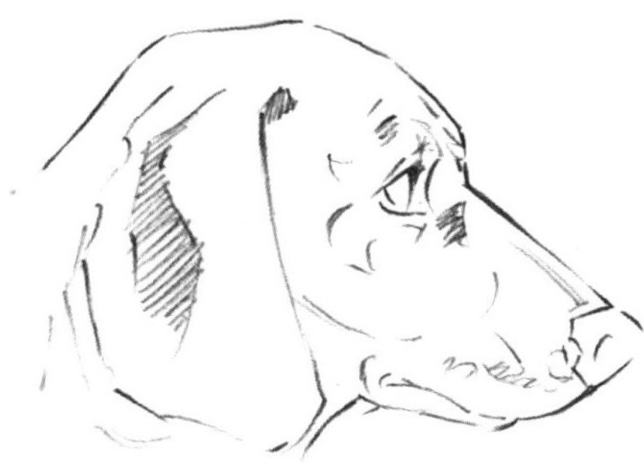

3 Apply shading to define the shape using the rounded tip and the broad side of an HB pencil.

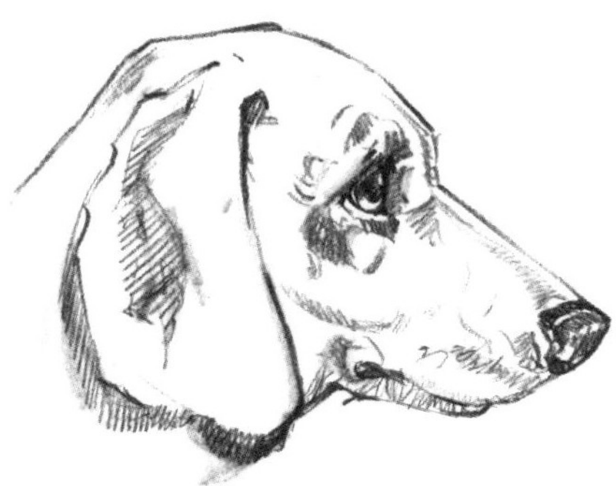

4 Use the tip and broad side of a sharpened pencil to draw individual sections of hair, gradually thickening the hatching. Use a well-sharpened 2B pencil for the darkest areas.

Use HB, 4B, and 6B pencils to fill in the outline below. Deepen shading in areas of shadow, such as inside the ears and around the mouth.

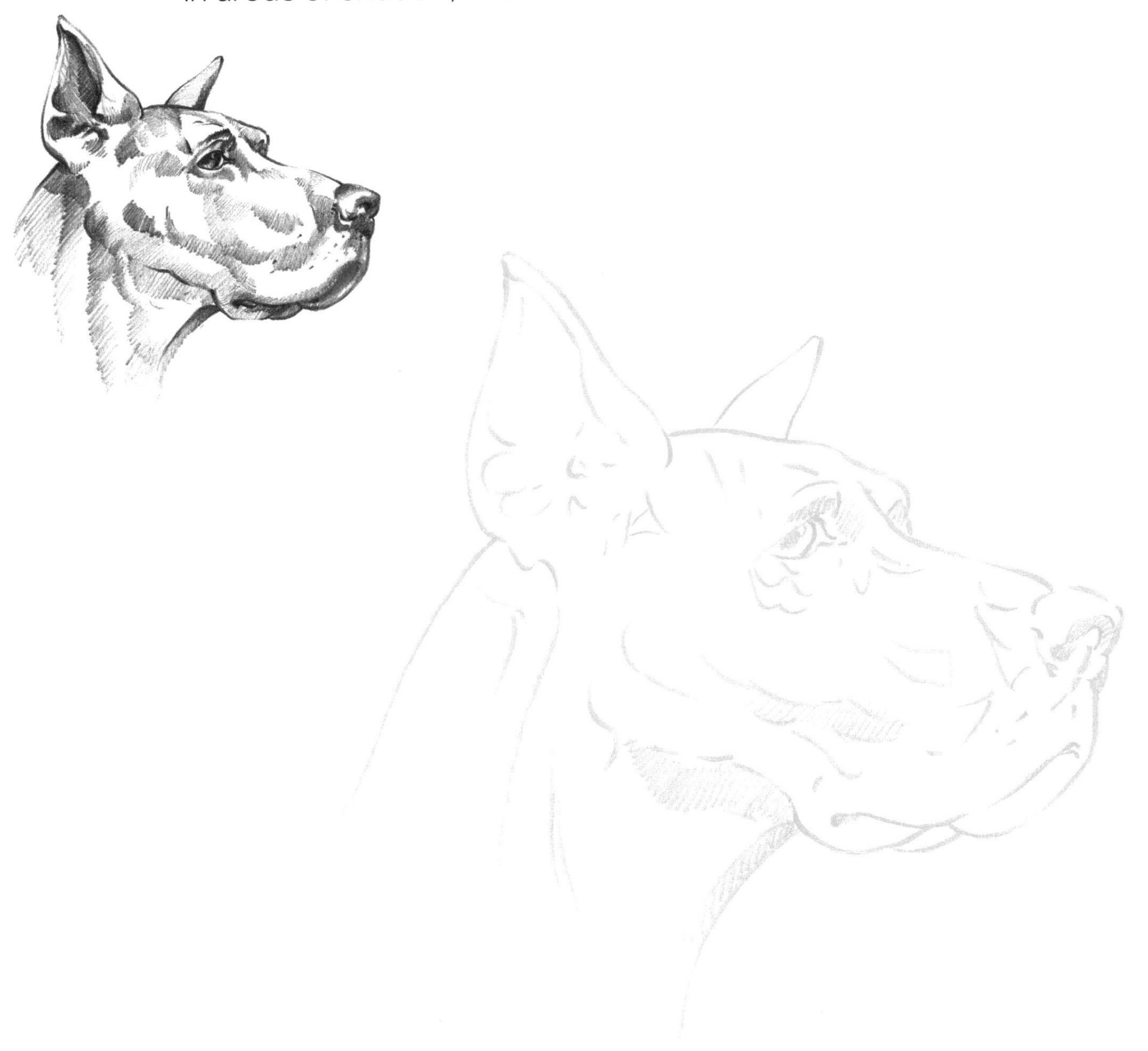

German Shepherd

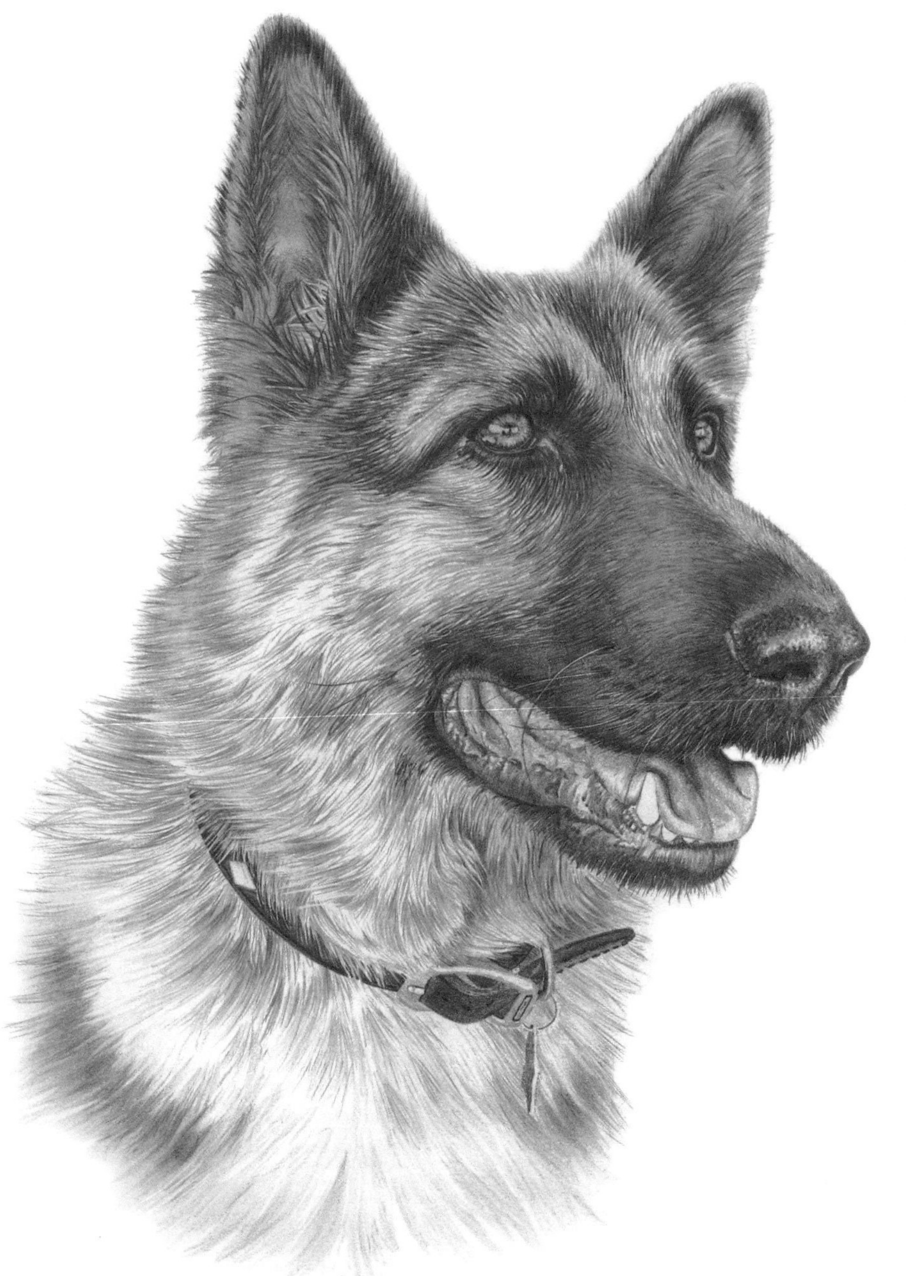

Capturing the likeness of an animal is a significant achievement in drawing. Such a portrait requires careful observation and a thorough understanding of shape and proportion. Take your time to study the subject. The German Shepherd's high-set ears make up almost half the height of its face. The long muzzle tapers toward the front to a blunt nose tip and slopes slightly downward on the bridge. The short fur on the face accurately traces the shape of the head and neck.

Indicate the direction of the fur growth with short strokes. For the darkest areas, use a 2B pencil. Leave highlights in the pupil, iris, and teeth. To create a smooth transition to the white background, smudge the pencil lines at the base of the neck with a blending stump.

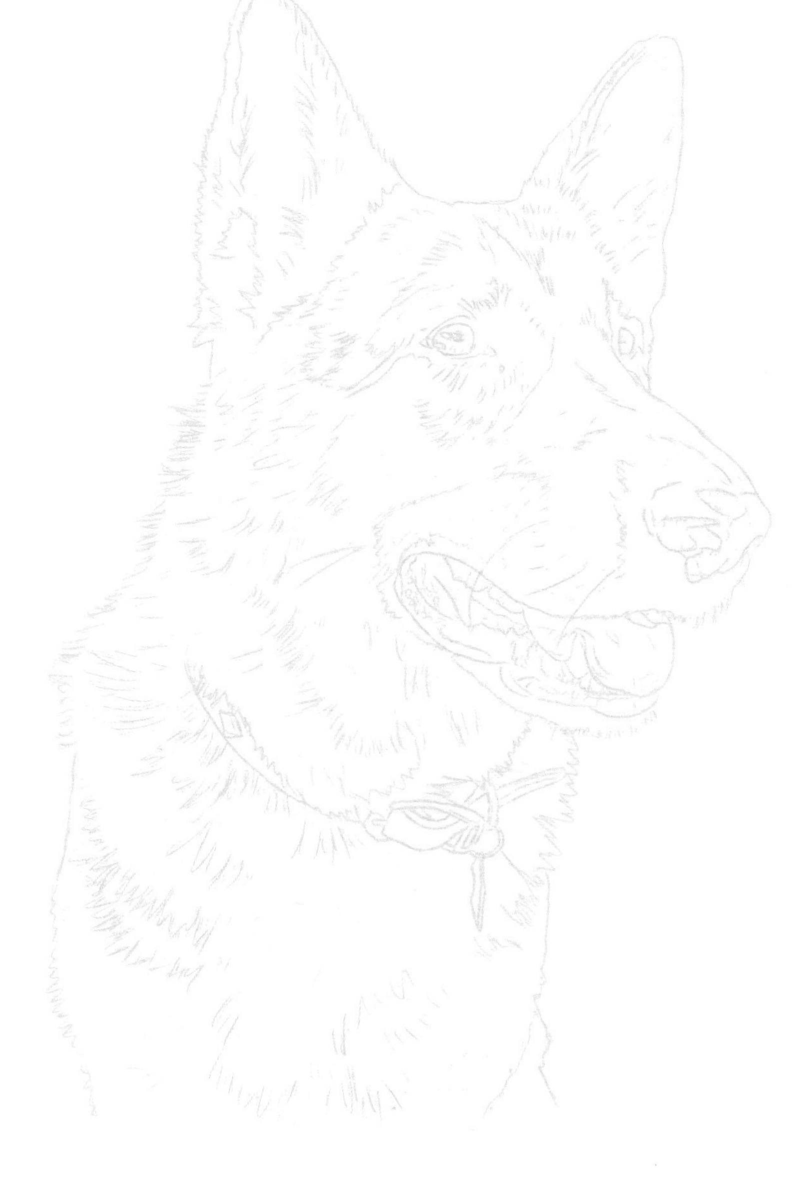

Adult Dog and Puppy

Adult dogs and puppies may have the same body, but their proportions are quite different. Proportion is the relationship between one part and another. Only when the proportions of a subject are correct does a likeness to the original emerge. A puppy is not simply a miniature dog. Puppies are more compact. Their eyes, ears, and especially their paws appear too large in relation to their body. Adult dogs are longer, narrower, and taller than puppies. The muzzle is noticeably long, and the teeth are large. Keep these differences in mind while drawing if your goal is to create a skillful portrait.

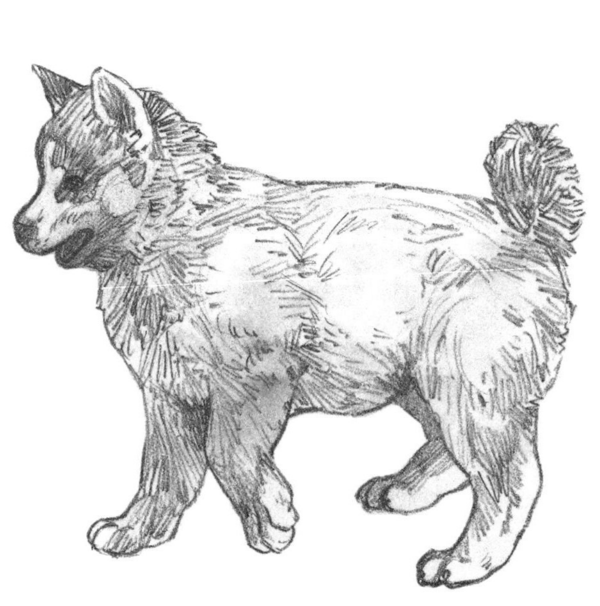

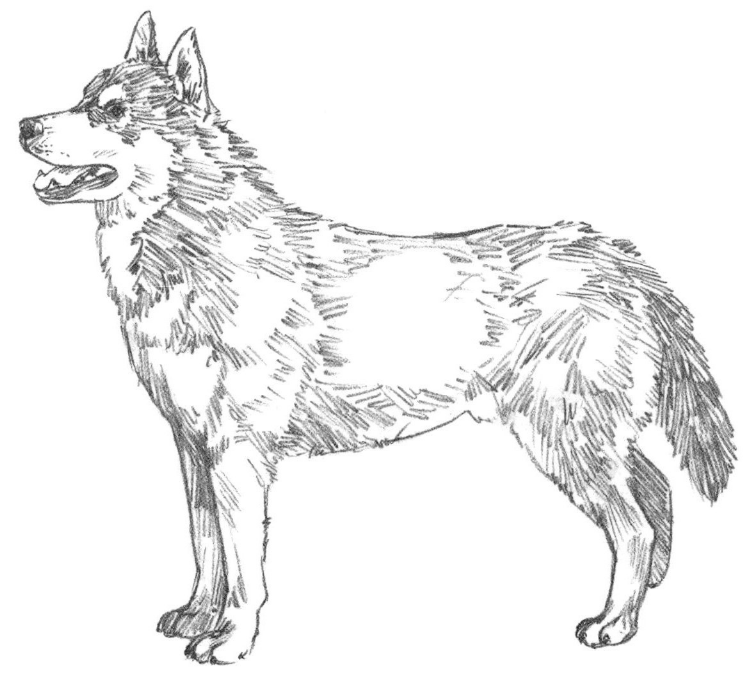

Develop this puppy using a variety of pencils to capture the details, including its wiry fur and compact body.

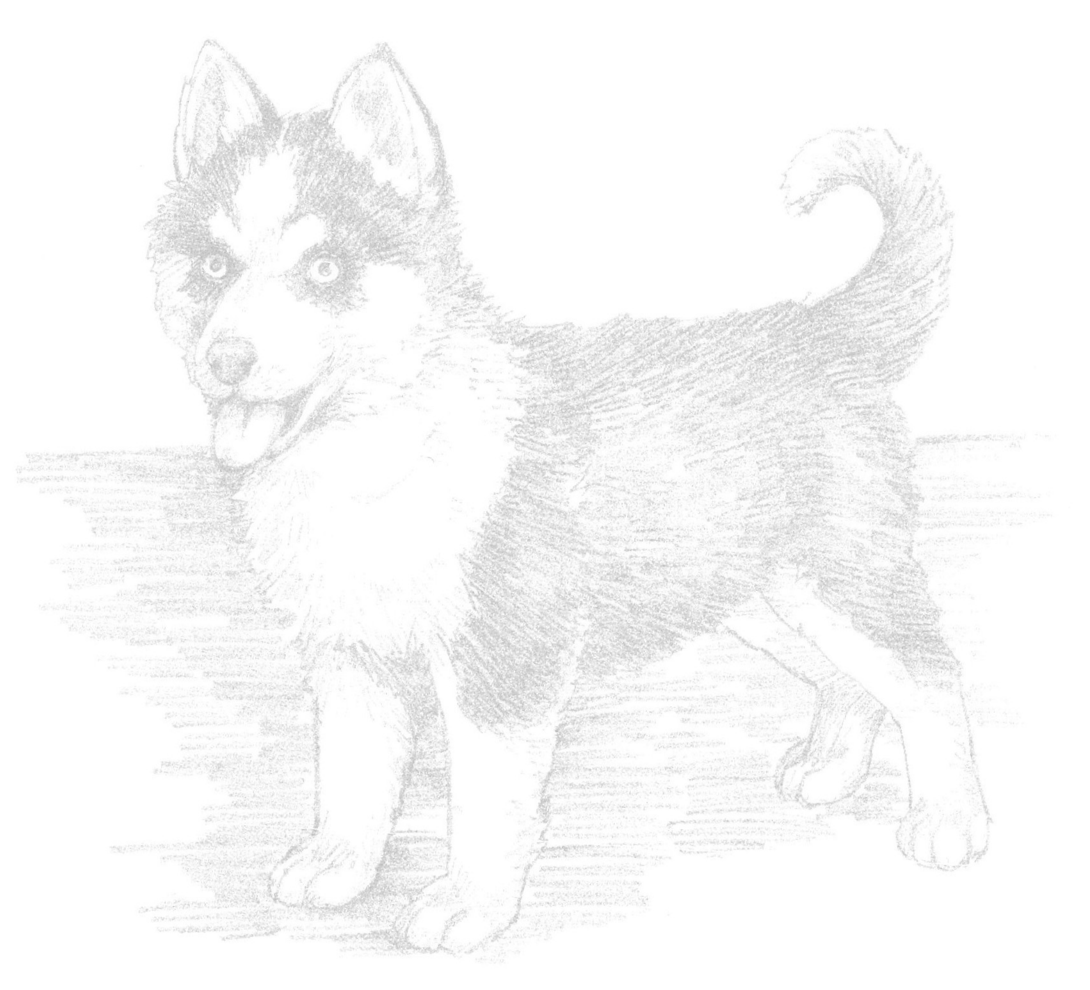

English Bulldog

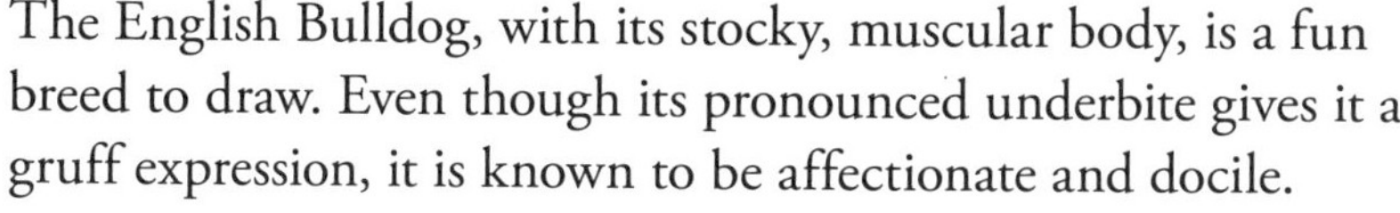

The English Bulldog, with its stocky, muscular body, is a fun breed to draw. Even though its pronounced underbite gives it a gruff expression, it is known to be affectionate and docile.

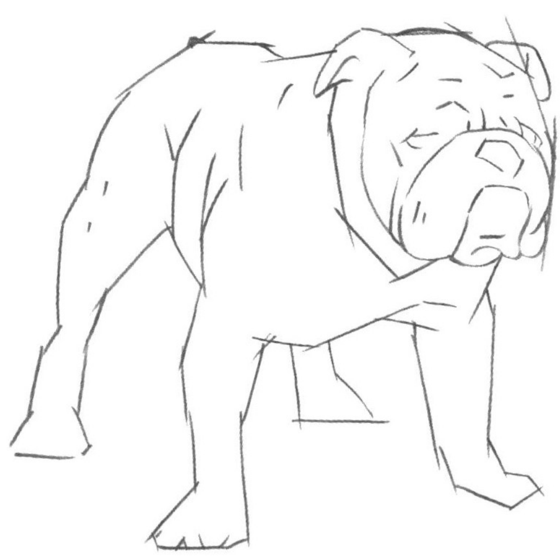

1 As you refine the shape, study the low placement of the eyes. Notice the flat nose that appears to be pushed into the face.

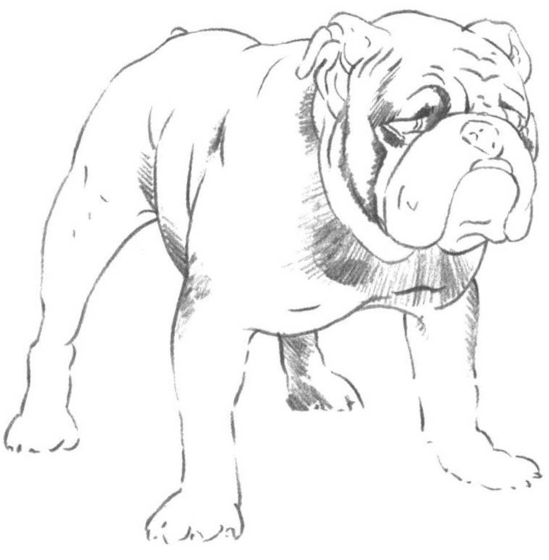

2 Begin shading with a sharp 2B pencil, developing the folds on the face and the contours and shadows along the body. Keep the pencil fairly sharp to make the folds distinct and the fur smooth.

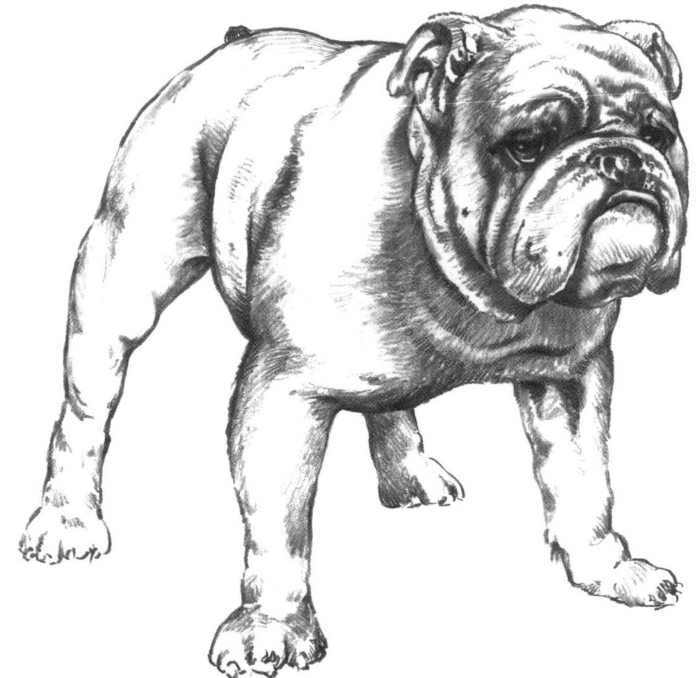

3 Use a sharp pencil to add the details in the eyes. As in all the drawings, work at your own pace, and don't rush when shading the fur. Your attention to detail will be apparent in the final rendering.

Trace the outline below, paying attention to the many folds in this breed's stocky body. Accentuate the folds with dark shading, applying strokes in the direction of hair growth.

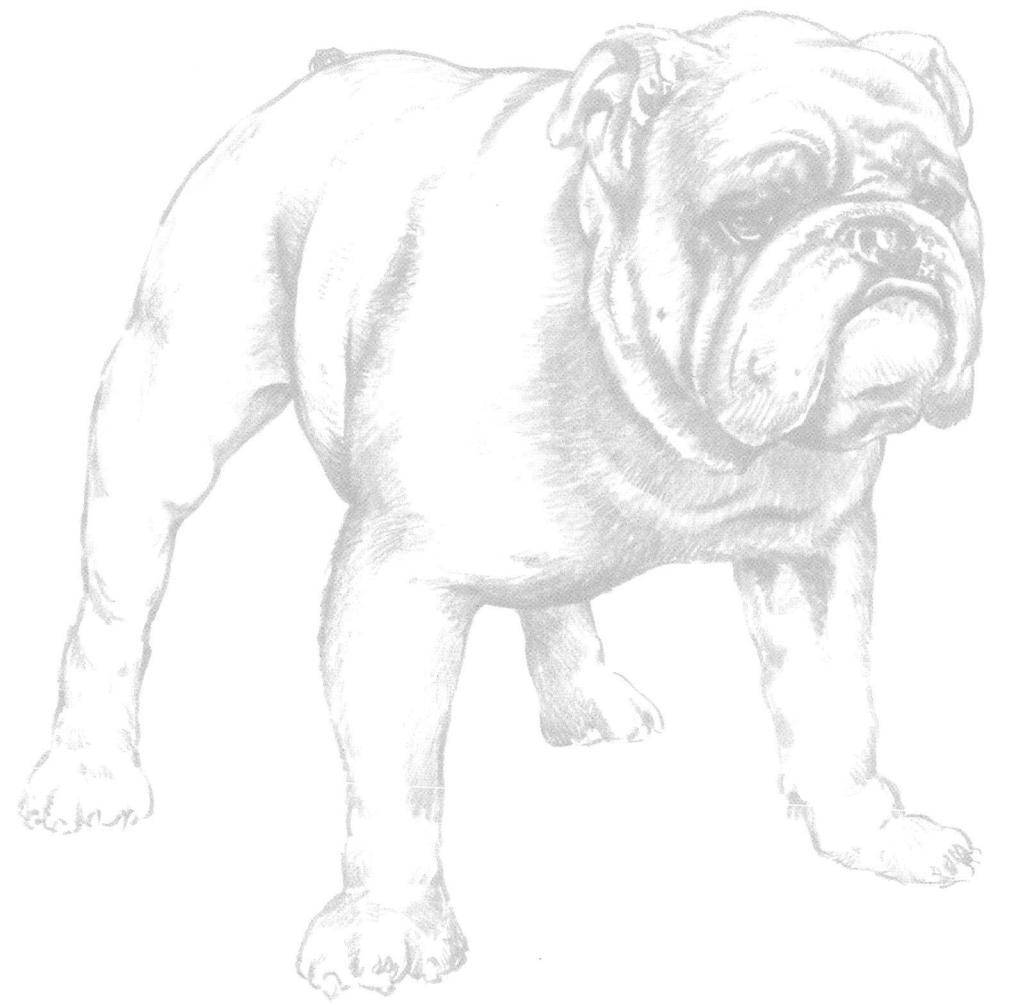

Doberman Pinscher

Doberman Pinschers are known for their sleek, dark coats. When drawing the shiny coat, be sure to sketch in the direction of hair growth—even in breeds with short, sleek coats.

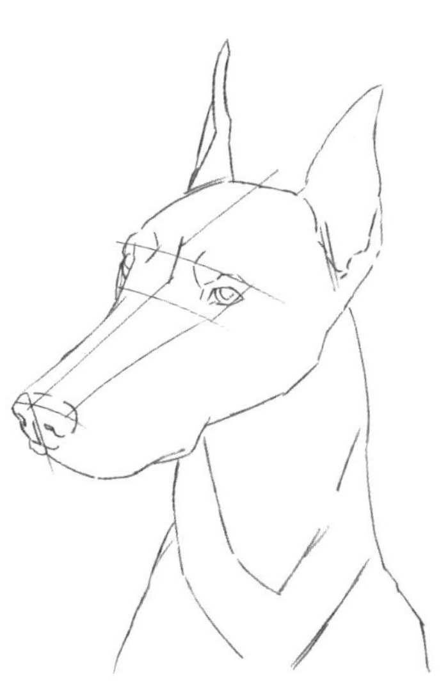

1 Block in the head and neck, and add guidelines for the face. Draw the eyes and nose.

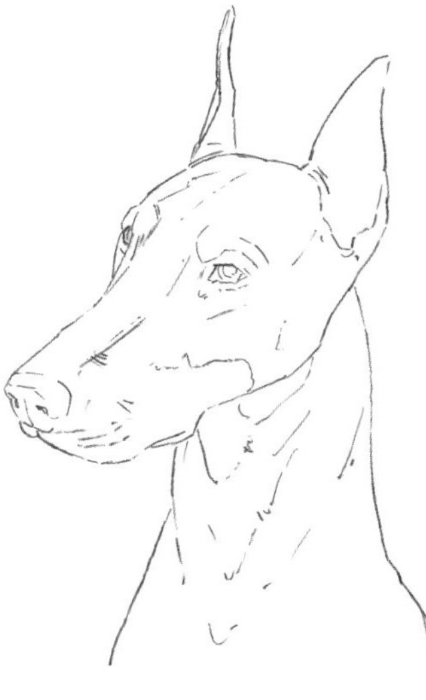

2 Erase any guidelines that are no longer needed. Then, draw a few short strokes to indicate a bit of fur.

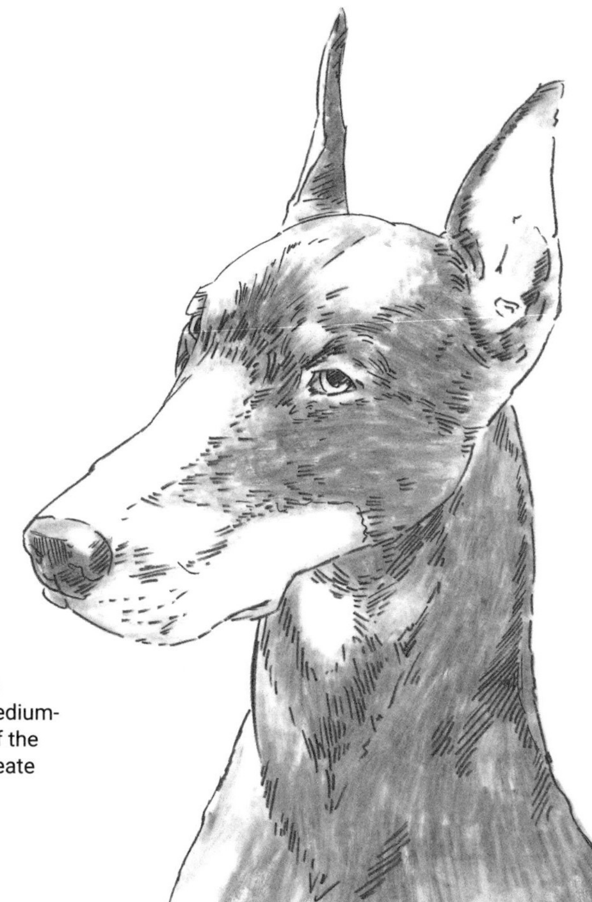

3 Now fill in the remaining darks. First, create some graphite dust by rubbing a pencil over a sheet of fine sandpaper. Then, pick up the graphite dust with a medium-sized blending stump, and shade in the dark areas of the dog's fur and nose. To avoid hard edges, blend to create soft gradations where the two values meet.

Practice shading using graphite dust and a blending stump.
Continue to add details to create a realistic portrait.

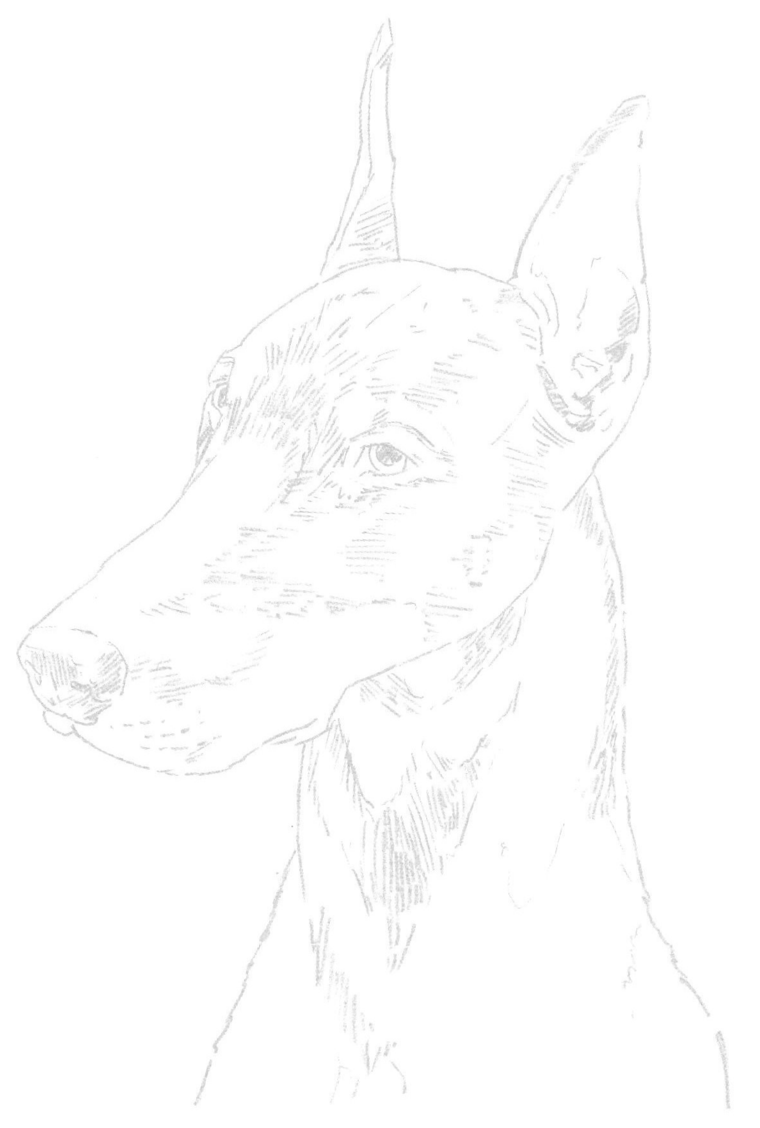

Focusing on Contrast

When working with a light-colored dog, it's particularly important to diminish the level of detail in the background. Light-colored dogs don't have much contrast in their hair, so the background elements can compete for attention. Refrain from adding too many background details to keep the viewer's focus on the dog.

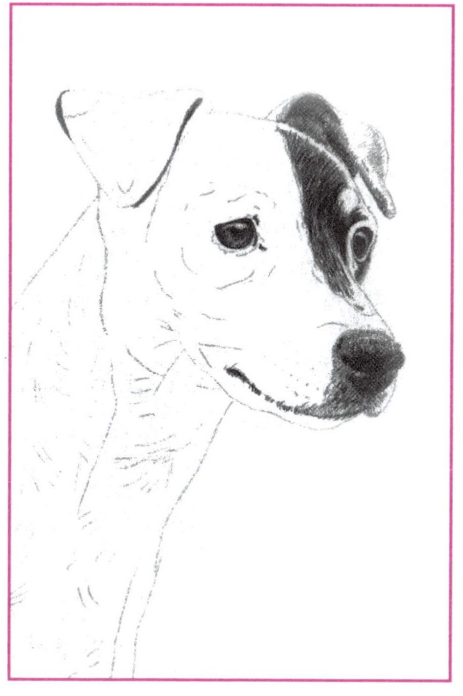

1 After developing a basic likeness, use a 5B pencil to block in the darkest areas, including the eyes, the shadow on the nose, the mouth, and edges of the ears. Darken the black patch around its left eye as well.

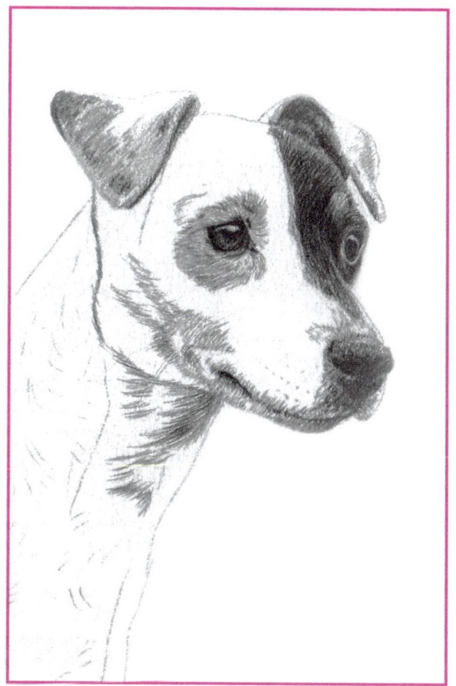

2 With a sharp H pencil, apply mid-tones to add hair around the eyes and on the mouth, cheekbone, jawline, and ears, applying short lines that follow the direction of hair growth.

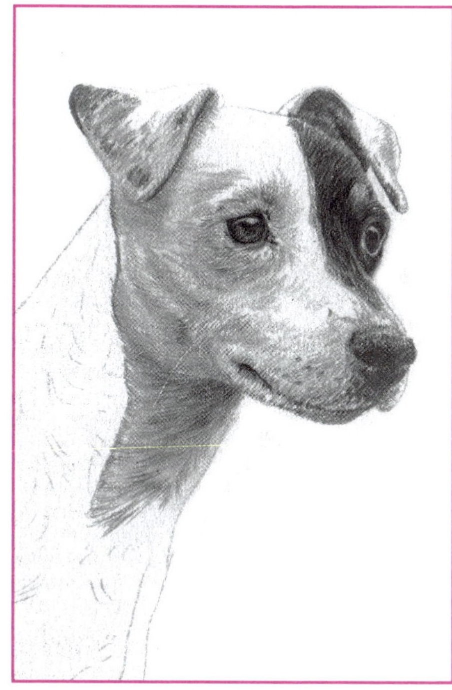

3 Use an H pencil and short strokes to add the lightest areas of hair over the face, gradually fading out the strokes toward the top of the head. Add mid-value dots near the mouth to mark where whiskers grow.

Using everything you've learned to this point, complete a finished portrait of this Jack Russell terrier. Use the additional space to practice techniques, such as rendering fur and shading.

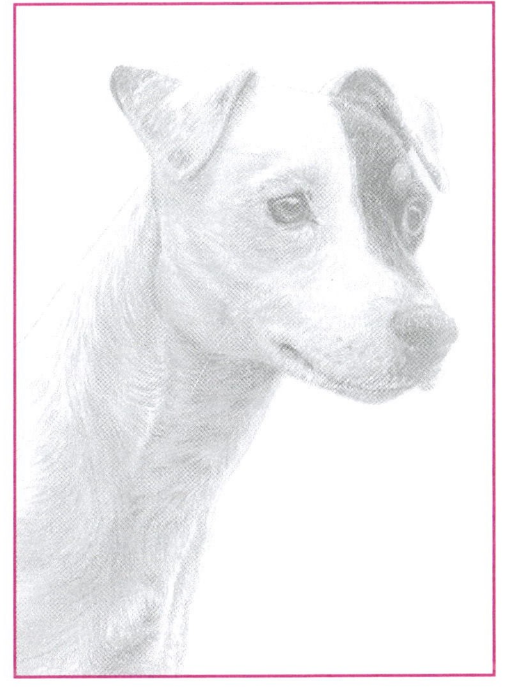

Wolf

The wolf has a relatively large head with a broad forehead, a long muzzle, and short, rounded ears that point forward. Its eyes are set close together and are slightly slanted.

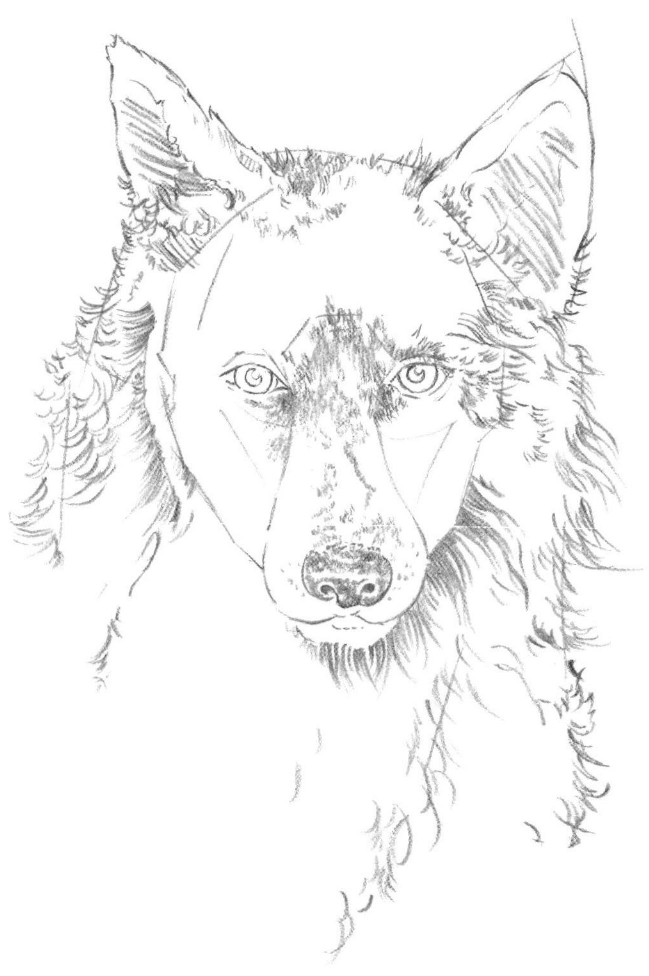

1 Detail the wolf's fur and face, including the eyes and nose. Leave some areas on the ears, forehead, and front of the snout white. Lift out light reflections with a kneaded eraser.

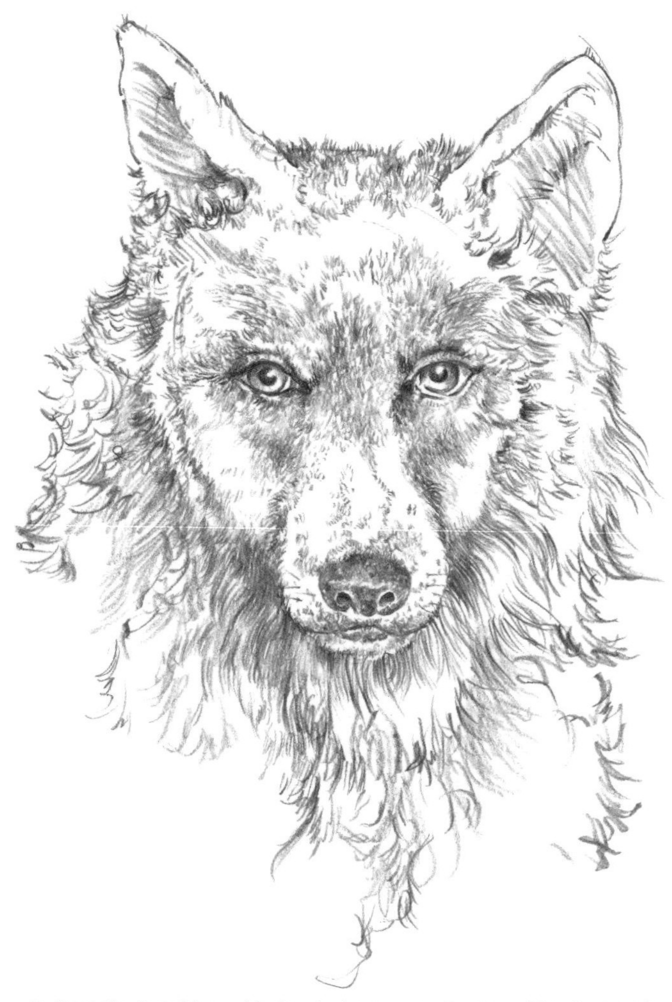

2 Start the hatching with the darkest tones in areas like the inside of the ears or under the muzzle. Create the fur using different shades of gray and different strokes and lines to render the fur as realistically as possible.

Draw a wolf below. Carefully develop the eyes, facial features, and fur using a variety of strokes and squiggles.

Cat Head

Most typical cats have a rounded head with a short face marked by protruding cheekbones and a short muzzle. Studying the underlying structure of the skull is helpful for drawing a realistic, proportional head.

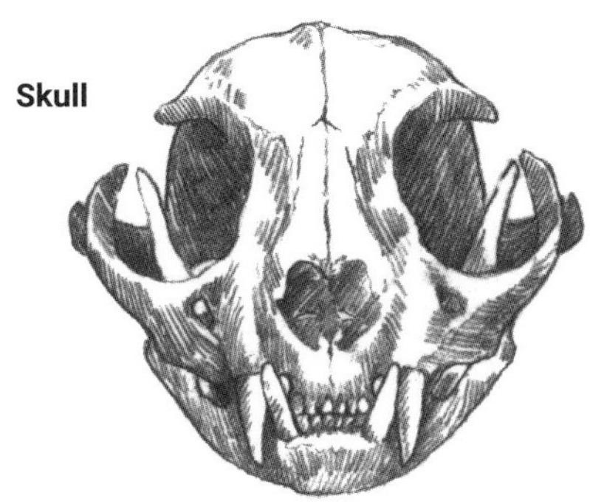

Remember the underlying form of the skull to help you keep the facial features in proper proportion.

Although all cats' heads are basically the same shape, profiles do vary among breeds. Be sure to study the shape of your subject's head before drawing it. Notice whether the cat's face is flat, pointed, or square. Look at the position of the nose compared with the eyes, and the eyes with the top of the head. Check the proportions of all the features before getting started. Begin by lightly roughing in the basic shape. Then refine the shape until you achieve a likeness to the subject. Draw your cat subject from different angles.

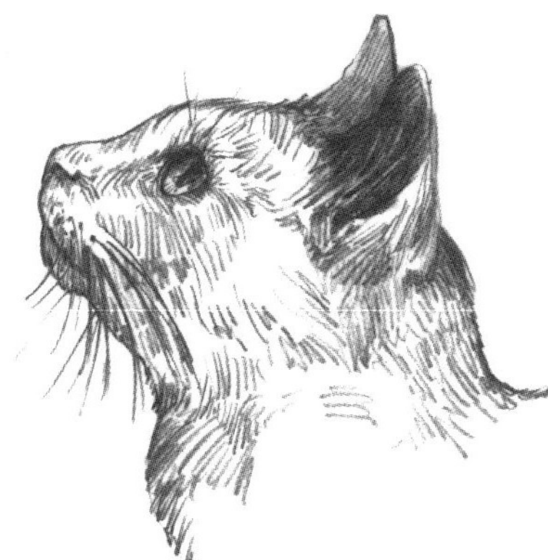

This cat has an angular profile, wedge-shaped nose, and large, pointed ears typical of short-haired breeds.

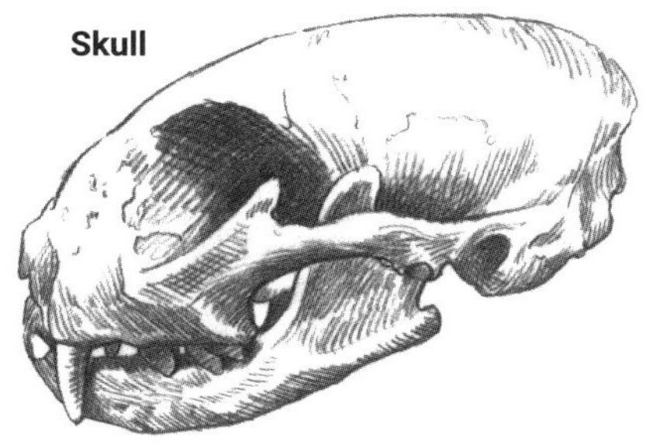

When rendering cats (or any subject), it is best to work from live models or photographs. Trying to draw from memory or imagination is much more difficult. Collect photos of cats and kittens from catalogs, magazines, and books, and keep them in a file for future reference.

Practice drawing some cat heads in the area below using reference photos—or draw from a live model if possible!

Cat Features

Cats have individual faces—and their facial features also reflect the characteristics of different breeds. Focus on mastering the individual features of the face, such as the ears, eyes, nose, and whiskers, before combining them to create a portrait.

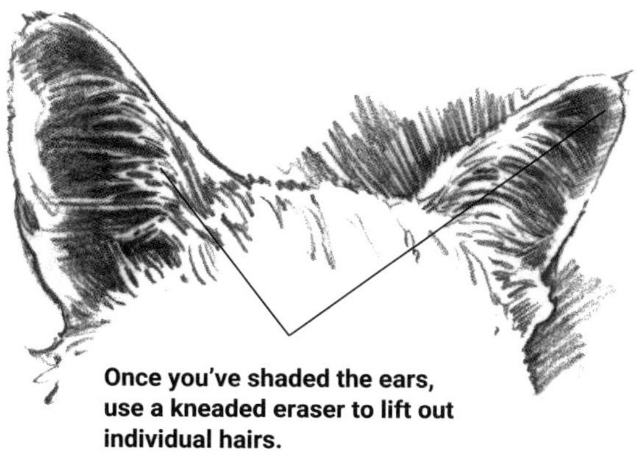

Once you've shaded the ears, use a kneaded eraser to lift out individual hairs.

Many cats have almond-shaped eyes. Sketch the eyes in proportion to each other. Here, the cat's head is turned at an angle, so the eye closest to the viewer will be slightly larger. Once you've nailed the basic shape, focus on the iris, individual hairs, and the fur around the eye.

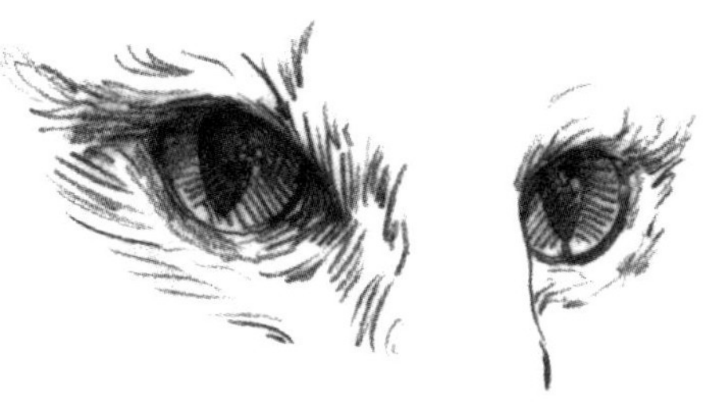

Sketch the ears as triangles using an HB pencil. Continue to shape and soften them so they look rounded and natural.

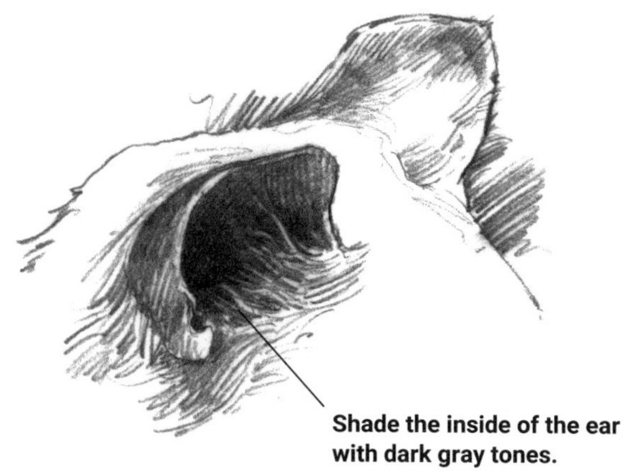

Shade the inside of the ear with dark gray tones.

Always draw hair in the direction of growth.

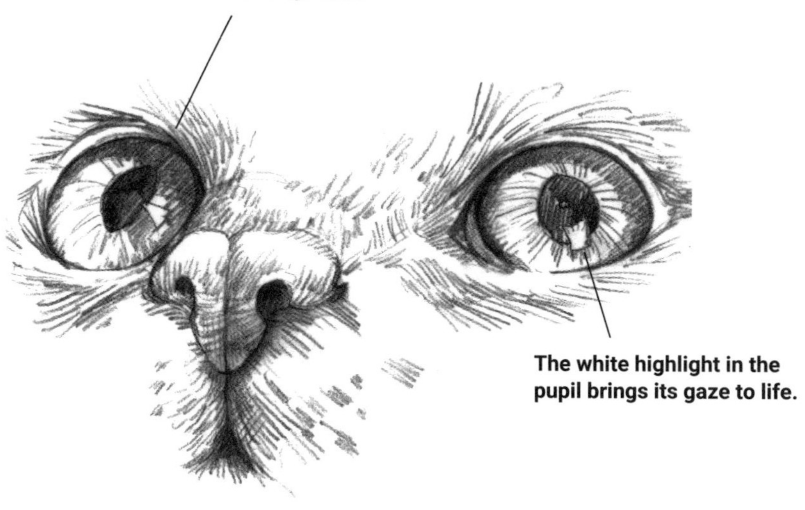

The white highlight in the pupil brings its gaze to life.

Cats have triangular noses, and their closed mouths look like an upside-down Y.

Draw the long, stiff whiskers with sweeping strokes using a sharpened pencil. Don't forget the dark spots on the muzzle!

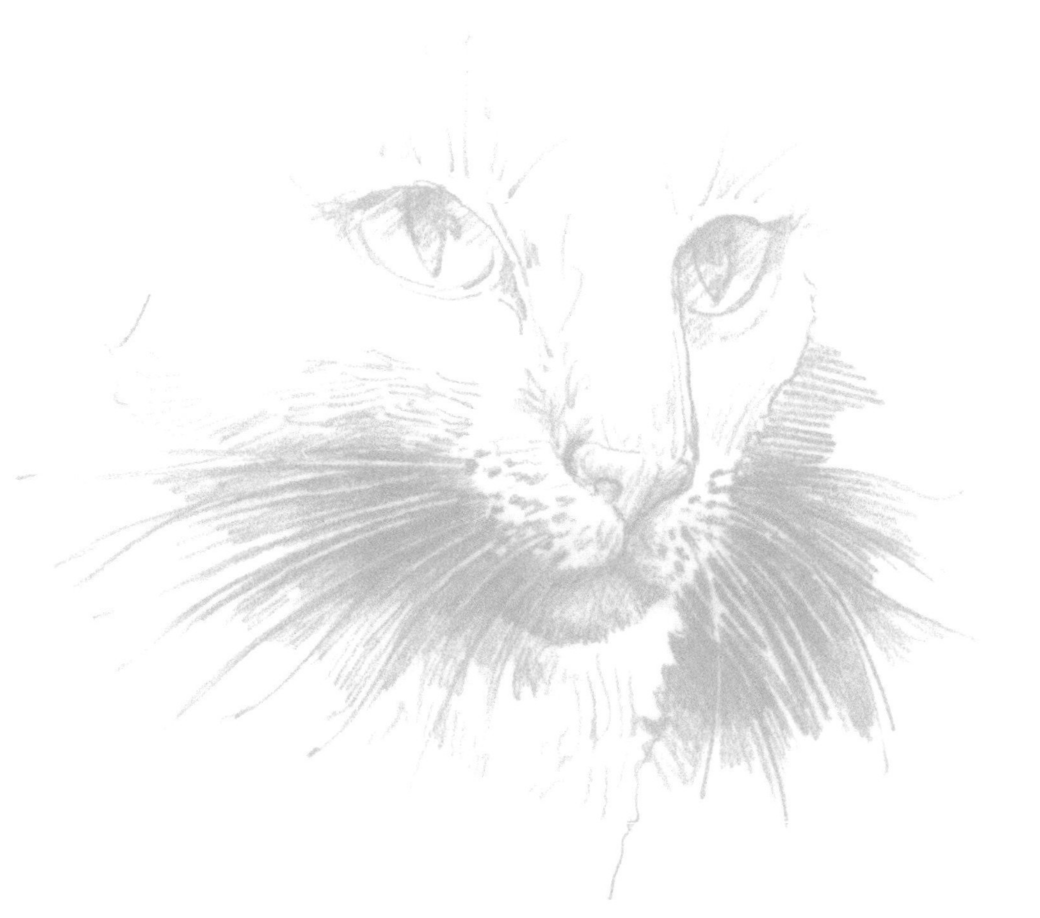

Cat Fur

Every cat breed has its own unique fur—long or short, soft or thick, striped or solid. You can easily depict different fur types using the techniques shown here. And you don’t have to draw every hair individually.

Solid-Colored Fur

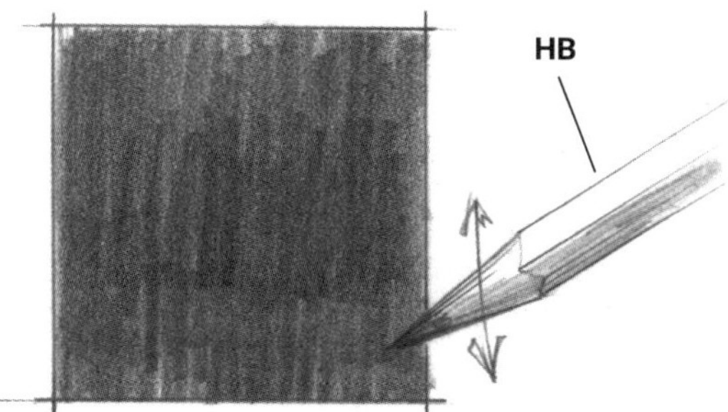

1 Cover the surface evenly with the side of an HB pencil and vertical strokes. Apply several layers.

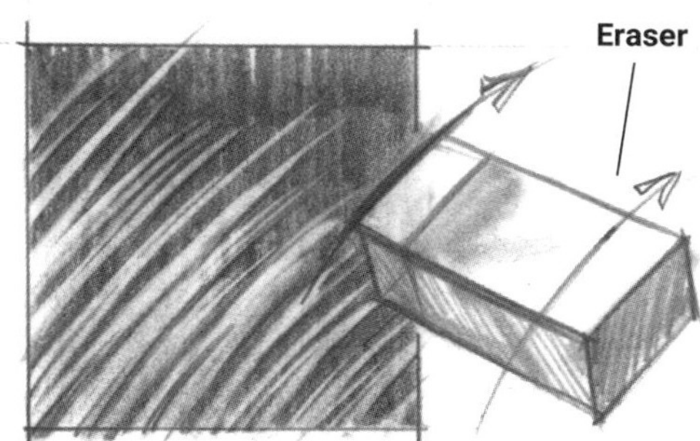

2 Erase individual light hairs in the direction of hair growth. Lift the eraser at the end to create a nice hair tip.

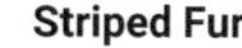

Striped Fur

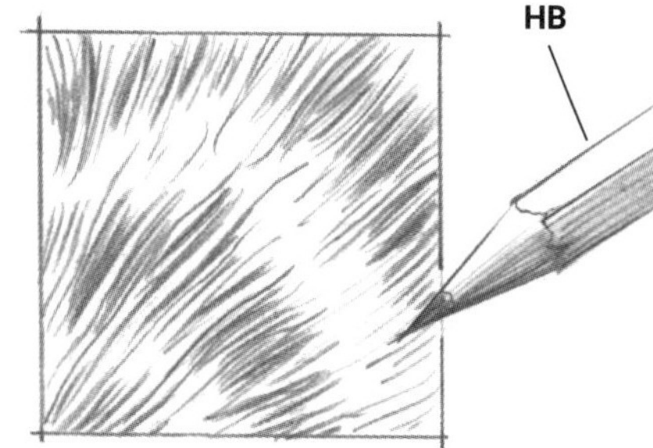

1 Using an HB pencil, draw the dark fur areas first.

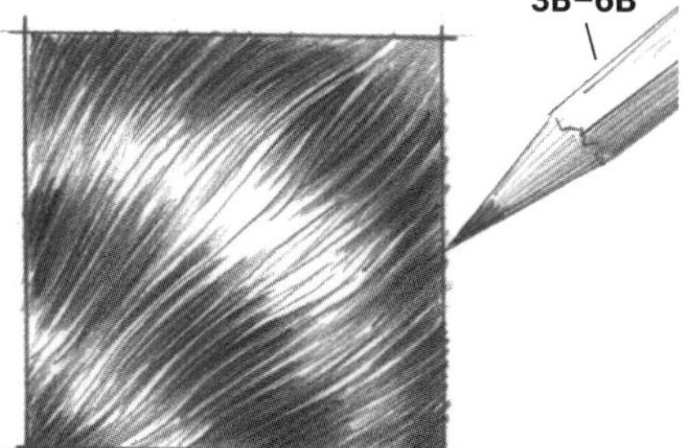

2 Work out the structure and details with pencils between 3B and 6B. Soften transitions with a blending stump.

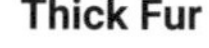

Thick Fur

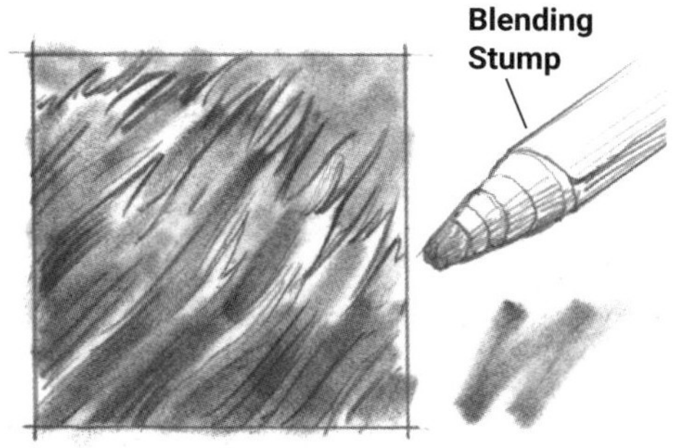

1 Apply thin lines with an HB pencil; then smudge some lines with a blending stump.

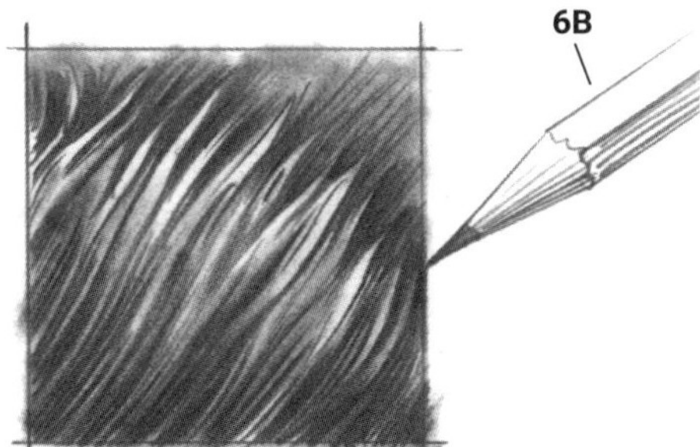

2 Using a sharp 6B pencil, rework the fur texture in the direction of hair growth. Lift out highlights with an eraser.

Using HB, 2B, and 6B pencils, an eraser, and a blending stump, draw whiskers and fur in the spaces provided.

Whiskers

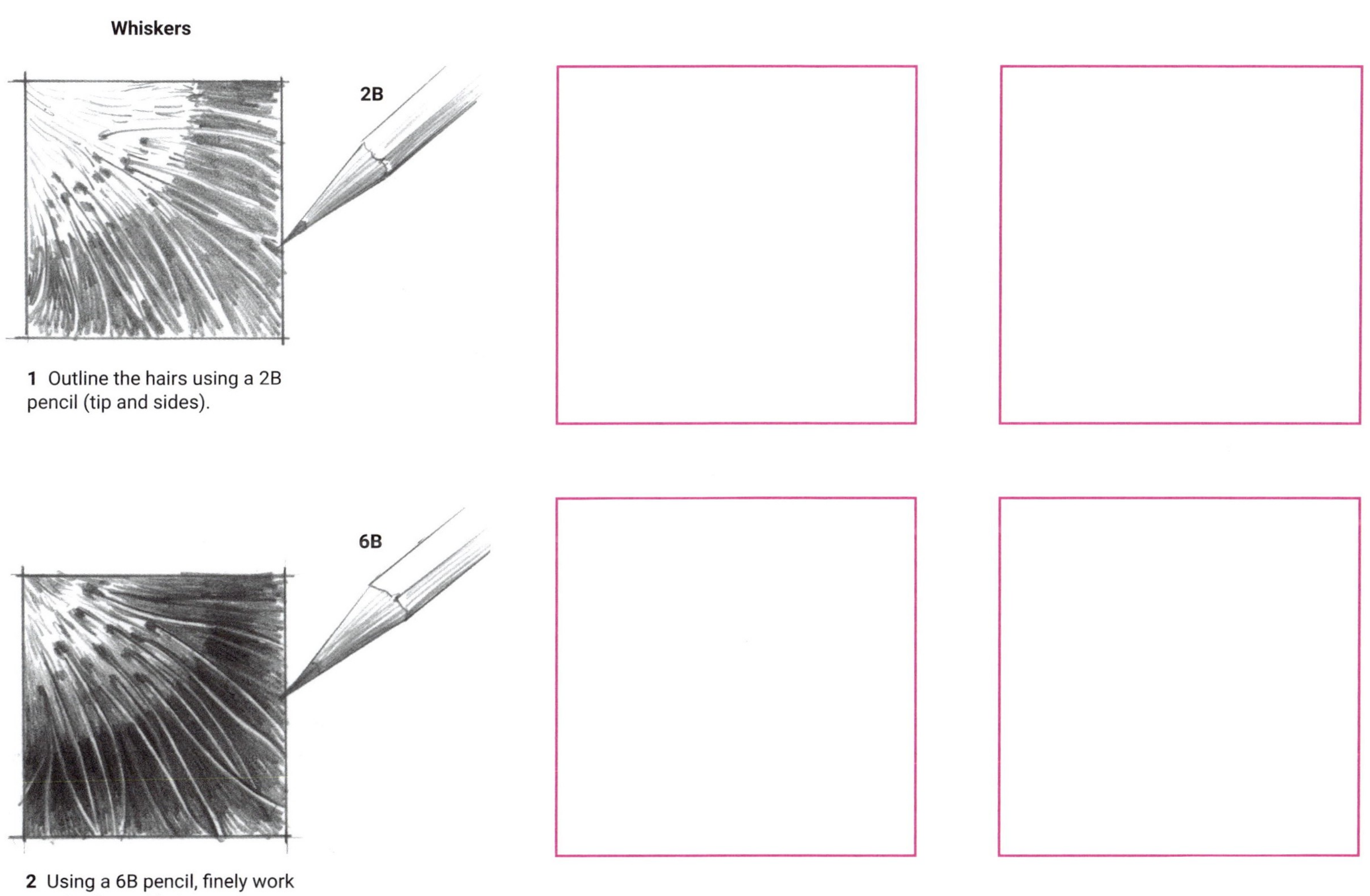

1 Outline the hairs using a 2B pencil (tip and sides).

2 Using a 6B pencil, finely work out the fur and hair.

Domestic Cat

Cats are among the most popular pets. This domestic tabby cat is particularly interesting due to its striped fur.

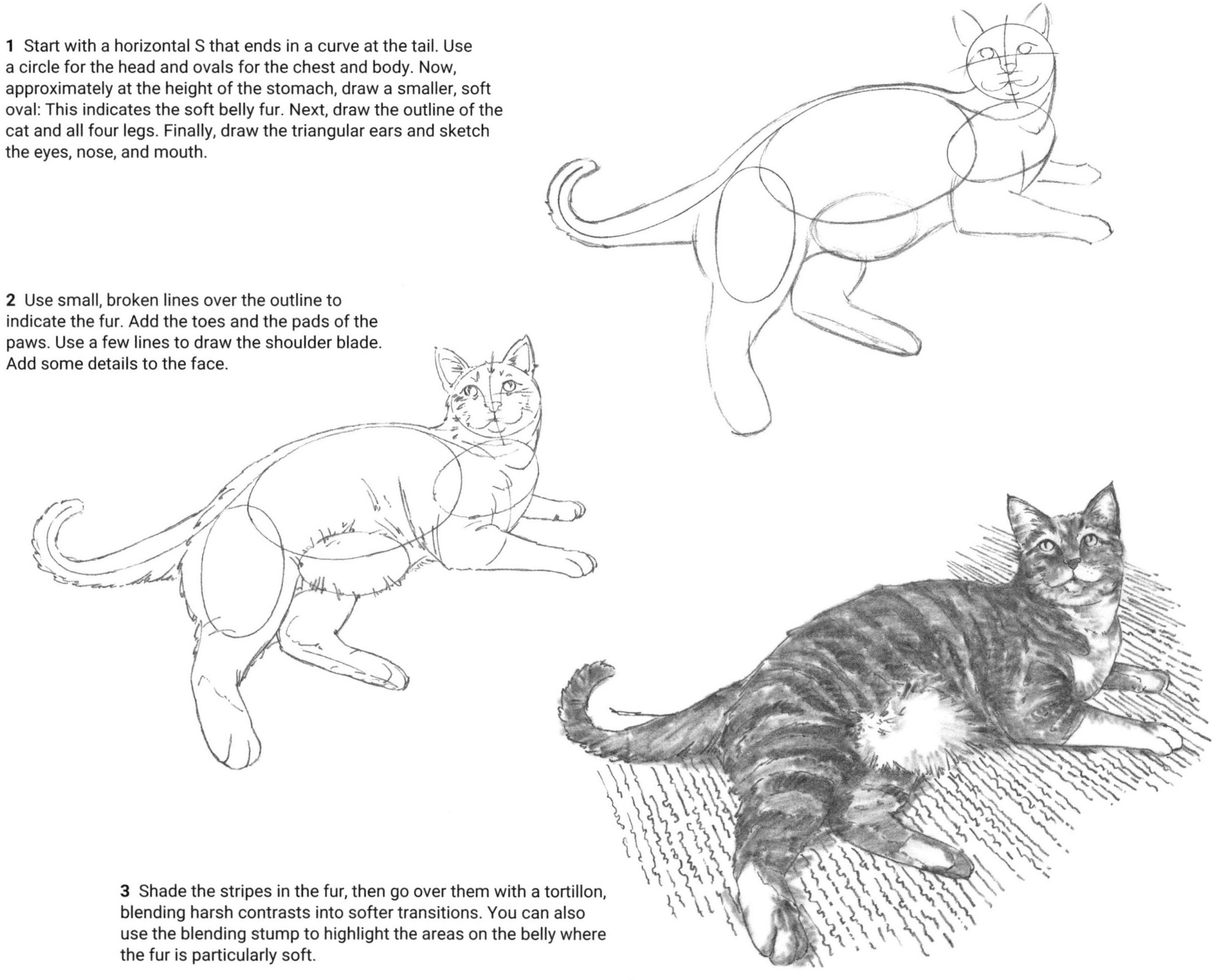

1 Start with a horizontal S that ends in a curve at the tail. Use a circle for the head and ovals for the chest and body. Now, approximately at the height of the stomach, draw a smaller, soft oval: This indicates the soft belly fur. Next, draw the outline of the cat and all four legs. Finally, draw the triangular ears and sketch the eyes, nose, and mouth.

2 Use small, broken lines over the outline to indicate the fur. Add the toes and the pads of the paws. Use a few lines to draw the shoulder blade. Add some details to the face.

3 Shade the stripes in the fur, then go over them with a tortillon, blending harsh contrasts into softer transitions. You can also use the blending stump to highlight the areas on the belly where the fur is particularly soft.

Use a variety of pencils, an eraser, and a blending stump to complete this drawing.

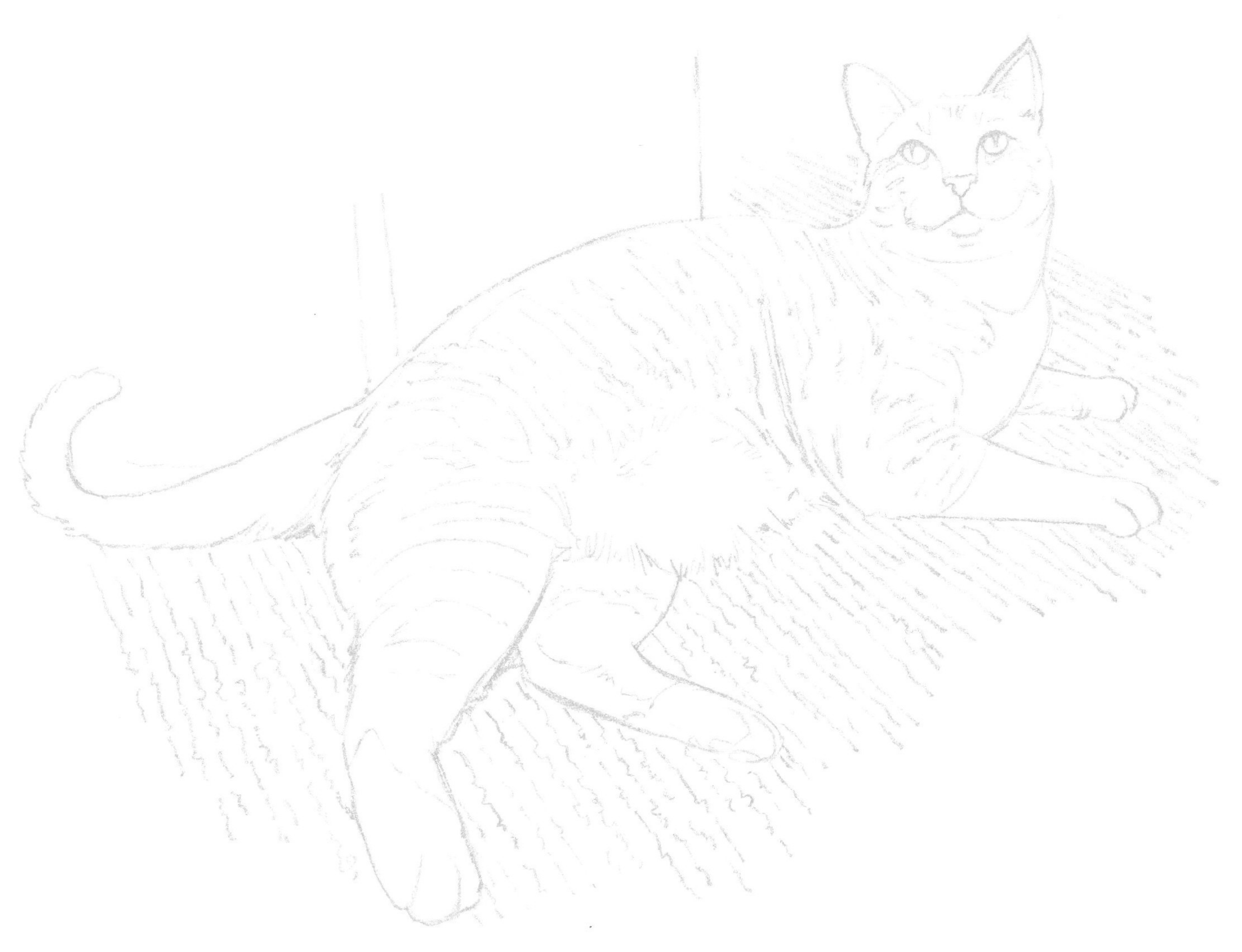

Grooming Cat

A cat grooming itself is an appealing subject—but it's quite a challenge to draw. As always, start with basic shapes and construction lines to create the outline. Work to ensure the body weight and features are in proportion before building out the details.

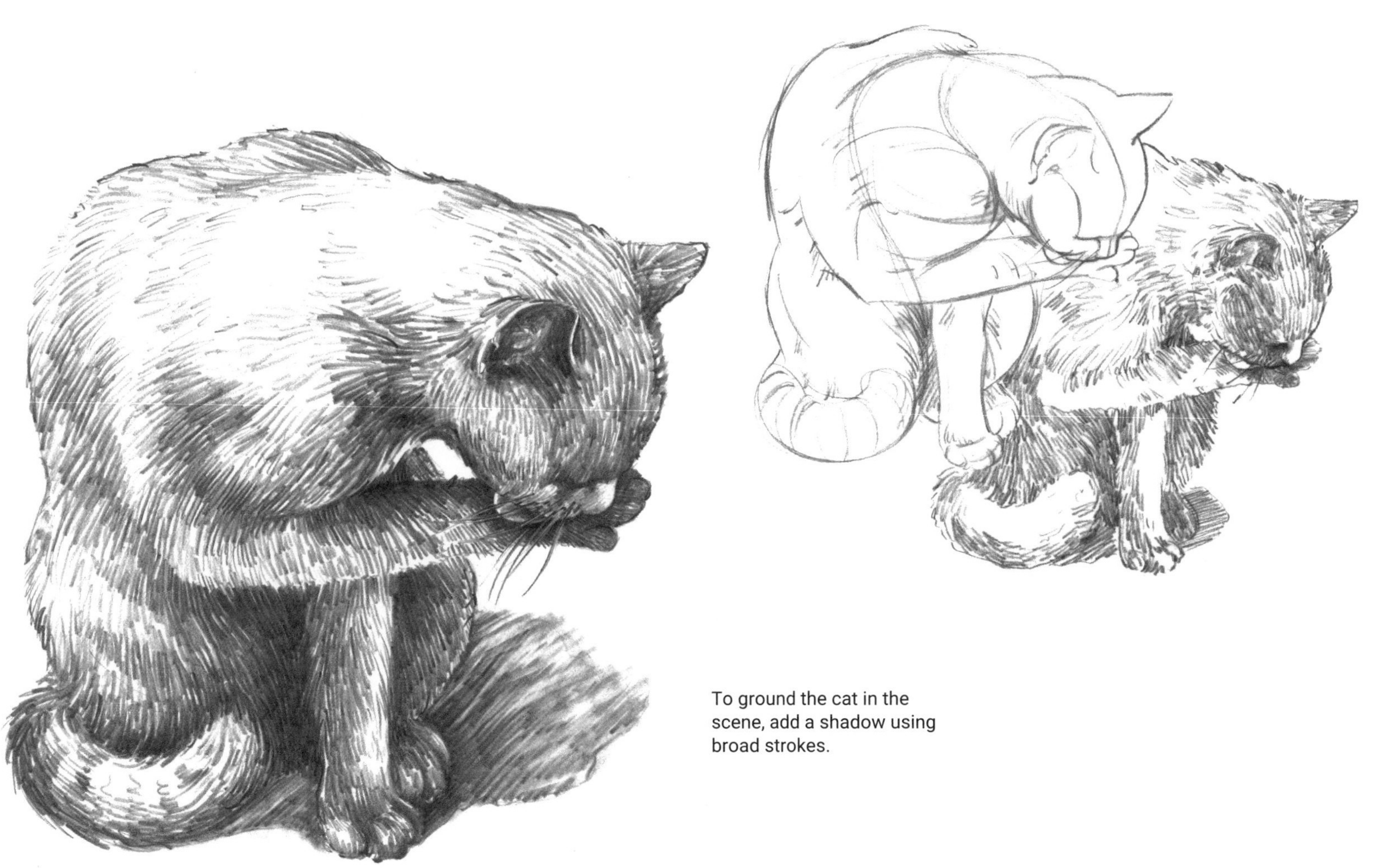

To ground the cat in the scene, add a shadow using broad strokes.

Even strokes create the impression of short, smooth, well-groomed fur. Use a 6B pencil to create dark areas of the fur. To add shine, vary the pressure and length of the strokes.

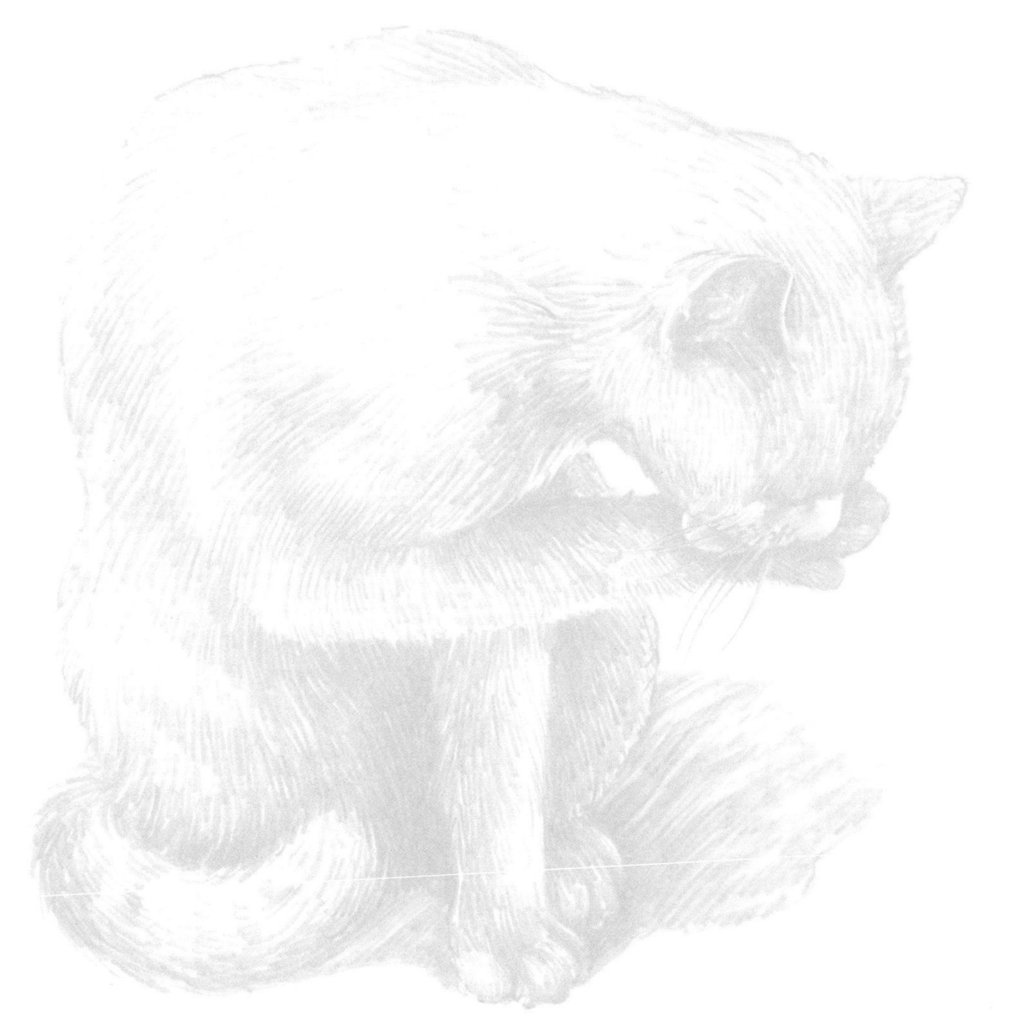

Short-Haired Cats

The cat is an agile animal. Its fine sense of balance allows it to prowl easily along narrow ledges or fences. This subject is slim and muscular with a narrow, wedge-shaped head, large ears, and long, thin tail.

Block in this pose carefully, using ovals for the chest and haunches. When you're comfortable with the body proportions, block in the legs and tail, as shown in step 1.

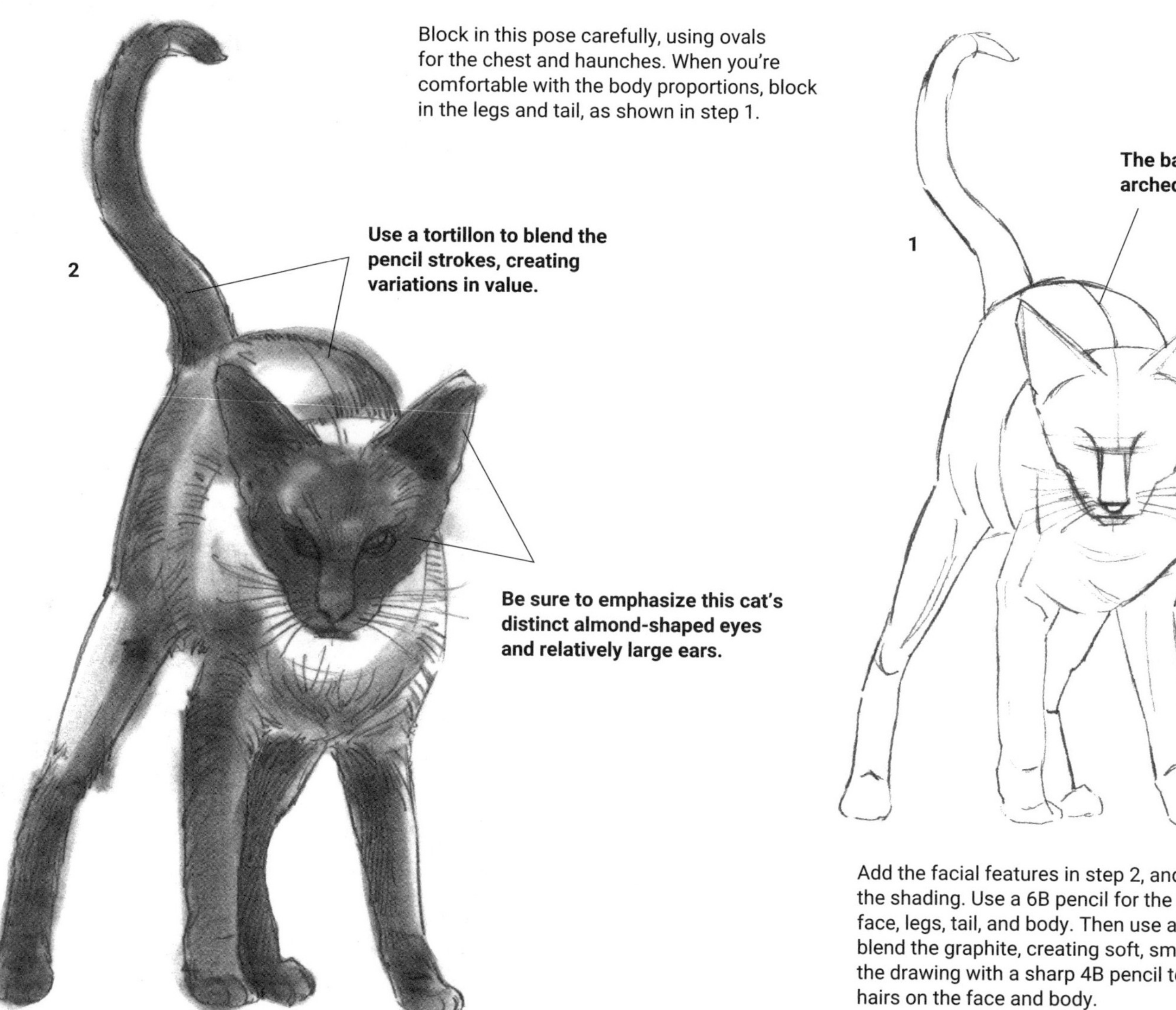

Add the facial features in step 2, and then develop the shading. Use a 6B pencil for the dark areas of the face, legs, tail, and body. Then use a paper stump to blend the graphite, creating soft, smudgy areas. Finish the drawing with a sharp 4B pencil to bring out the hairs on the face and body.

Trace the outline below, and then fill in the features and the shading of this cat. Take your time when applying shading.

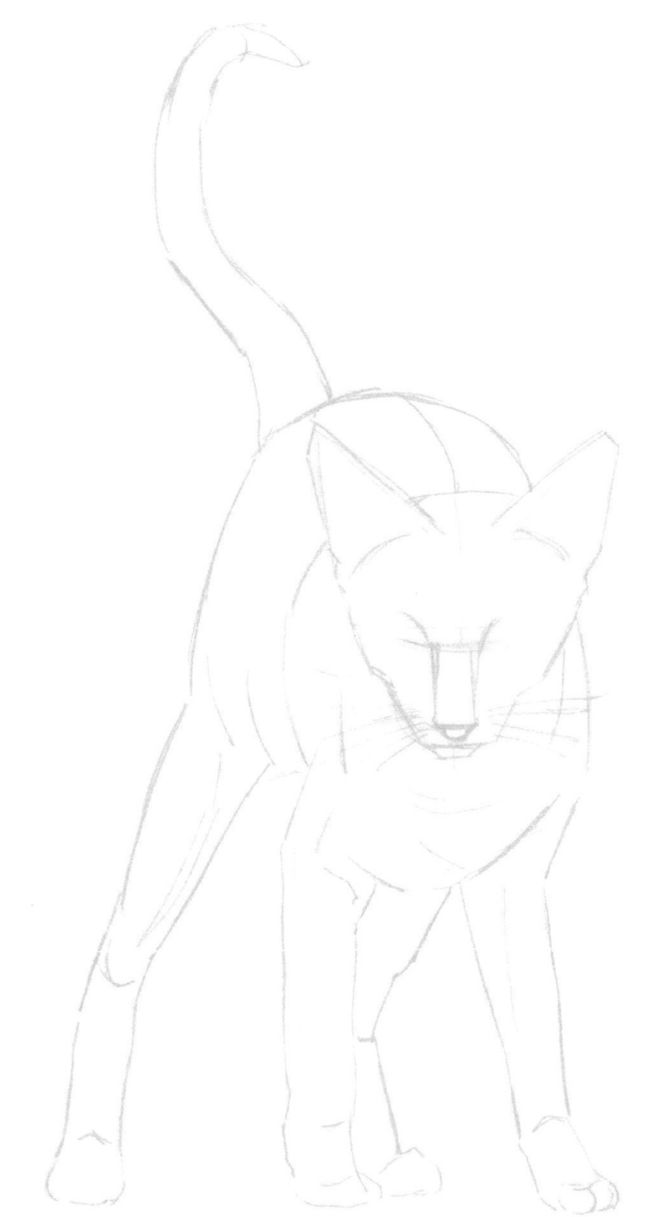

Rabbit

The rabbit has short, soft fur, which you can create using hatching and crosshatching. Use a variety of pencils for this portrait.

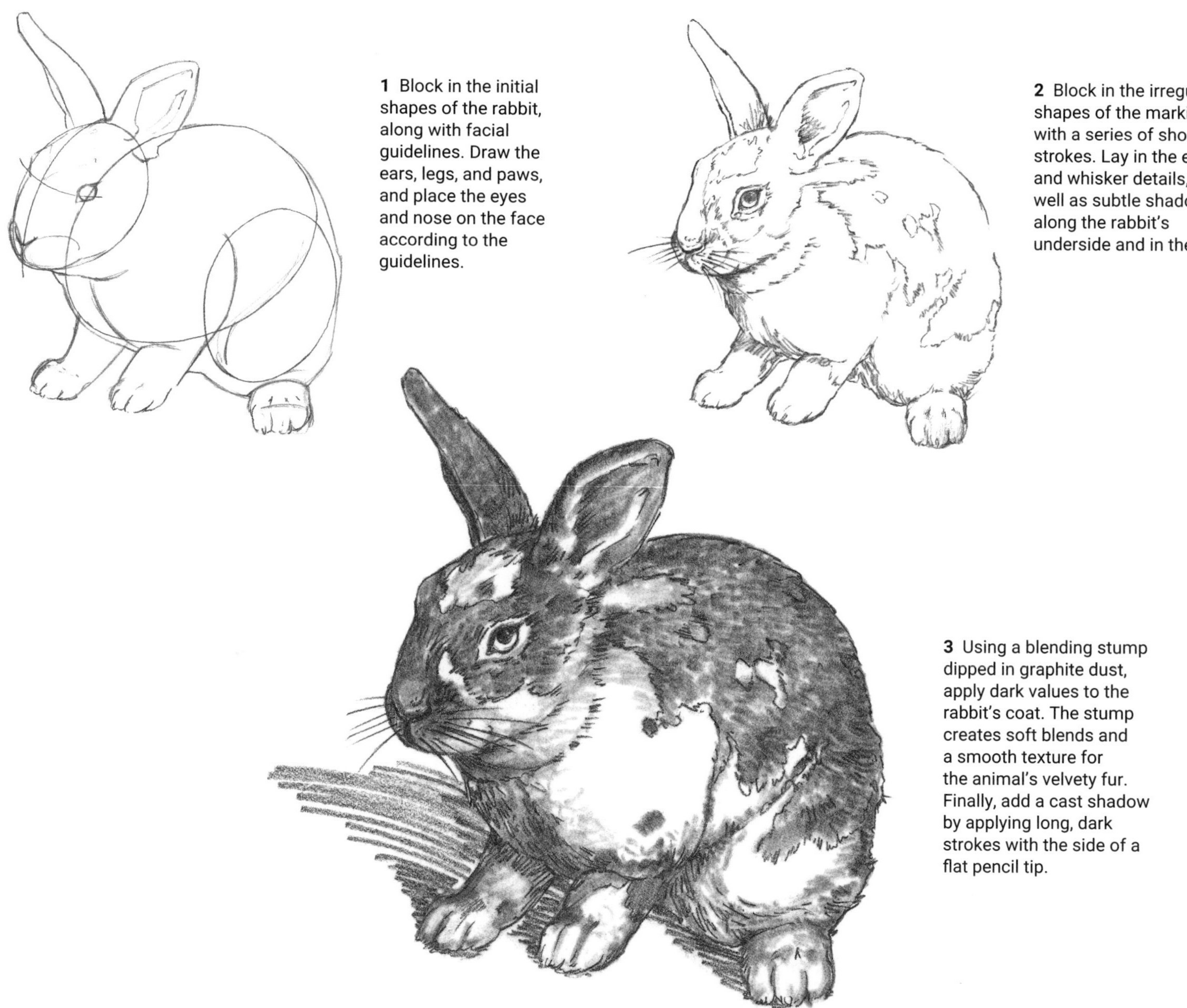

1 Block in the initial shapes of the rabbit, along with facial guidelines. Draw the ears, legs, and paws, and place the eyes and nose on the face according to the guidelines.

2 Block in the irregular shapes of the markings with a series of short strokes. Lay in the eye and whisker details, as well as subtle shadows along the rabbit's underside and in the ear.

3 Using a blending stump dipped in graphite dust, apply dark values to the rabbit's coat. The stump creates soft blends and a smooth texture for the animal's velvety fur. Finally, add a cast shadow by applying long, dark strokes with the side of a flat pencil tip.

Fill in the details of the rabbit using the outline below. Be sure to make the light and dark areas of the fur as vibrant as possible.

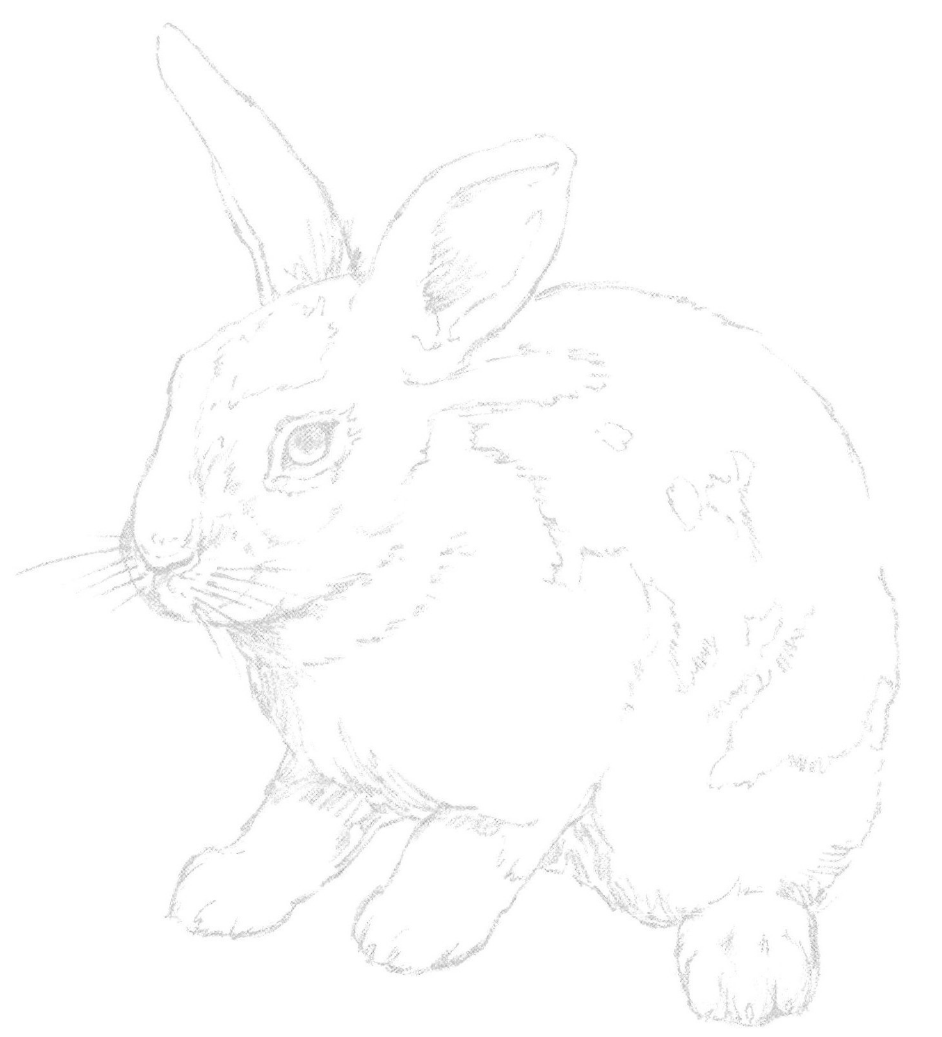

Guinea Pig

These balls of fluff have soft, silky coats; tiny little paws and ears; whiskers; and cute, curious eyes. A series of short hatch marks is enough to indicate fur in this project. Leave a tiny speck of white in the eye to show a glimmer of life.

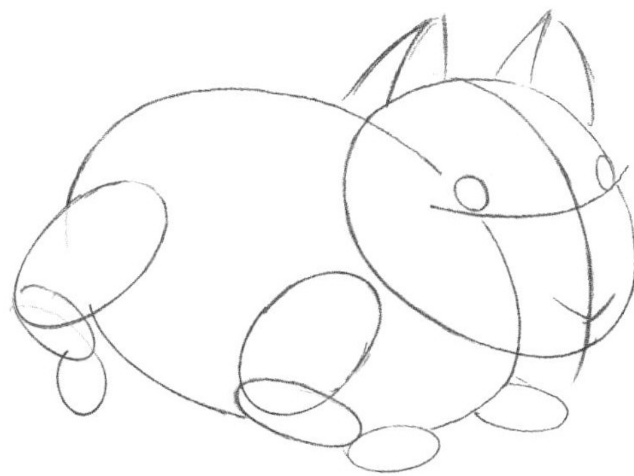

1 Establish the underlying structure, indicating the legs and paws with a series of ovals. Add the position of the ears and place the eyes just above the horizontal guideline.

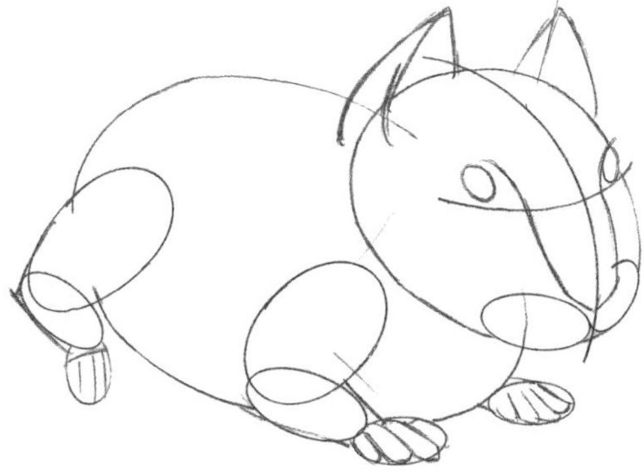

2 Begin to define the toes on the paws. Draw the shape of the nasal area with a U-shaped line. Then use small ovals to define the cheek pouches.

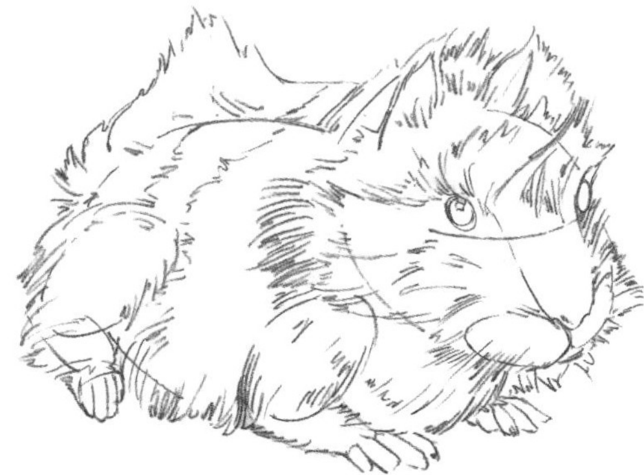

3 Begin to render the thick, furry coat around the basic structure, applying short strokes of varying thicknesses. It's much easier to work out the direction of fur growth and the overall shape of the animal when you know what is underneath.

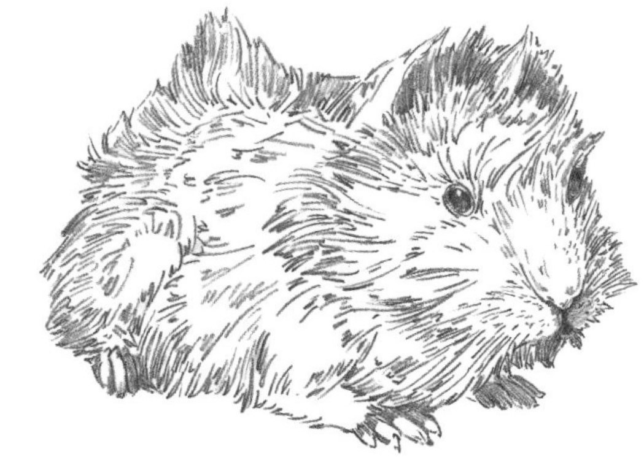

4 Erase any guidelines and continue to develop the fur. With the broad side of a pencil, stroke light shadows around the edges of the guinea pig to suggest its roundness.

Use a series of hatching marks and then apply shading with the side of a pencil to create the fur on the guinea pig.

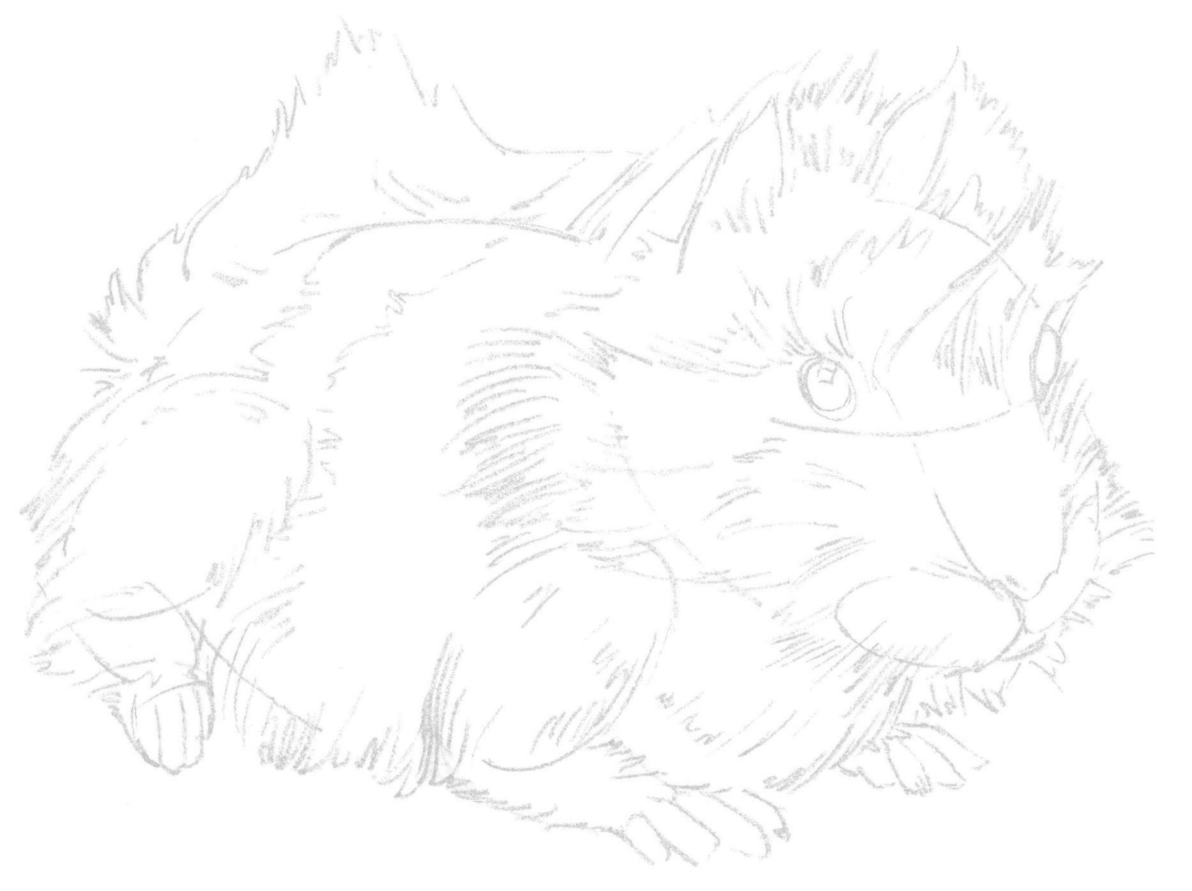

Ferret

The ferret is not a wild animal, but it was bred from wild polecats and belongs to the marten family. Typical features include an elongated body, strong legs, round ears, and a rounded snout.

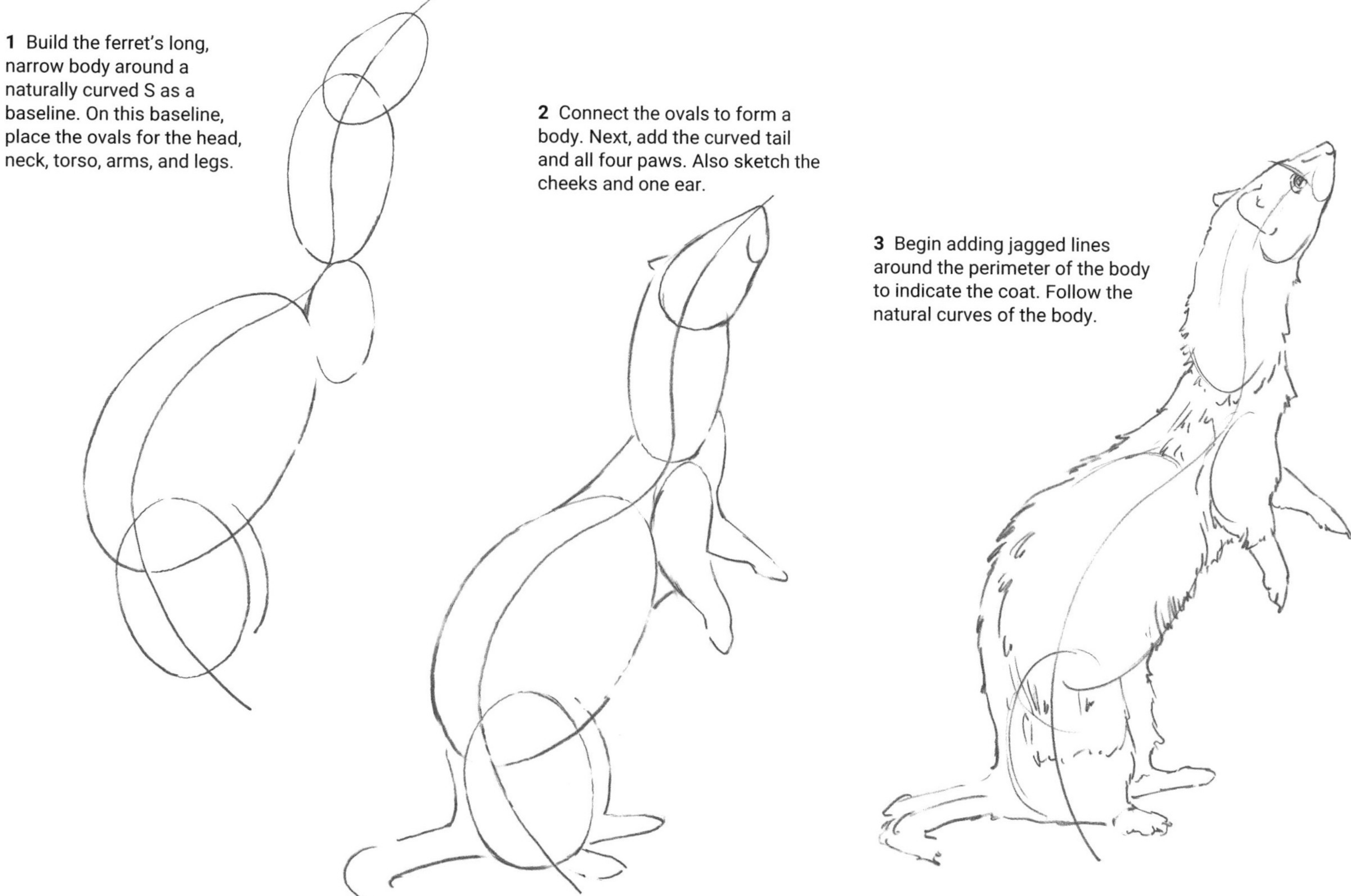

1 Build the ferret's long, narrow body around a naturally curved S as a baseline. On this baseline, place the ovals for the head, neck, torso, arms, and legs.

2 Connect the ovals to form a body. Next, add the curved tail and all four paws. Also sketch the cheeks and one ear.

3 Begin adding jagged lines around the perimeter of the body to indicate the coat. Follow the natural curves of the body.

Place the darkest strokes close together on the background limbs. This will make them appear to recede slightly, which enhances the spatial effect of the drawing.

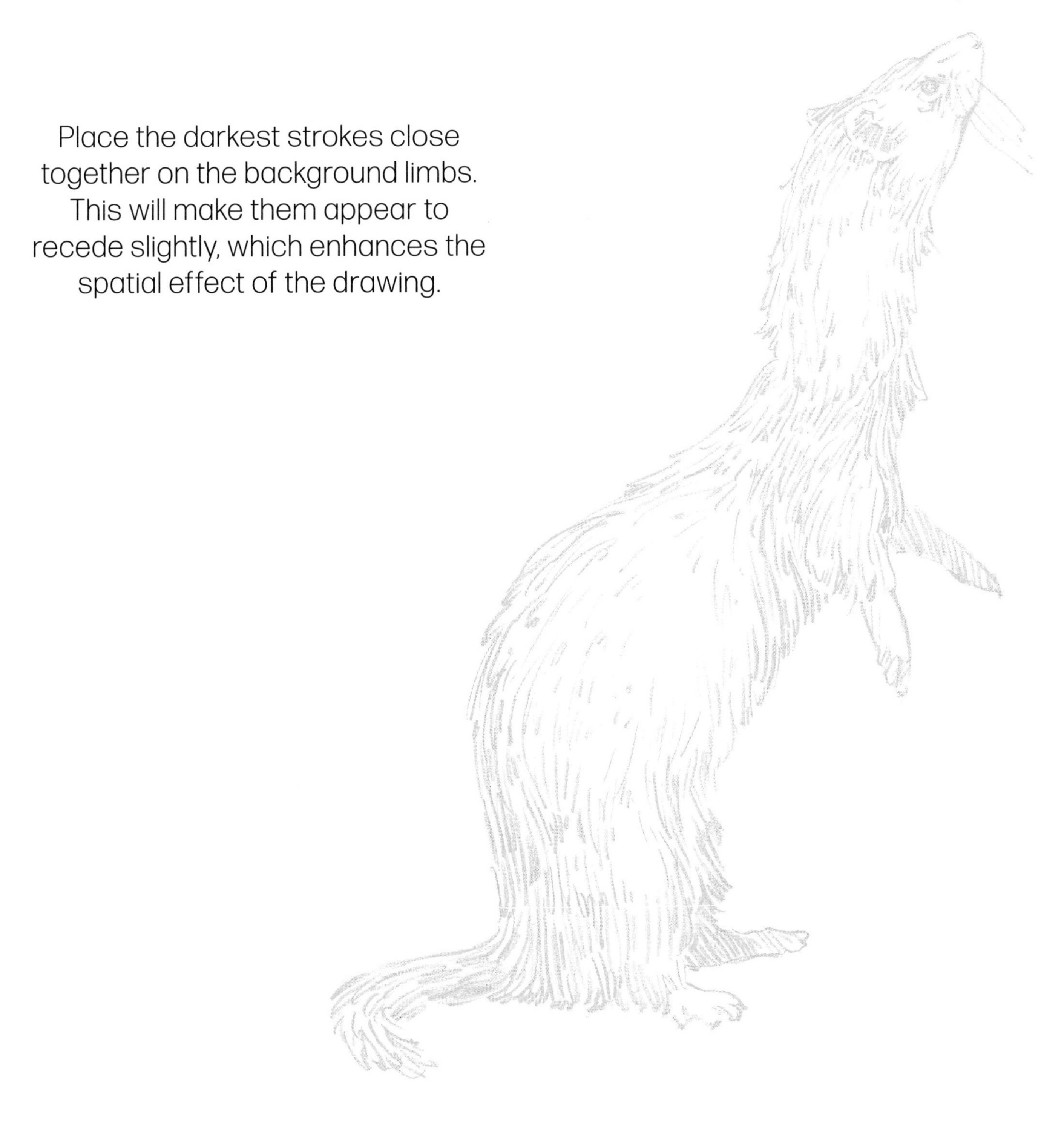

Giraffe

With the giraffe, the proportions must be right. Consider how it would look if the legs were too short or the neck too thick! Use the head as a measurement to draw the basic structure of the animal in the correct proportions. For example, count how many heads the neck is long.

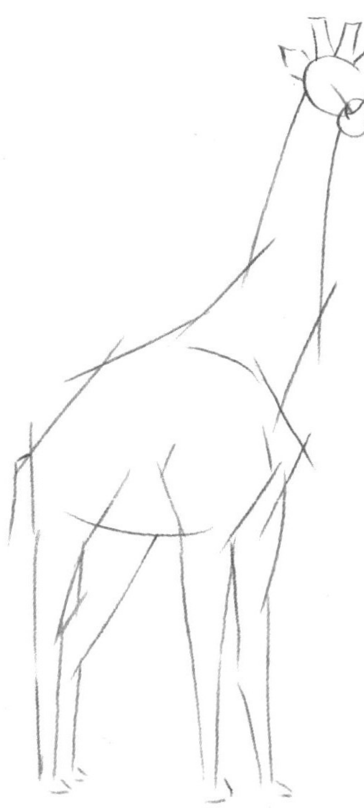

1 Start with a basic outline of the form. In particular, the neck should not be longer than the legs, and the back should slope at a soft angle.

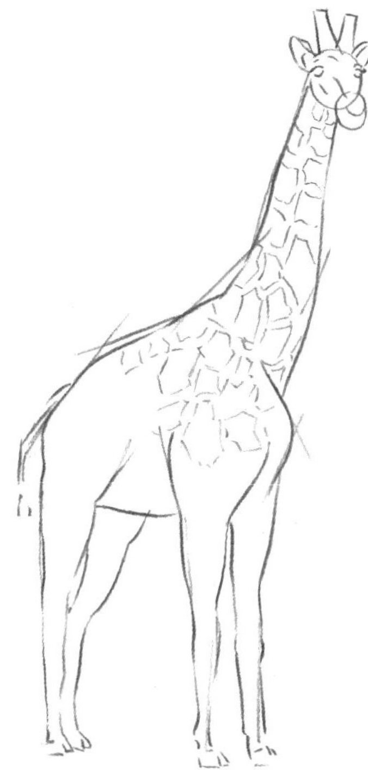

2 Begin to add the pattern and indicate the facial features. Note how its spots are large and irregularly shaped.

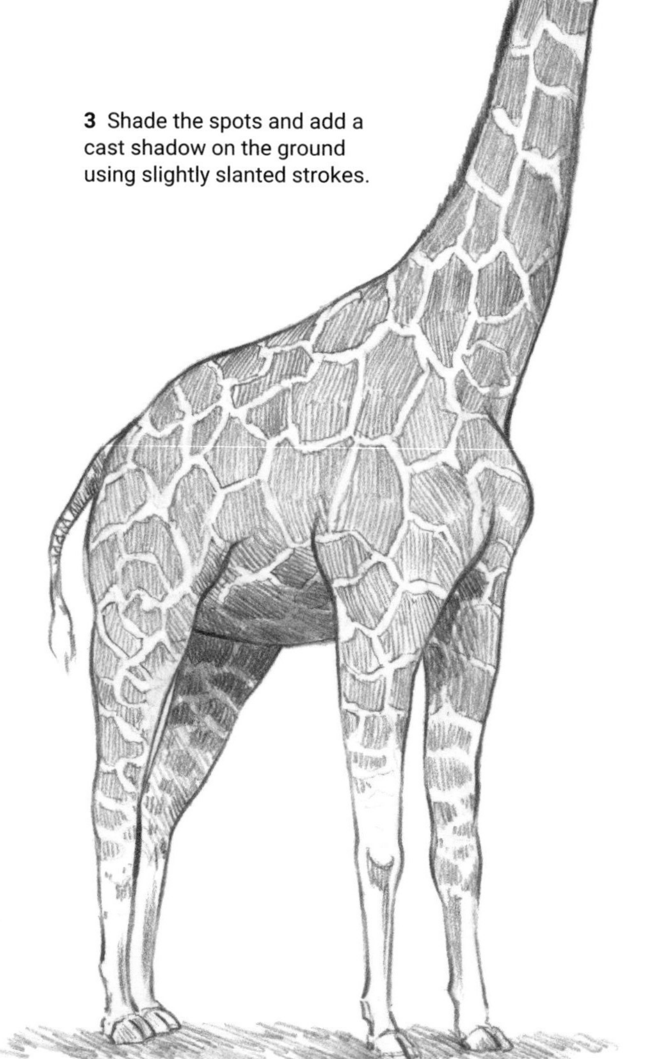

3 Shade the spots and add a cast shadow on the ground using slightly slanted strokes.

Complete the facial details and spots. Using a 2B pencil and short, small strokes, draw in the short mane.

Face and Head

First, draw a large circle for the head and two smaller circles for the muzzle; then add the ears and horns. Draw the curved jawline, the eyes and eyelashes, and the inside of the ears. Using a soft pencil, add shading to the face.

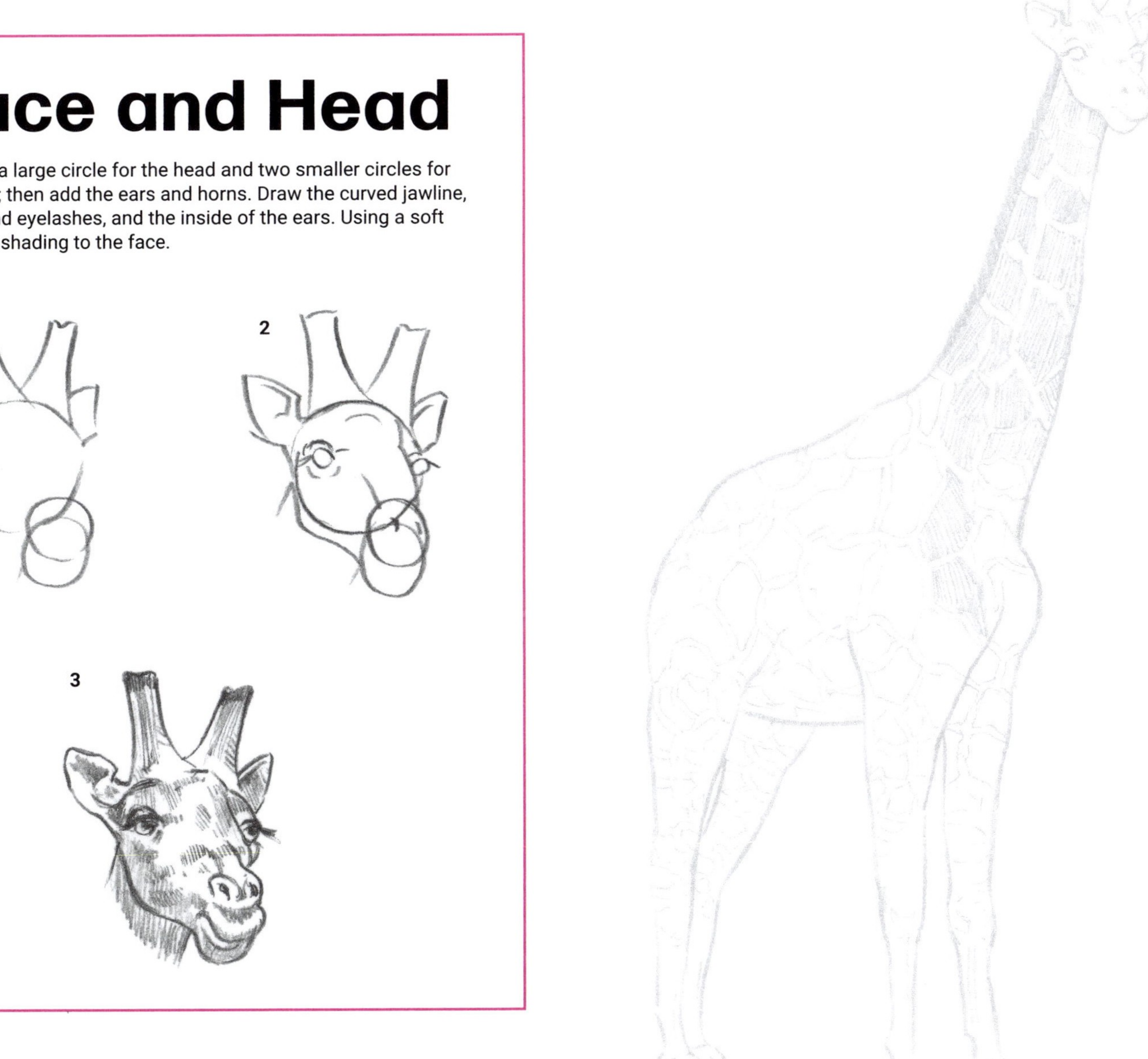

Giant Panda

A panda is easy to draw if you work step by step, starting with circles for the head and body. Then add ovals for the arms, legs, and paws, as well as the eyes, nose, and bamboo leaves. Use soft, short strokes to make the bear's fur look thick and fluffy.

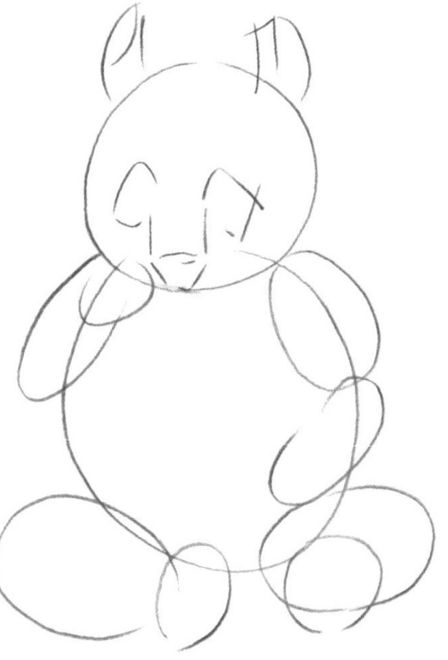

1 Draw a circle for the head and a larger oval for the belly. Use smaller ovals to create the legs, upper and lower arms, and feet. A few strokes define the position of the eyes, ears, and nose.

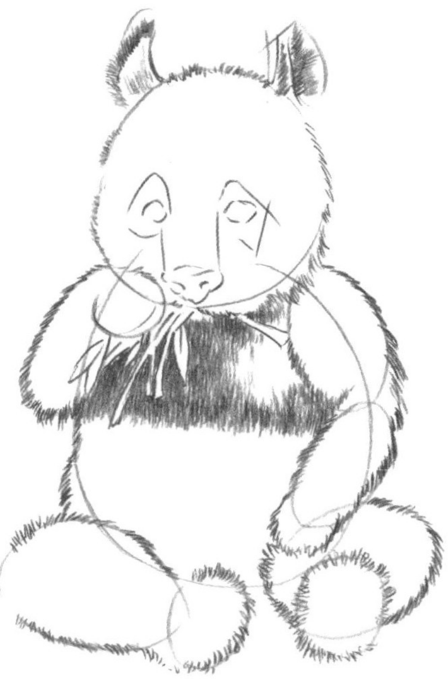

2 Sketch the eyes, nose, and bamboo branch. Using short, soft strokes, cover the panda with fur. Using an HB pencil, draw the dark fur on the chest, following the direction of fur growth.

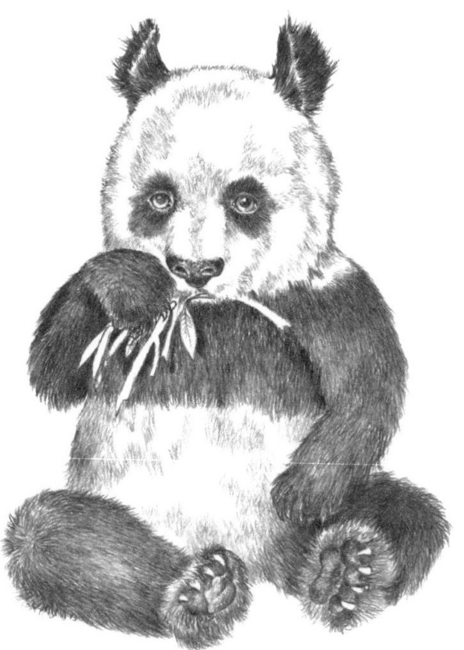

3 Continue to draw the fur with soft, short strokes. Don't worry about shading the fur evenly. Light and dark areas will add shape to the form. Complete the feet, claws, nose, and eyes.

Shade in the darkest areas of the fur. Then soften the lines with a blending stump. Draw a few contours that reveal the bear's stocky shape.

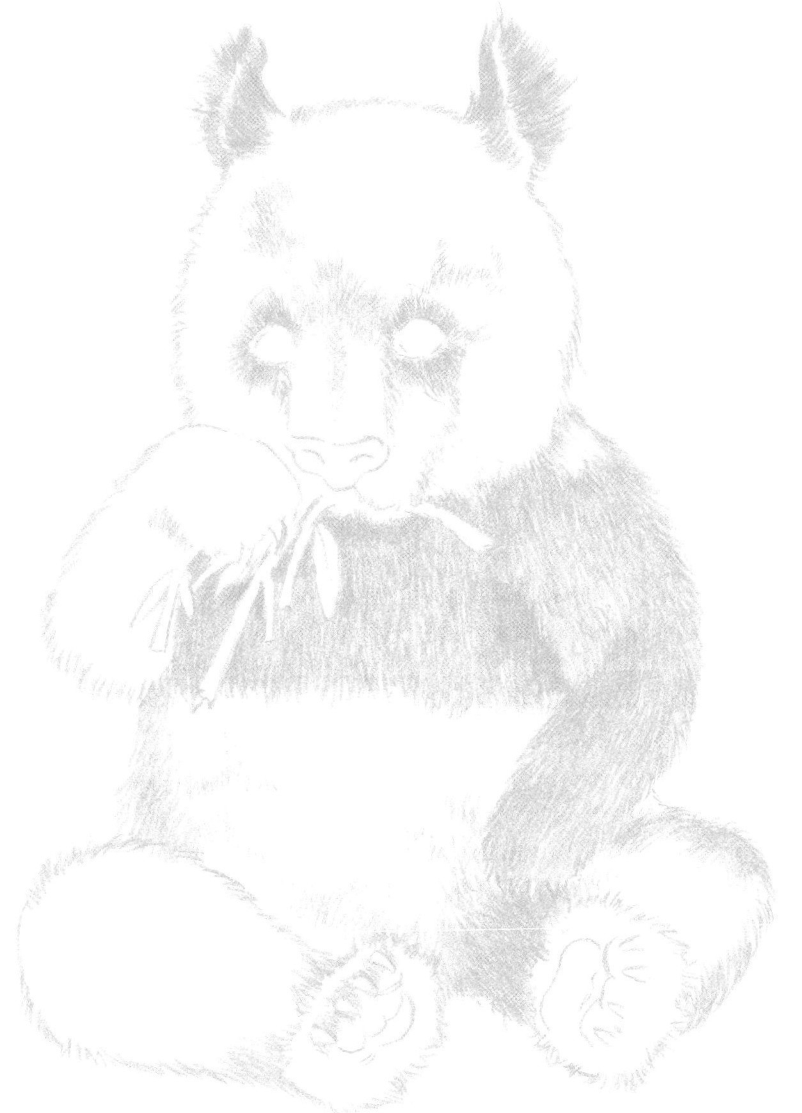

Baboon

Baboons are some of the most fascinating primates. Its distinctive features include a long, dog-like snout, closely set eyes, a powerful jawbone, and thick, rough fur.

1 Using a sharp HB pencil, start with the rough outline of the head and construction lines for the main facial features. Then add the outlines of the body, arms, and legs, and finally, the curves for the tail.

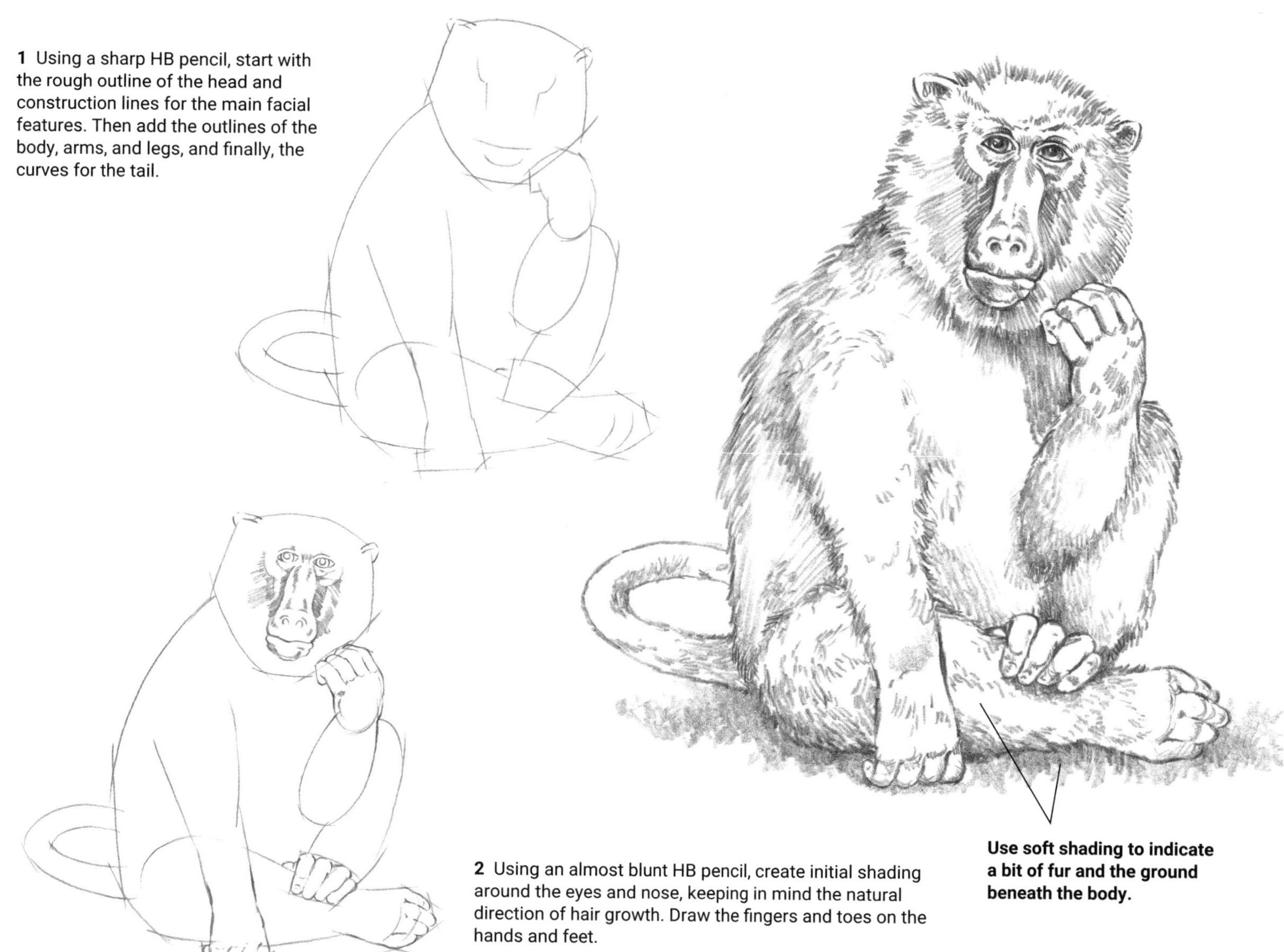

2 Using an almost blunt HB pencil, create initial shading around the eyes and nose, keeping in mind the natural direction of hair growth. Draw the fingers and toes on the hands and feet.

Use soft shading to indicate a bit of fur and the ground beneath the body.

Draw the mane and the fur on the back with short, parallel strokes.
Finish by hatching the darkest areas, leaving the highlights white.

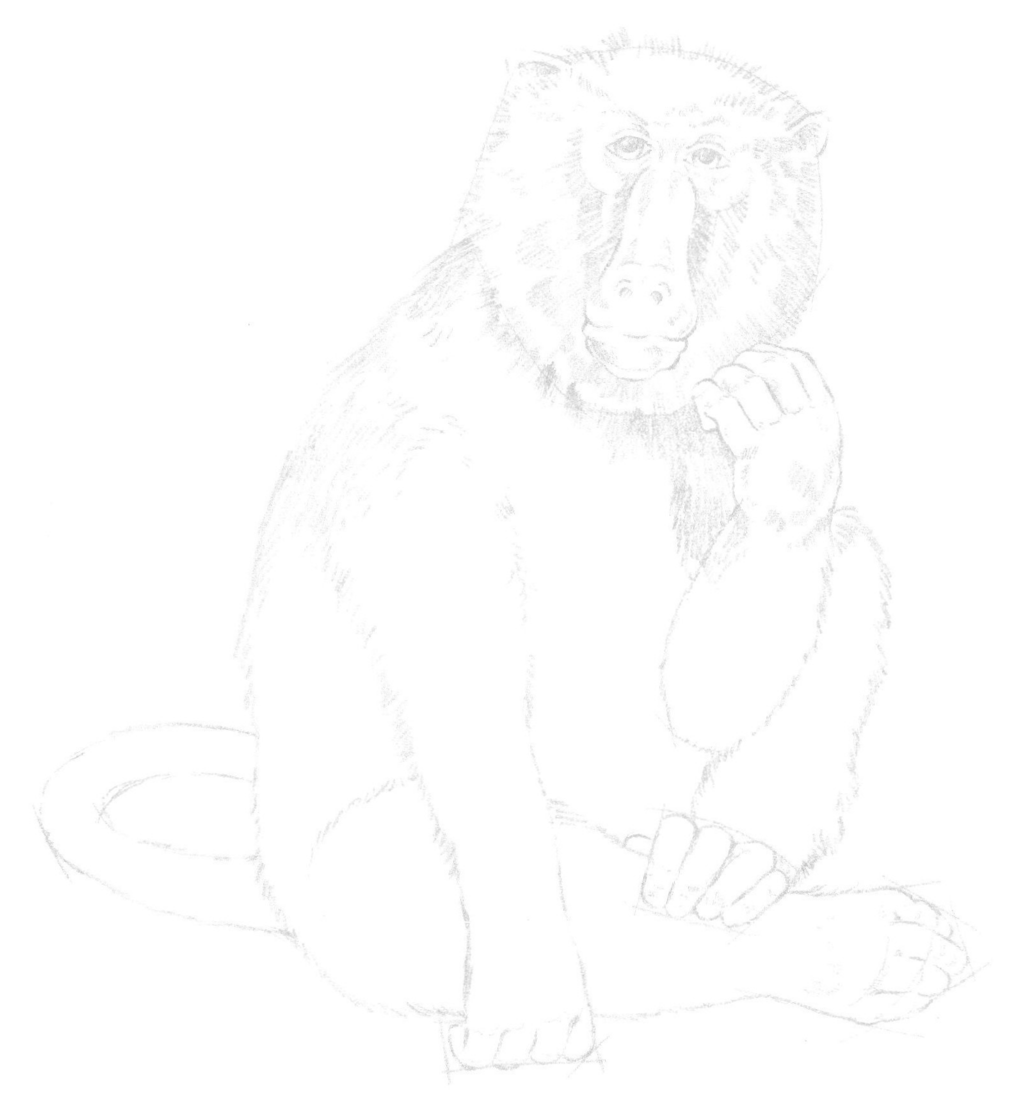

Chimpanzee

Notice how alternating dark and light shading techniques for the fur helps create dimension in this portrait of a chimp.

1 Start with overlapping ovals for the body. Add guidelines for the face. Then, sketch in the eyes, nose, and mouth. Next, draw short strokes that follow the direction of hair growth to outline the body. Rough in the hands and feet.

2 Soften the outlines with uneven, curved strokes and dashes. The outlines should not be solid and smooth; they should suggest the hairy texture of the chimp's coat. Draw the hands and feet inside the guidelines established in step 1.

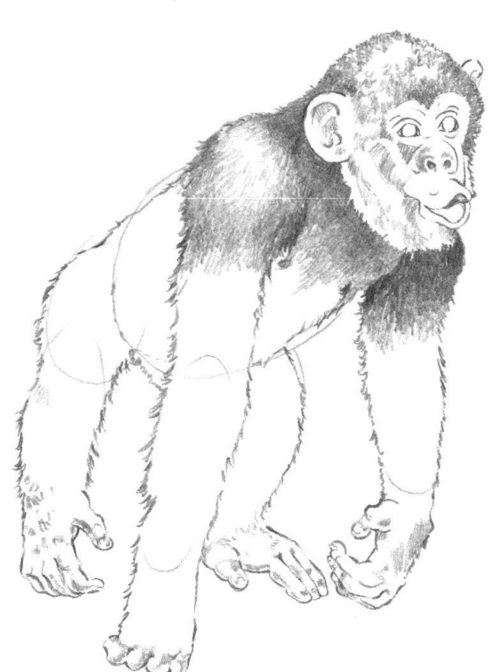

3 Add shading and the final details to the face, filling in the eyes and the mouth.

Your turn! Using the skills you have learned, fill in the shading on the chimpanzee, and complete the facial features.

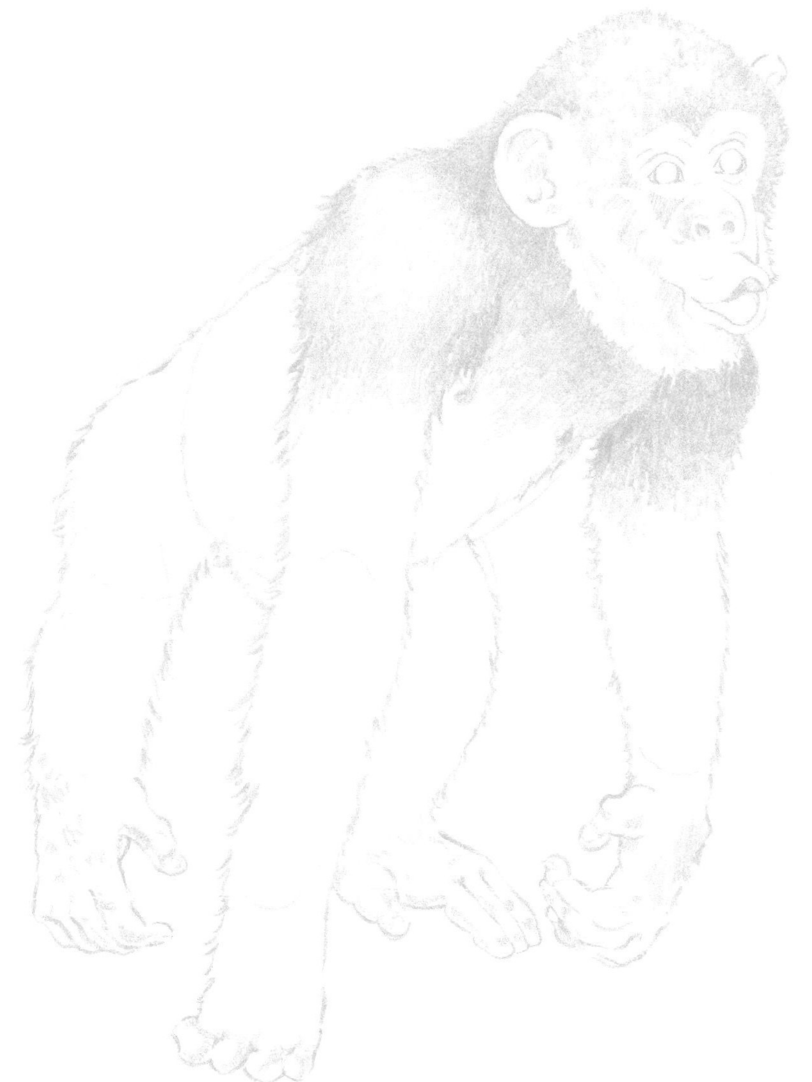

Antelope

With their slender, graceful physique and curved, ringed horns, antelopes make for a lovely drawing subject.

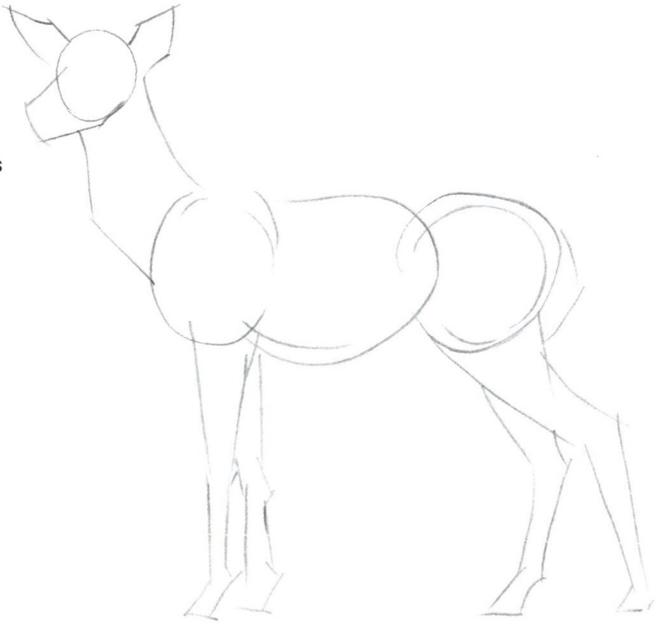

1 Start with the basic shapes for the muzzle, head, neck, chest, belly, and rump.

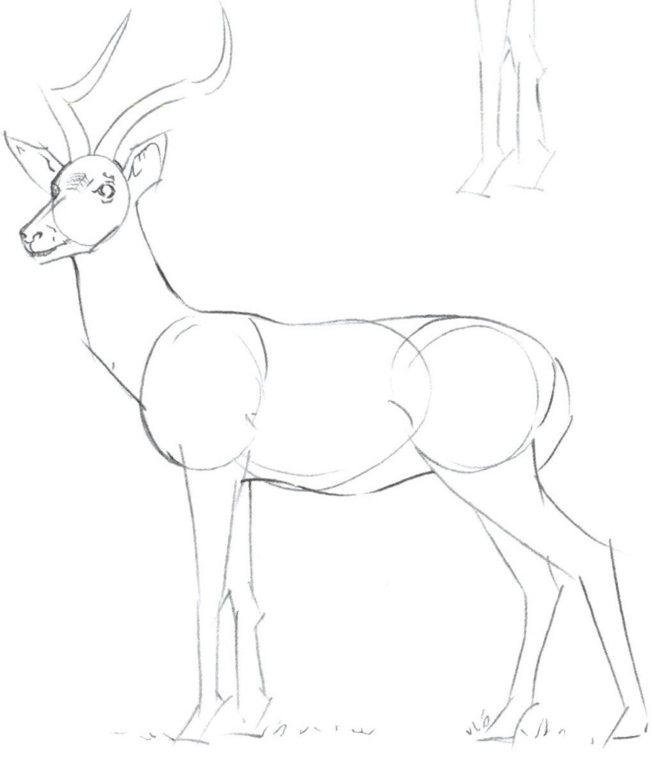

2 Shape the outline until it starts to resemble the animal. Add the horns and facial details. Add a few strokes to indicate blades of grass, which help anchor the antelope in the frame.

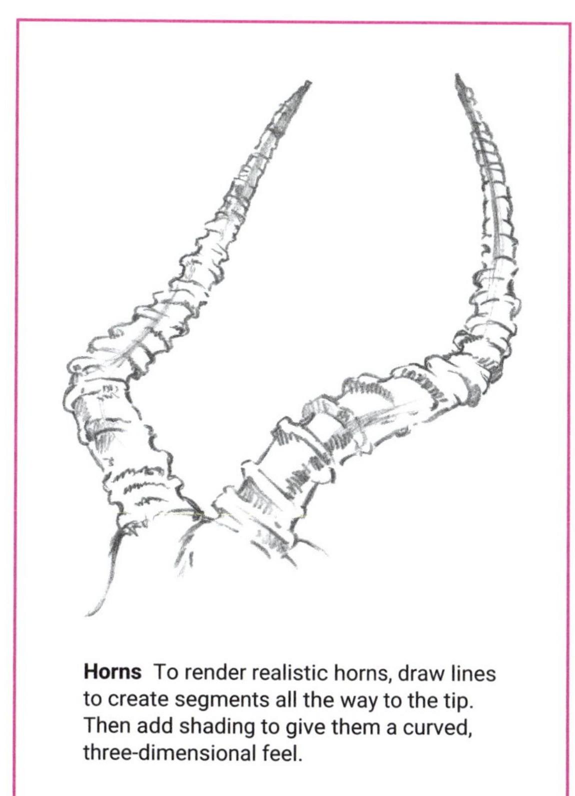

Horns To render realistic horns, draw lines to create segments all the way to the tip. Then add shading to give them a curved, three-dimensional feel.

It only takes a few strokes to make the face, horns, and body stand out. Add shading to the belly and the upper inner sides of the legs with dark hatching marks.

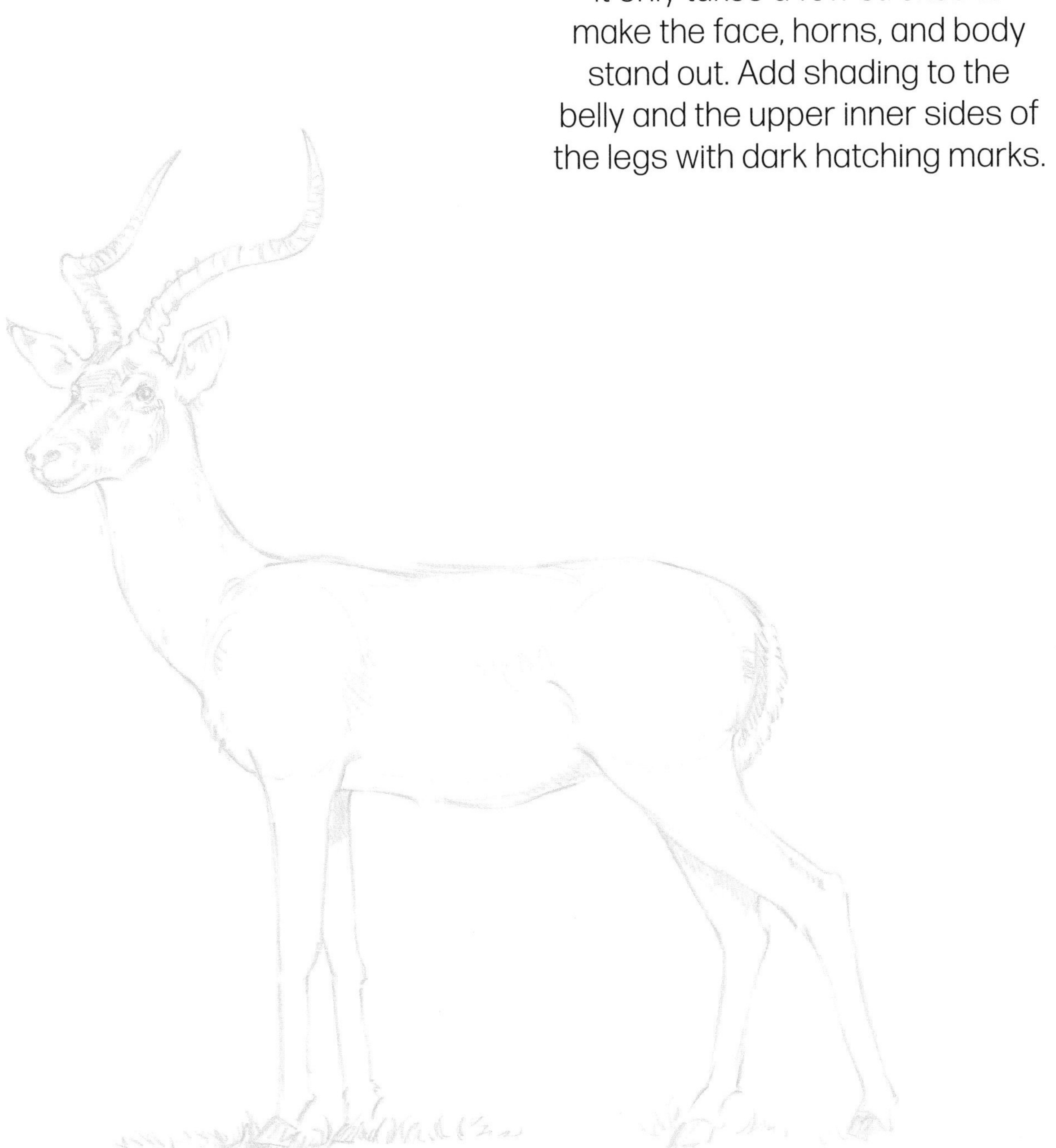

Koala

Koala bears have such character. Their round, compact bodies are easy to block out using ovals and circles. When drawing a koala, experiment using a variety of techniques to render its coarse, wiry fur and the varied textures of the nose, claws, and eyes.

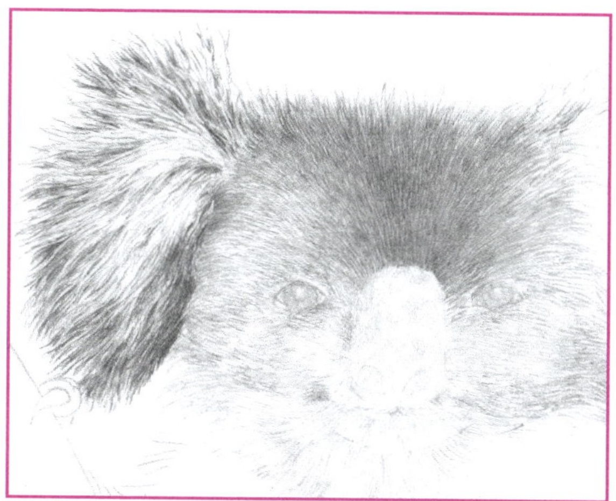

1 Start with the basic shape of the head. Then use a 2B pencil to draw the fur using short, quick strokes. With an HB pencil, darken the forehead above the nose. Use a 2H to build up the fur around the ear, cheeks, chin, and mouth. Draw the iris in each eye with a 2H, and add some tone to the nose.

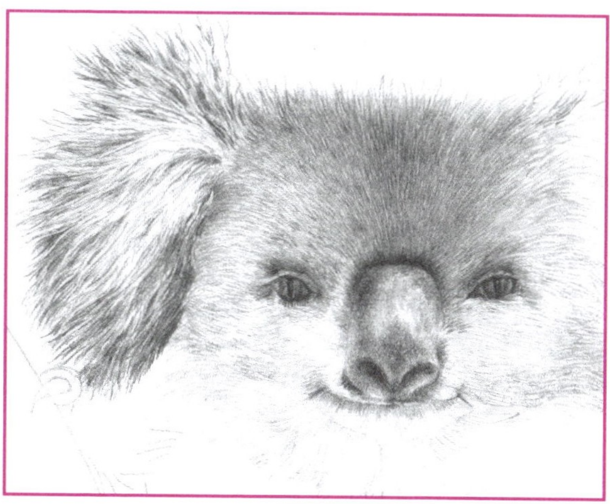

2 With a dull HB pencil, add circular strokes to the nose, leaving some areas white. Switch to a 2B and use short strokes above and below the nose to create more contrast and to darken the nostrils. Using an HB, create short lines in the mouth and under the nose, and darken the pupils. Draw eyelids and brows with short, directional strokes. Use the 2B to darken the irises and areas around the eyes.

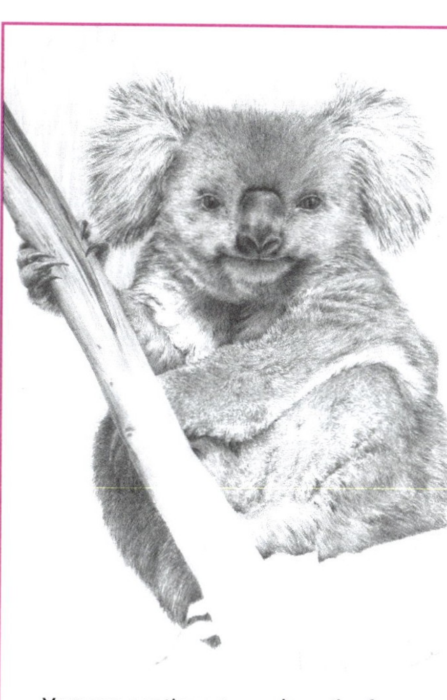

You can continue to work on the face, or develop the rest of the bear and include a tree branch. Remember to keep the background lighter so that the focus remains on the bear.

Use this outline to build out a portrait of a koala bear. Take your time and use all of the tools at your disposal to create a realistic final drawing.

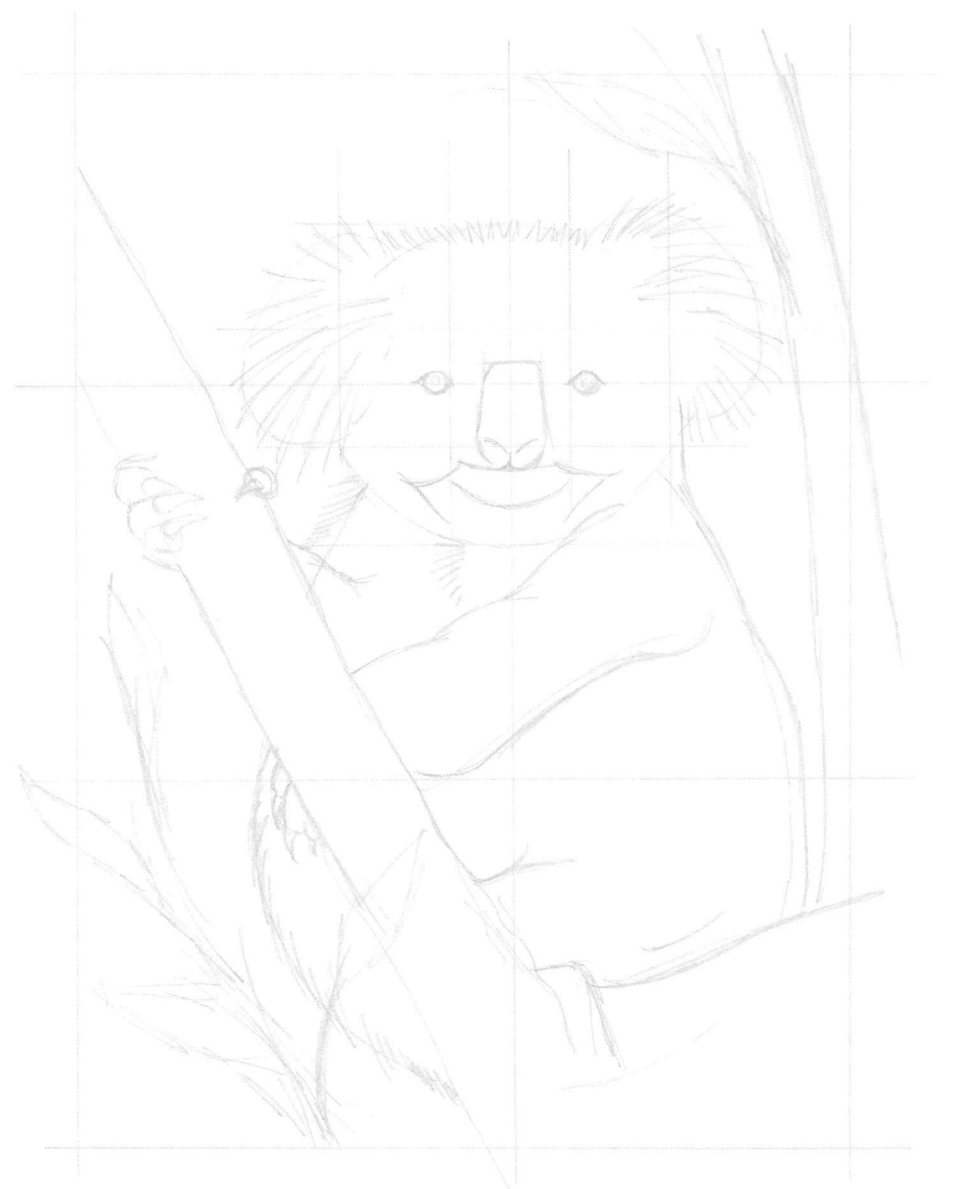

Kangaroo

Kangaroos have disproportionately large eyes, ears, and feet, and a strikingly long tail. The more attention you pay to the details, the more lifelike your drawing will be.

1 Block out the body using light lines. Develop the facial features and use an HB to begin shading. Continue the line work down the neck, alternating between HB and 2H pencils. With a sharp 2H, work down the forearms and the back, following the direction of the fur.

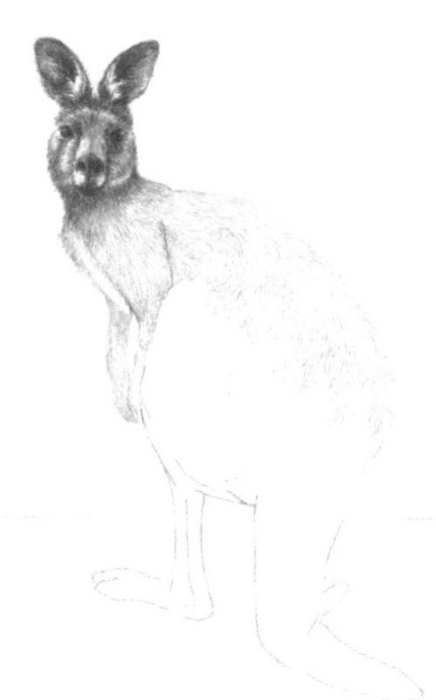

3 With a sharp HB, work lightly over the entire body and head, defining and sharpening the tones. Next, emphasize the paws, deepen the tone under the shoulder and neck, and add more fur across the hip and back. Use a kneaded eraser to lighten the highlight on the leg.

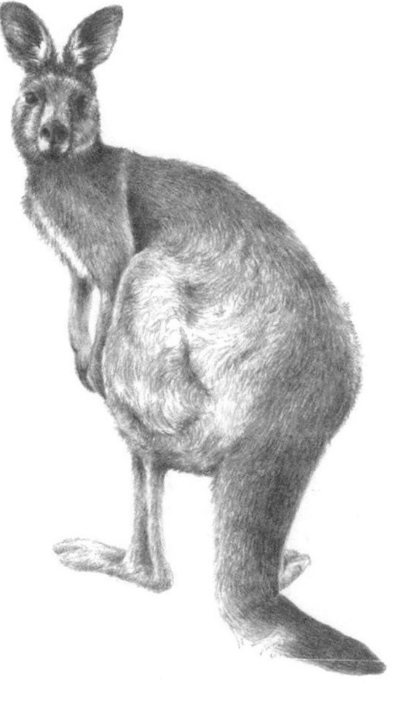

2 Use a sharp HB to add a second layer of fur. Where the fur is darker, the strokes are closer together; where the fur is lighter, the strokes are farther apart. The fur is longer and wavier on the kangaroo's back, so your pencil strokes should reflect this. Use a sharp 2B to darken the fur, adding form and tone.

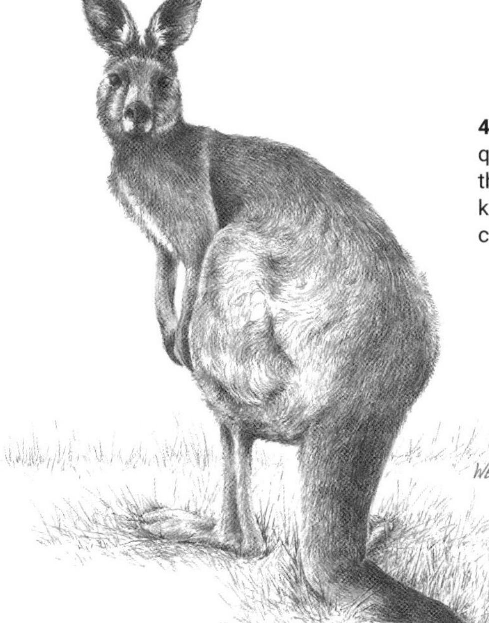

4 Add grass using loose, quick strokes. Darken the areas where the kangaroo's body is in contact with the ground.

Practice layering and shading techniques on the outline below.
Create the form beneath the fur using short, curved strokes.

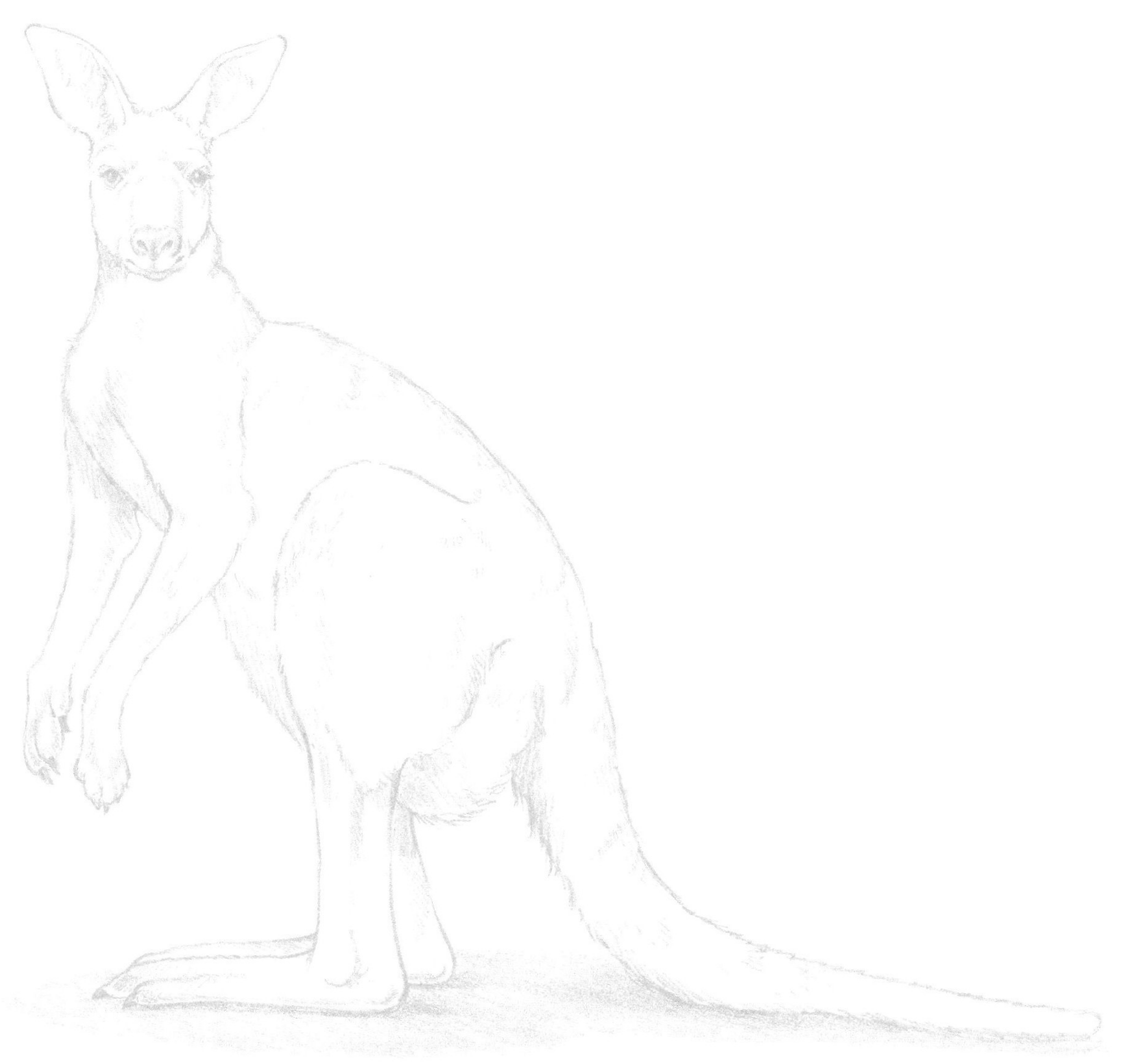

Parrot

All parrots have an upright posture and a powerful beak. Their vibrant and bold colors are particularly striking, so once you've completed your sketch, bring it to life using colored pencils.

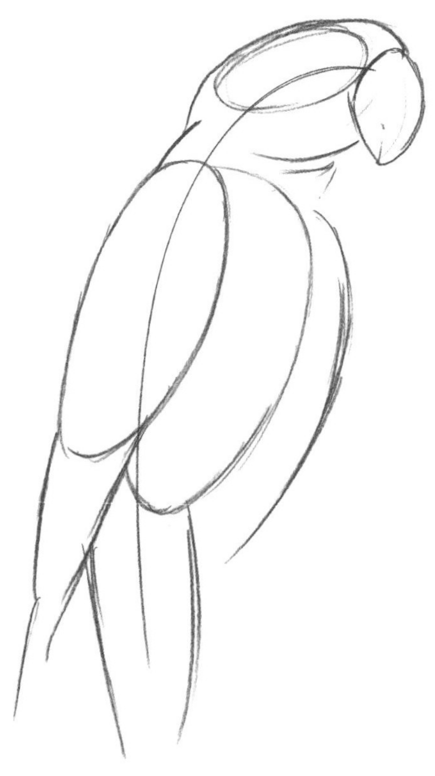

1 First, use an HB pencil to draw an arc from the beak to the tail. On this first line, use ovals and inward-curving lines to build the beak, head, chest, wings, and tail.

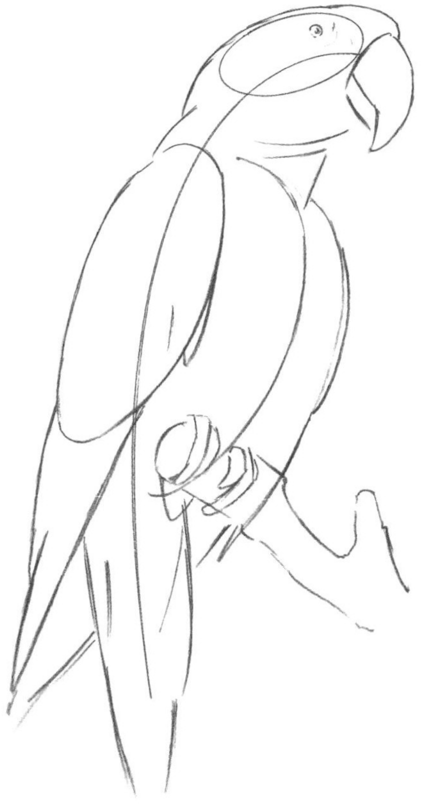

2 Sketch the claws and a thick branch so the parrot doesn't "hang" in the air. Draw the eye and the precise lines of the beak, which has an upper and lower half.

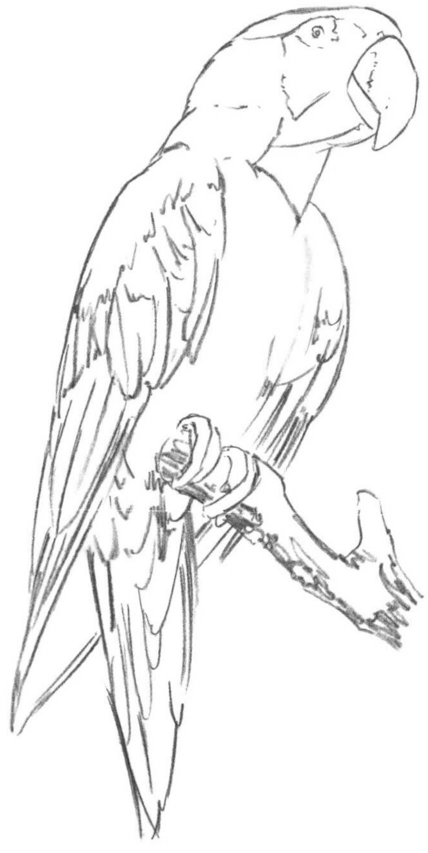

3 Erase all unnecessary construction lines. First, give the branch more shape by hatching the underside and at the ends. Then, focus on the outline and the feathers.

Shade in the outline here with colored pencils. Use varying pressure to create different effects that will emphasize the vibrancy of this beautiful bird.

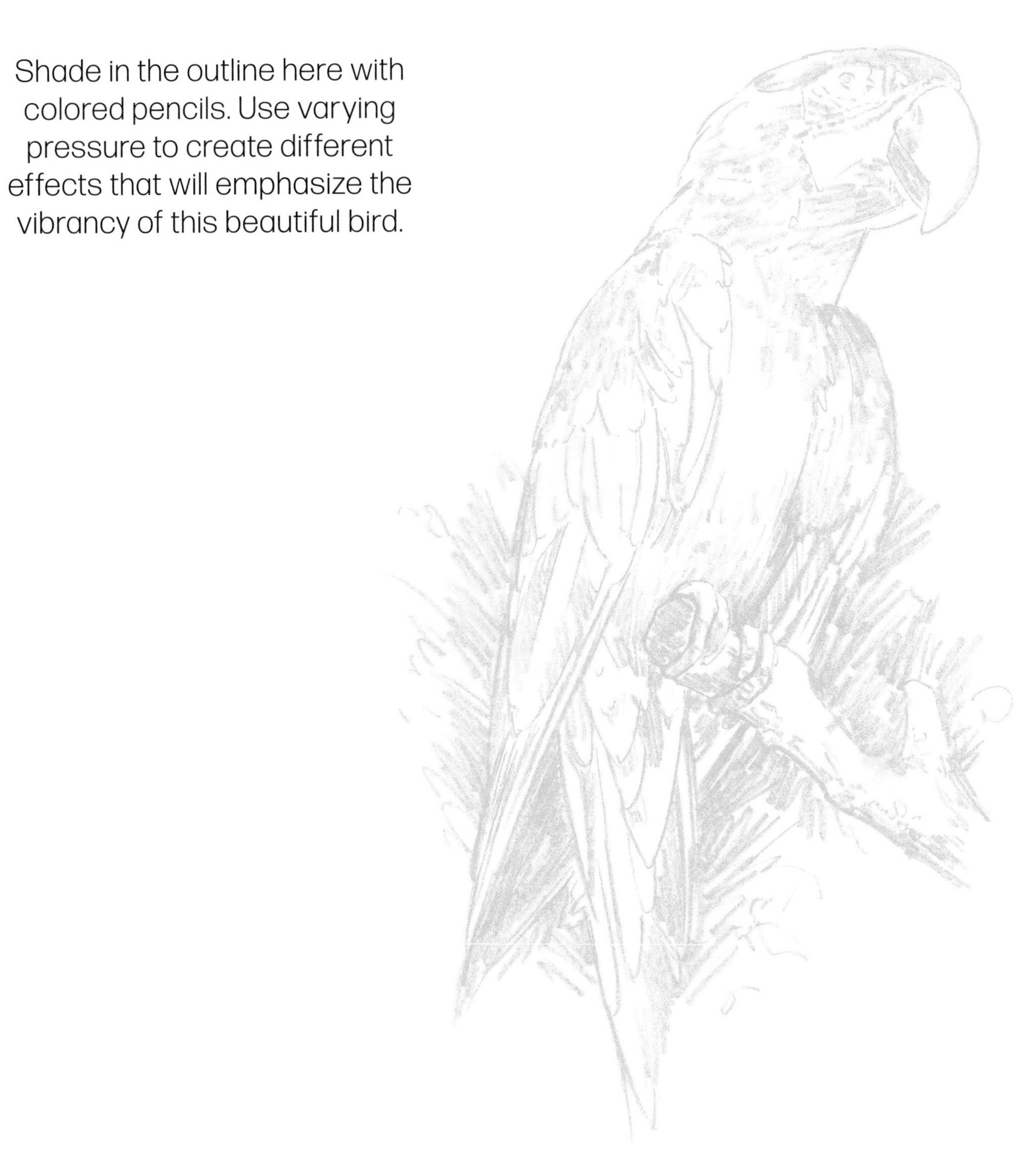

Python

Pythons are found primarily in Africa, South Asia, and Southeast Asia. At nearly twenty feet long, they are among the largest snakes in the world.

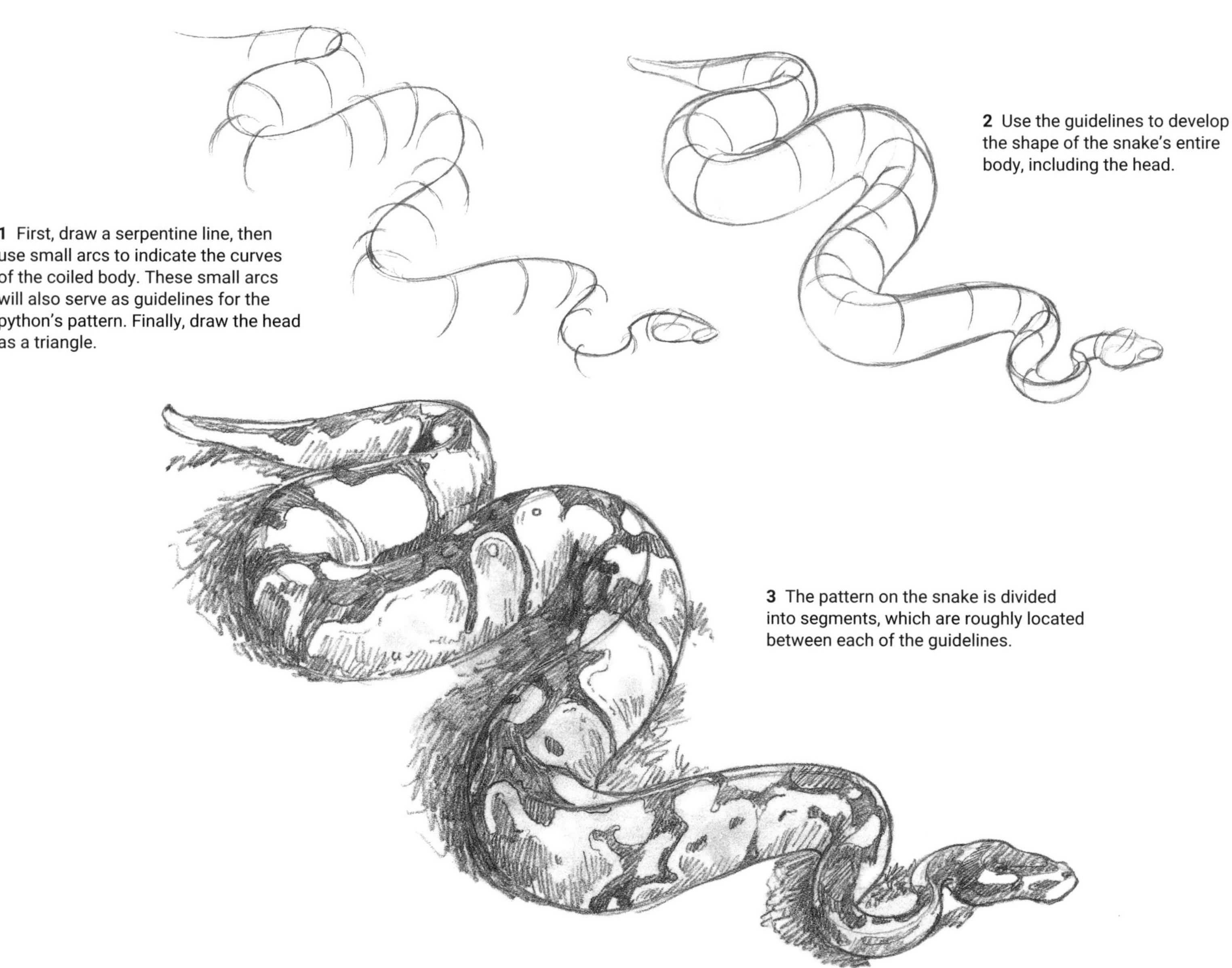

1 First, draw a serpentine line, then use small arcs to indicate the curves of the coiled body. These small arcs will also serve as guidelines for the python's pattern. Finally, draw the head as a triangle.

2 Use the guidelines to develop the shape of the snake's entire body, including the head.

3 The pattern on the snake is divided into segments, which are roughly located between each of the guidelines.

Fill in the dark areas with a sharp 2B pencil, and use light hatching in the spots to emphasize the curved body shape. Use short, heavy strokes to create the cast shadow on the ground.

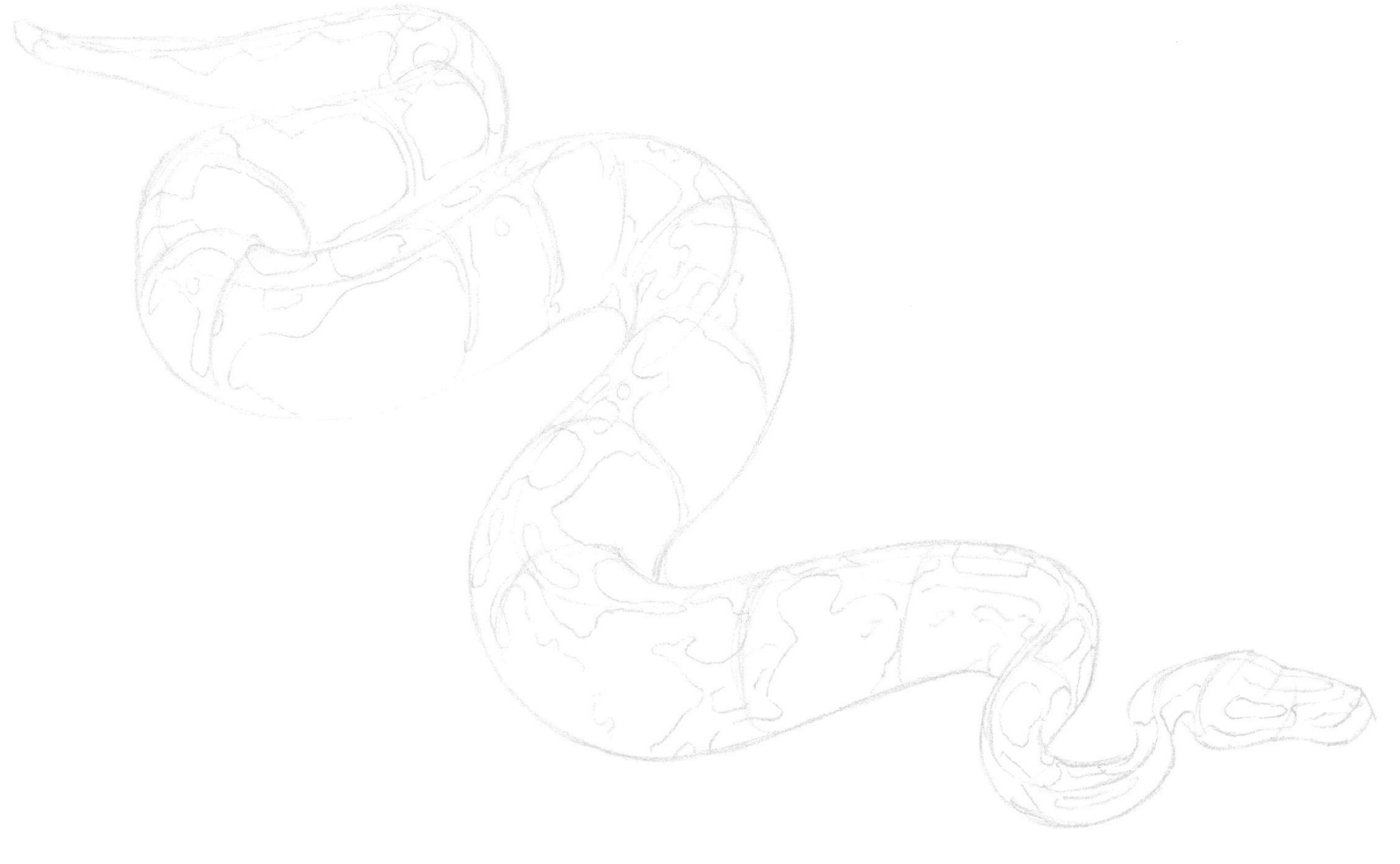

Polar Bear

With its oval-shaped body, rounded ears, and angular snout, the polar bear makes for a good beginning drawing project. Start with broad, rounded shapes to block in this bear's massive frame. Then develop the details as you go.

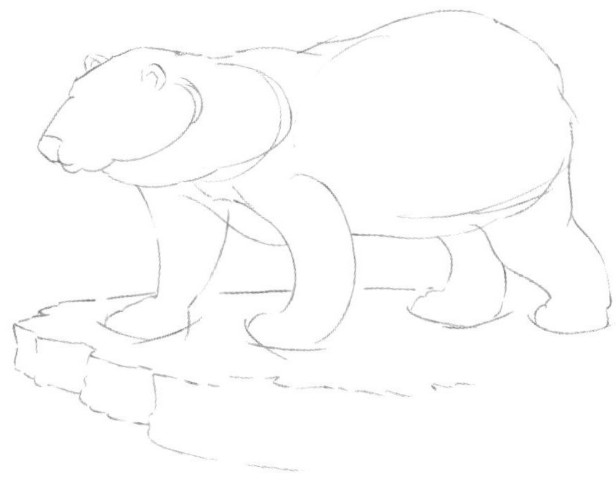

1 Sketch the general outlines of the body, head, and legs, paying careful attention to proportions. Add the ears with two semi-circles and block in the squarish nose. Sketch the thick ice floe beneath the bear's feet.

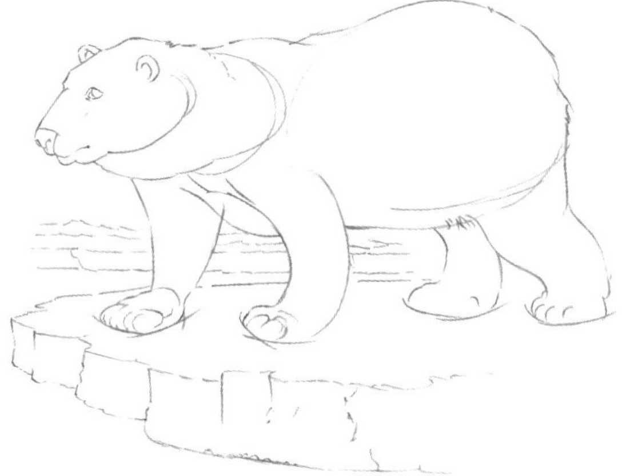

2 Place the eye and begin building the feet with circular strokes. To suggest the mass of ice in the background, add four broken horizontal lines behind the ice floe.

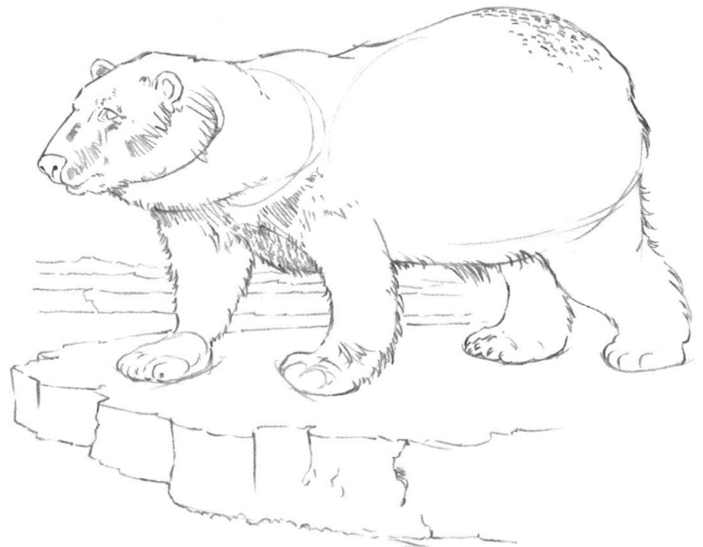

3 Begin shading the bear with short strokes that follow the direction of hair growth. Apply shading to only a few areas, including the underside, the back, and the face—just enough to suggest texture but still maintain the white of the coat.

Use the side of a sharp HB pencil to shade the water and the bear's cast shadow and a rounded tip to add ripples of water and shading on the ice floe.

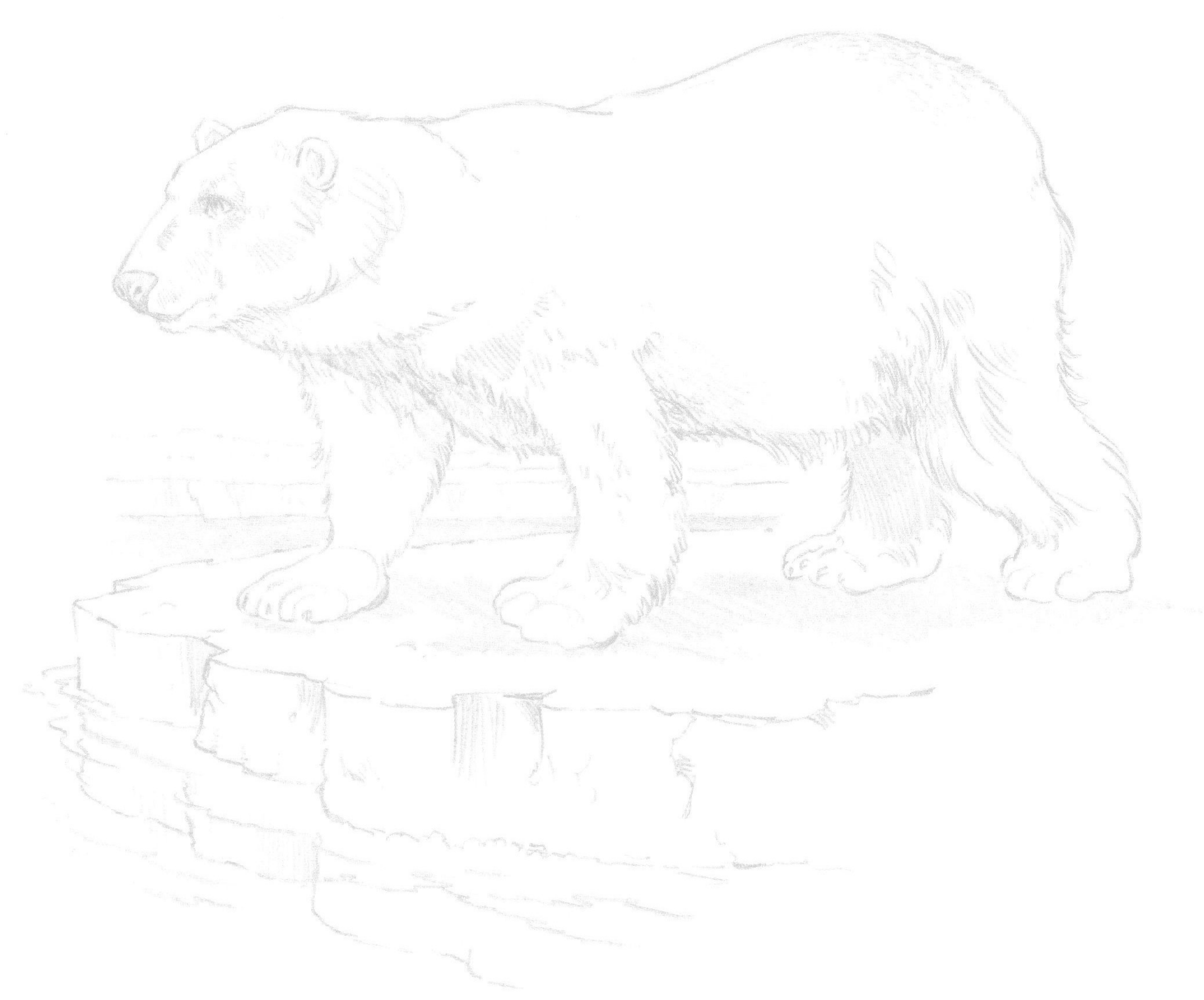

Penguins

Penguins are birds, but they cannot fly. However, they are excellent swimmers and divers. Their stocky-looking bodies, with their streamlined shape and narrow but powerful flippers, are adapted to life in the ocean.

1 Draw four long ovals for the bodies. Add smaller ovals for the heads and use triangles for the beaks. Rough in the legs and a few lines to indicate the ground beneath their feet.

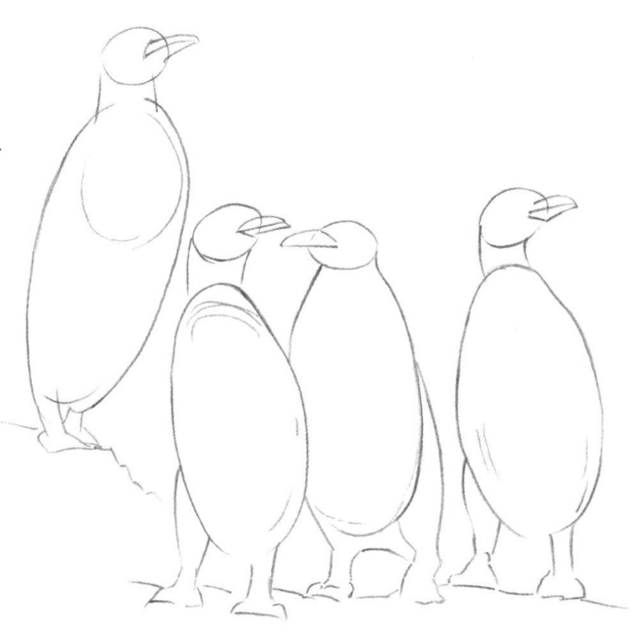

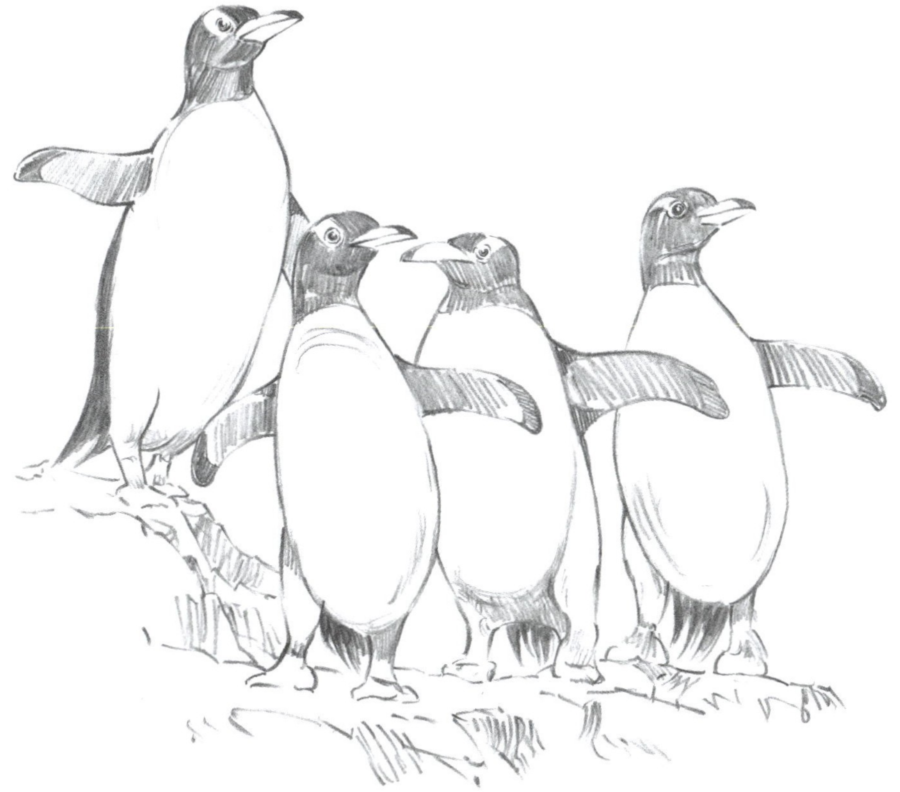

2 Use hatching to shade the dark parts of each penguin. Use a simple circle for each eye, leaving a white highlight. Add a few additional squiggly lines to fill in the rocks.

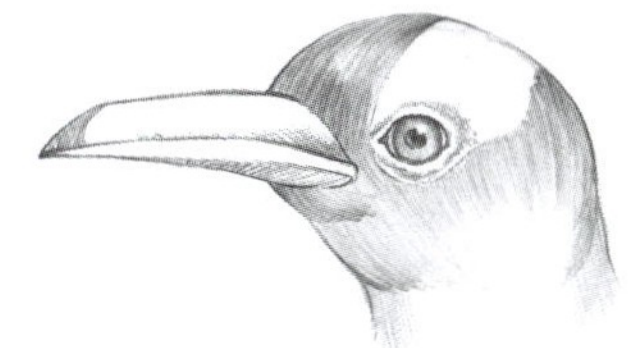

Drawing Different Species

The markings on the head vary from species to species. This gentoo penguin has a white stripe that begins on the lower eyelid and runs across the head. The eye itself is surrounded by a delicate, irregular gray border.

Shade the eyes, wings, and tails with a 2B rounded pencil. Use delicate, ridged, and wavy lines to create the rock. Then, shade the heads and beaks with parallel strokes.

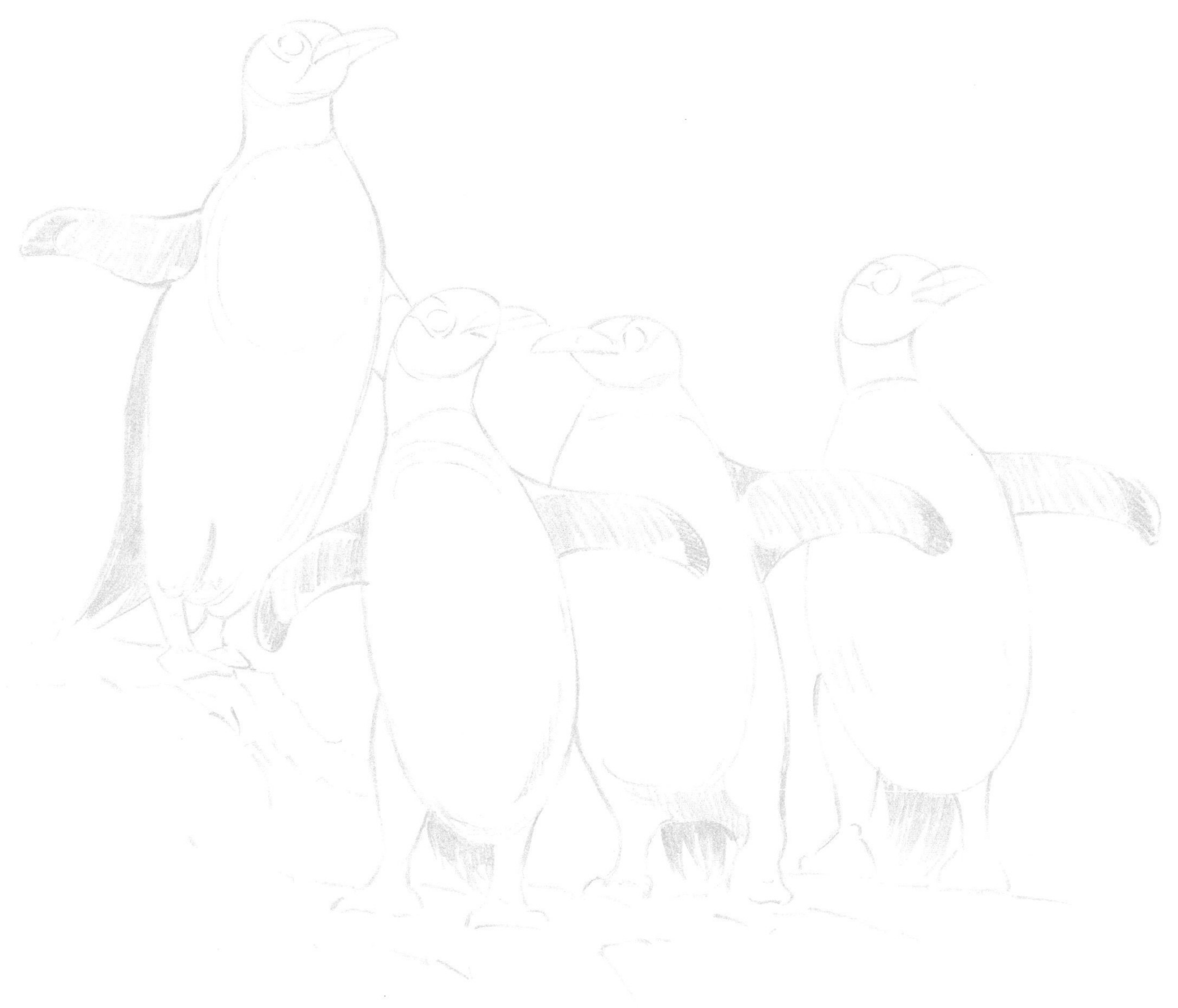

Bison

The bison is the largest land mammal in the Americas. Its dense fur is dark brown—almost black in winter. The head, forelegs, hump, and shoulders are covered with longer hair, while the fur on the flanks and backside is much shorter.

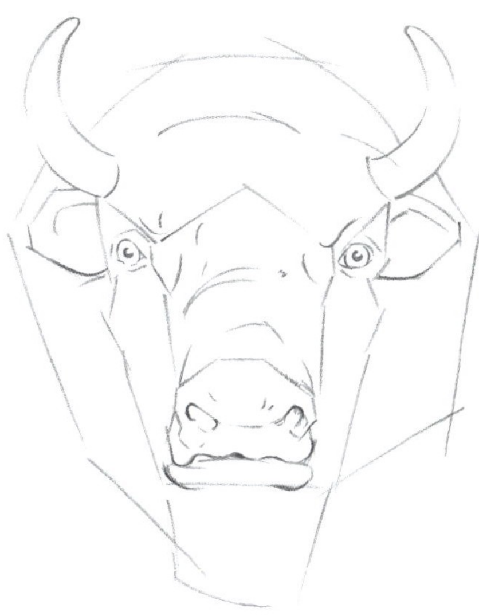

1 Block in the head and face. Then, add the bison's eyes, ears, and nostrils. The ears start directly below the horns and end at the lower eyelids. The eyes are wide apart, and they begin slightly outside the width of the muzzle. Shape the nose and muzzle in more detail.

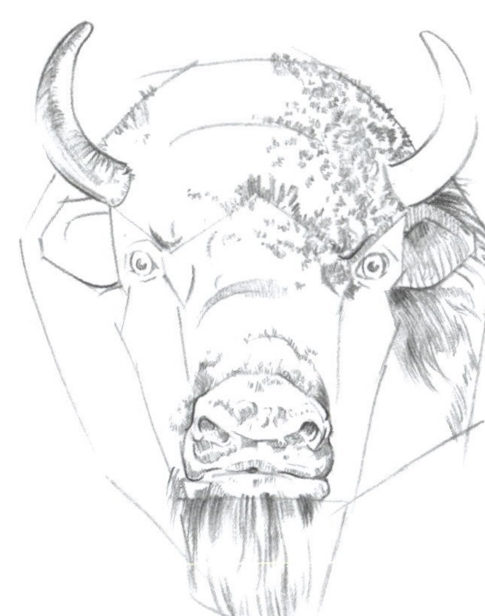

2 Begin shading the head, neck, and face. Draw the chin hairs with long wavy lines. With a rounded-tip pencil, draw the curled fur on the face and head. Shape the horns with semicircular lines.

Eye in Detail

First, lightly sketch the eyelids, pupil, iris, and eyebrows (step 1). Darken the pupil, leaving a highlight, and add some light shading around the eyelid (step 2). Shade the remaining parts of the eye, and use a blending stump to soften any harsh lines and abrupt transitions (step 3).

1

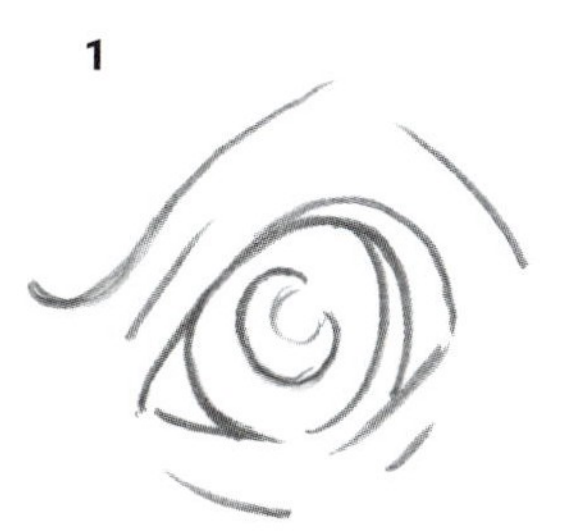

2

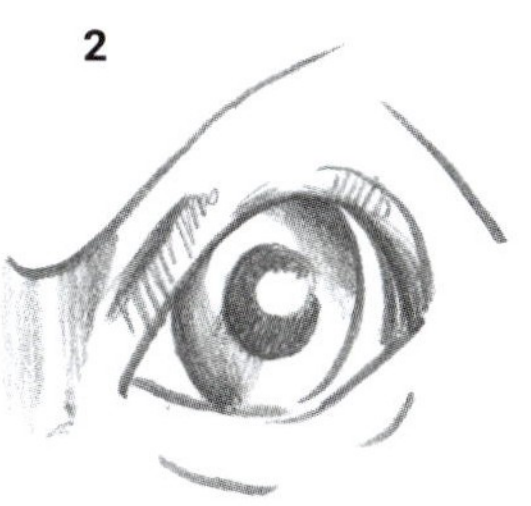

3

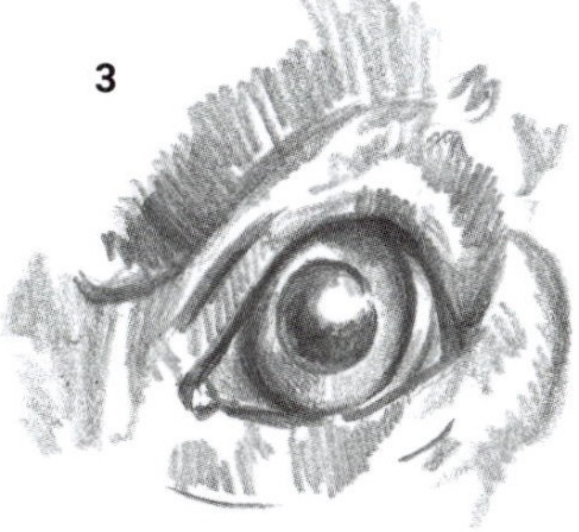

Practice working with sharpened and rounded-tip pencils to create the various textures of the bison, including its short, long, and curly fur, horns, and muzzle.

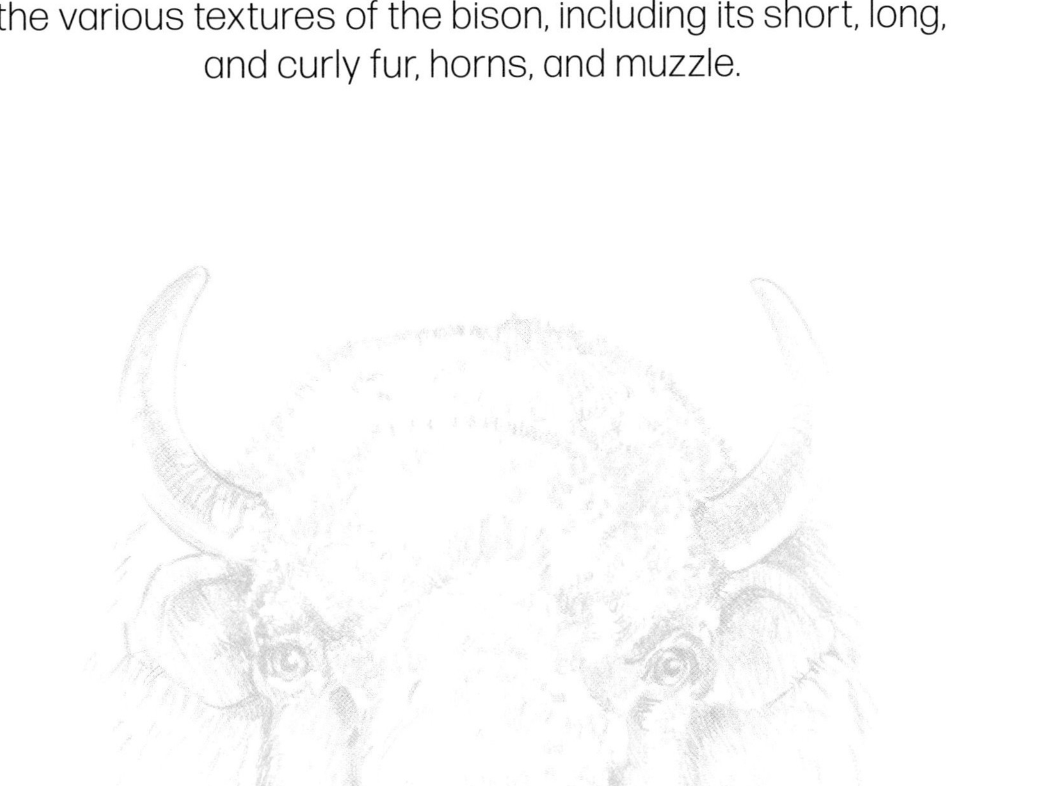

Asian Elephant

Large animals are great subjects for drawing wildlife. The big, round forms are easy to see. The Asian elephant differs slightly from an African elephant in that it has a smaller body and ears, and a more rounded back, among other minor differences. The head and body are sparsely covered in wiry hair, and their tusks often have been cut short to prevent damage to their surroundings.

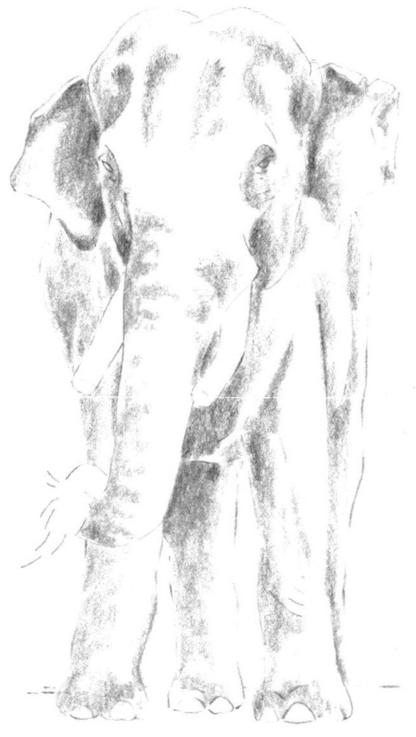

1 Block in the shape, and create a soft, smooth tone before adding the rough, cracked texture. Using a 2B pencil, make small circular strokes to fill in the darkest shadow areas.

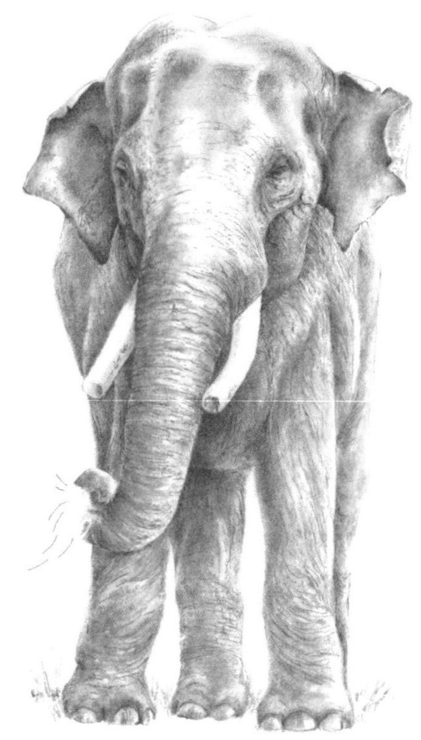

2 Working over the head, ears, and a bit of the trunk, add wrinkles using a sharp HB pencil. Sharpen the edges of the curls in the ears and use circular strokes around the eyes and brows. Continue adding wrinkles and creases. Develop the toes and trunk, and darken the ends of the tusks.

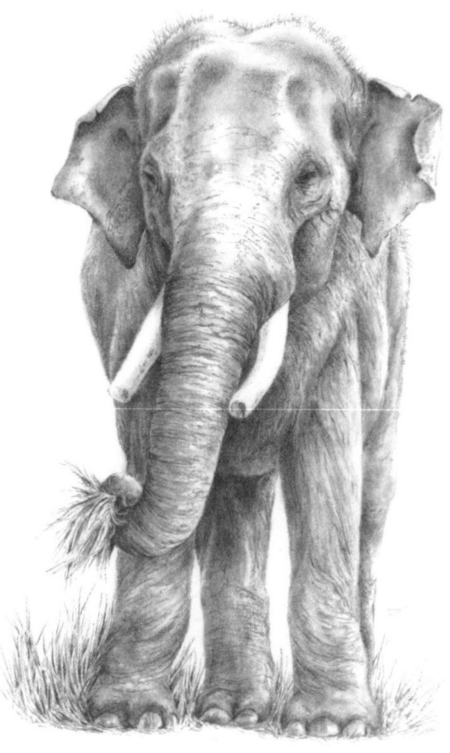

3 With a 2B pencil, continue to build up the skin. Deepen the darkest tones, and add some dark hairs on the elephant's head and back. Draw a few blades of grass on the ground and at the end of the elephant's trunk. Then, use a sharp 2B to fill in dark areas between strokes, giving the grass some depth. Add further detail to the feet and toes.

Build up the texture of the elephant's skin using a variety of shading techniques. Use a kneaded eraser to lift out highlights on the head, tusks, body, and trunk.

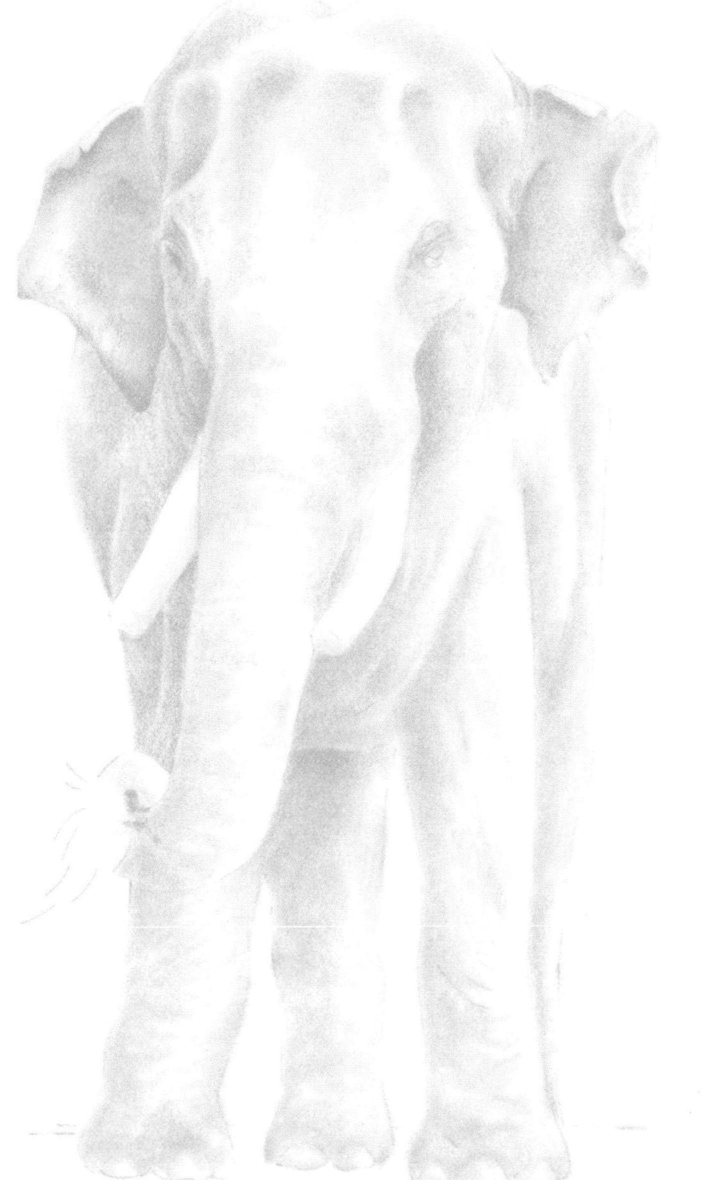

Horses

Familiarity with the horse's anatomy and musculature will help you make your drawings look realistic. Generally, areas with large, smooth muscles will be shaded lightly, whereas the areas of smaller overlapping muscles will require more complex shading. Study the illustrations to see how the muscles and tendons wrap around the horse's skeletal structure.

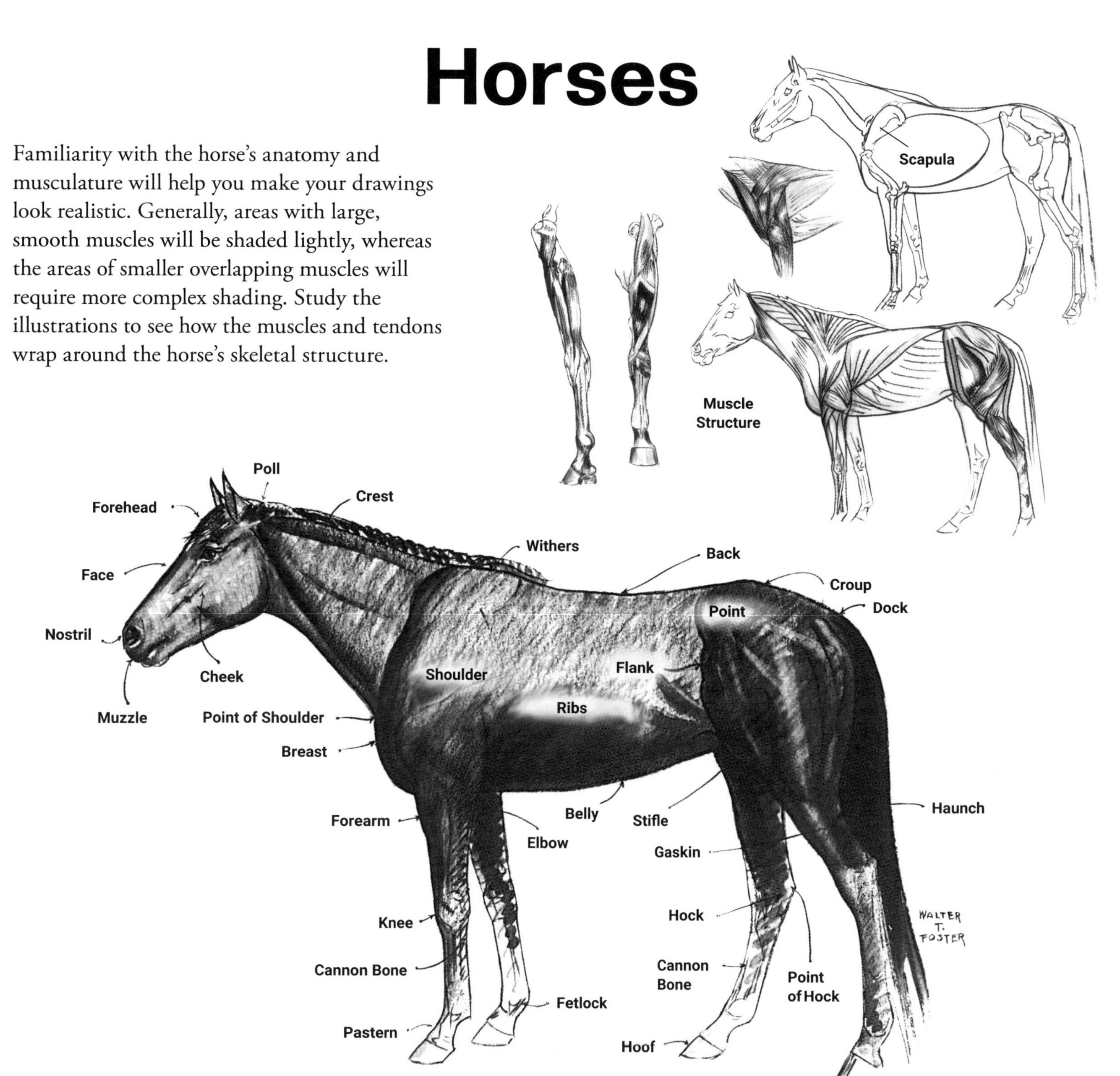

Trace the outline below to learn how to draw a horse in a side view.
Once again, notice how the horse can be measured using
its head size as a system of measurement.

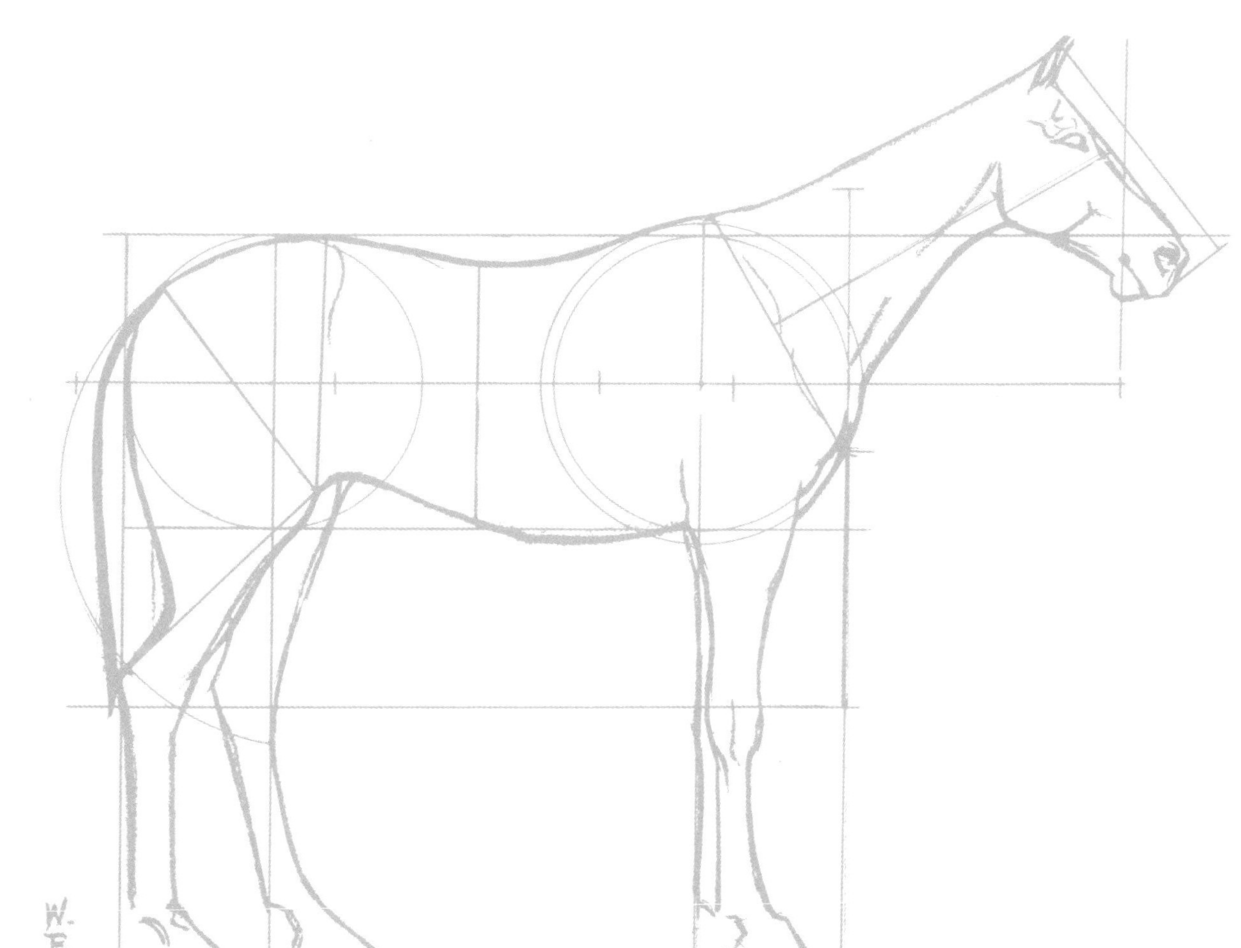

Horse in Profile

At the beginning of the drawing, it's important to get the proportions right, because once the shading and details have been added, changes become difficult. Sketch the basic shape with several construction lines first to establish the position of the horse.

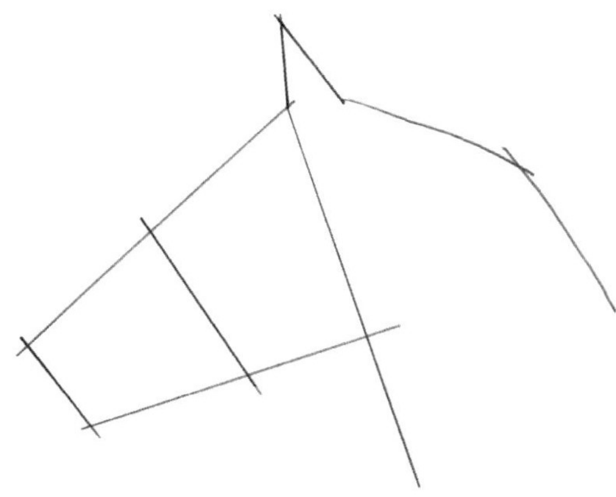

1 First, draw only the basic shape of the horse's head using an HB pencil and light pressure. Then add the muzzle, ear, and neck with quick, slanted strokes—paying attention to the correct angle. Then divide the head vertically down the middle. You will need this guideline later for the jaw outline.

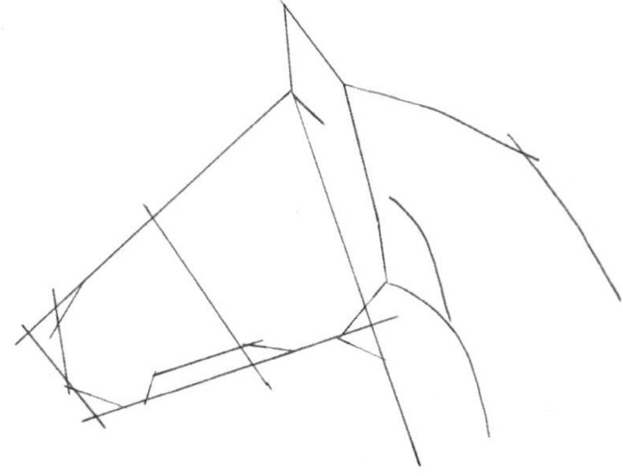

2 Still using straight lines, outline the shape of the mouth. Pay particular attention to the places where the construction lines intersect. Then, with several lines extending to the base of the ear, define the approximate jawline and outline the neck shape with several curves.

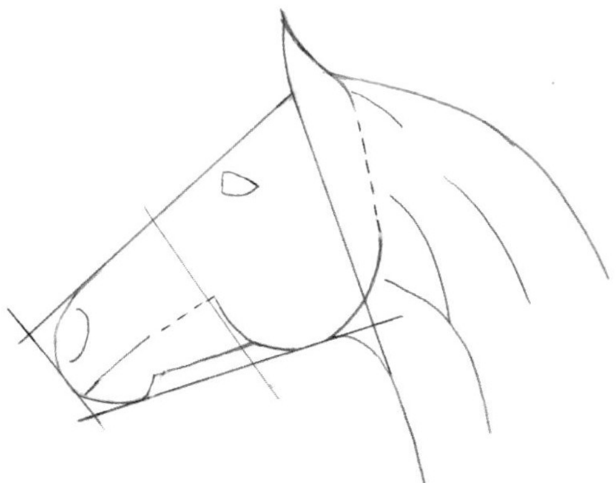

3 Develop the neck, mouth, and jaw. Carefully draw the eye and nose, then indicate the mouth with a line. Use dashed lines to check the accuracy of the proportions and angles.

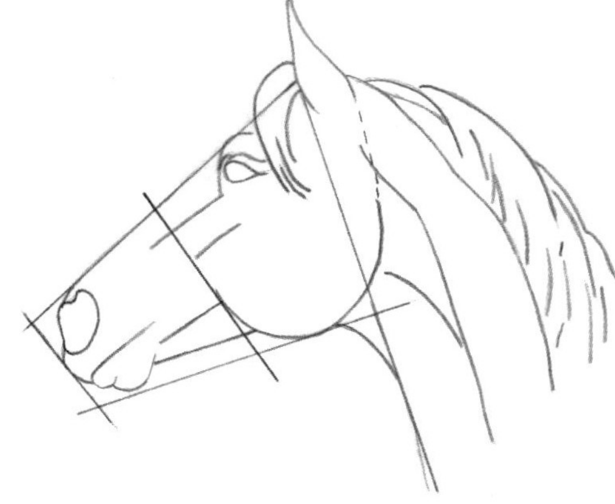

4 Work out the soft areas around the muzzle, and indicate the mane and forelock with a few strokes following the direction of hair growth.

Follow the steps above to block out a horse in profile. Then, use the skills you've learned to complete the details and add shading to bring your portrait to life.

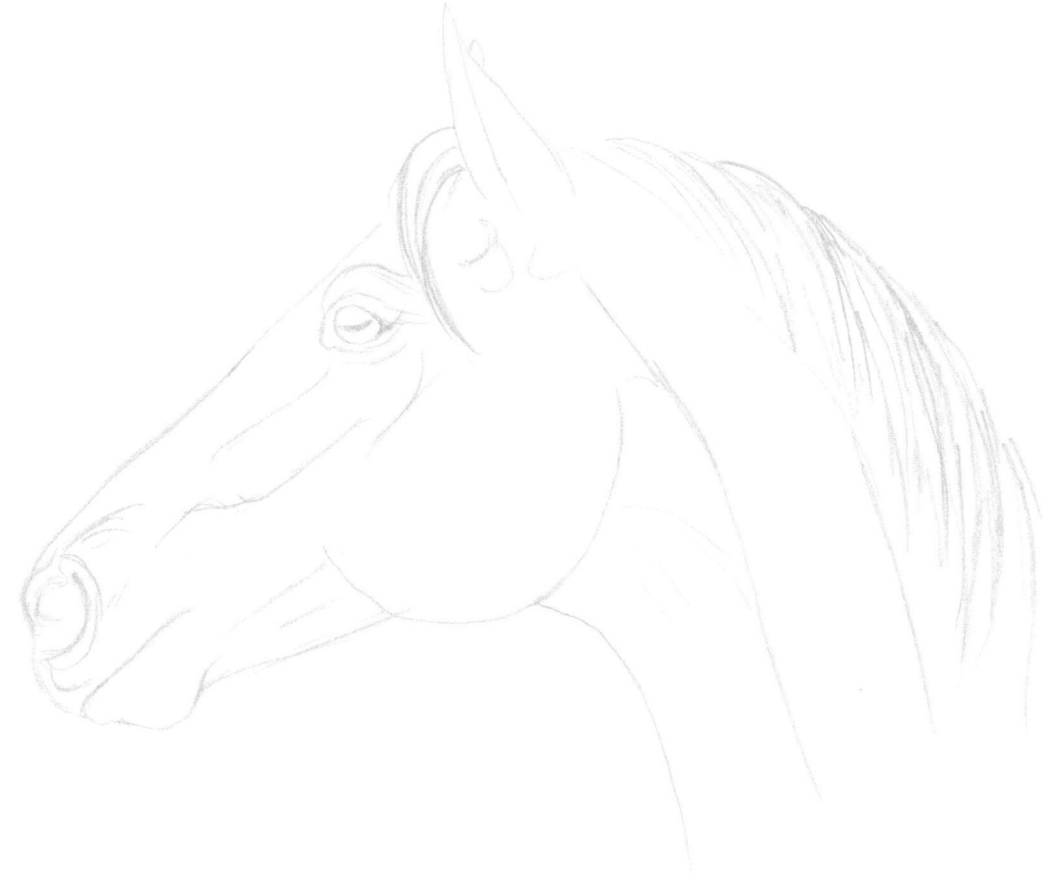

Drawing Horses

Horses are wonderful creatures, and they are a great joy to observe and draw. In this portrait, the key is to capture the warmth and intelligence reflected in their large eyes.

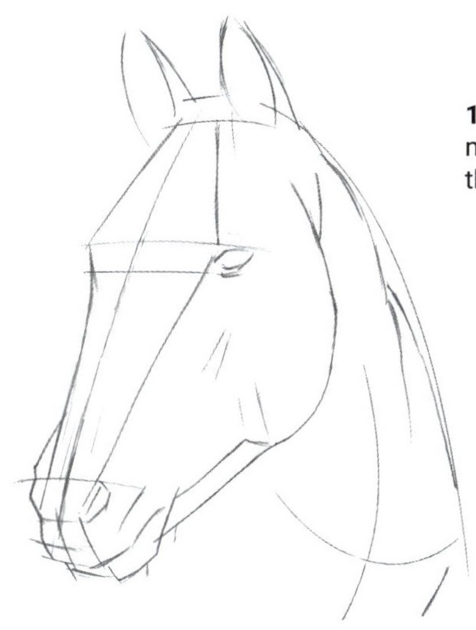

1 Draw the ears, nostrils, and mouth and further elaborate the neck and chin.

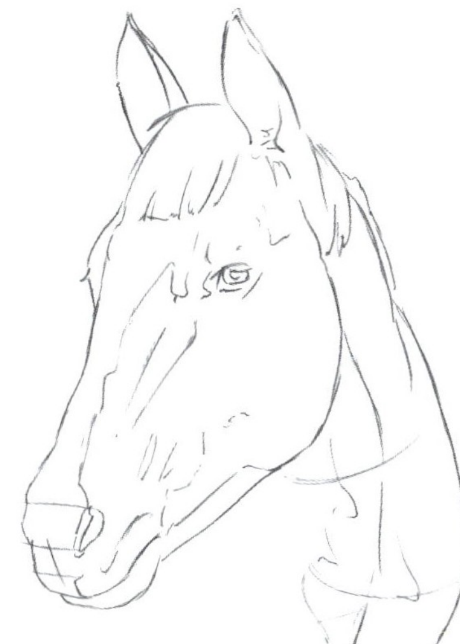

2 Erase all the construction lines that you no longer need, and draw the forelock. Lightly indicate the facial features, but add more detail on the eye.

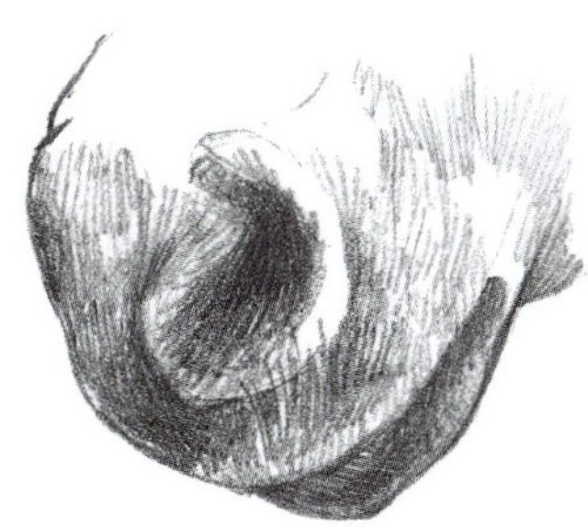

Mouth A horse's mouth and nostrils are soft and round. Draw these contours and then add hatching before shading the nostrils and the upper lip. Lift out highlights with an eraser.

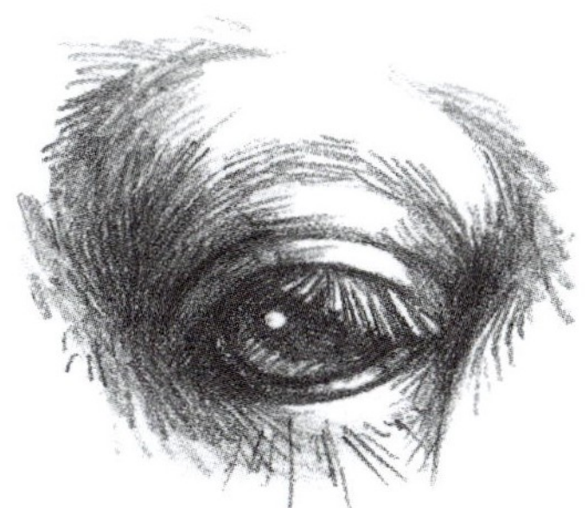

Eye To make the eye appear lively and warm, draw a light oval under the dark pupil and leave a white area in the pupil for the highlight.

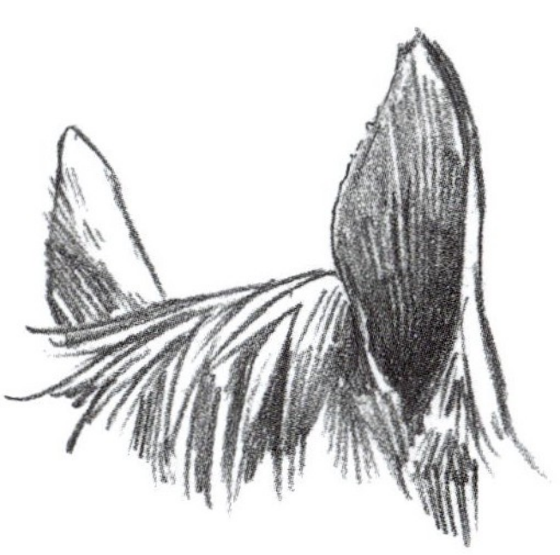

Ears Use several long strokes to draw the forelock. Shade the ears with parallel strokes that are darker at the bottom and become lighter toward the edges.

Use a sharpened pencil to add light shading in the direction of hair growth. Carefully draw the eyes, ears, and nostrils, and then sketch the forelock.

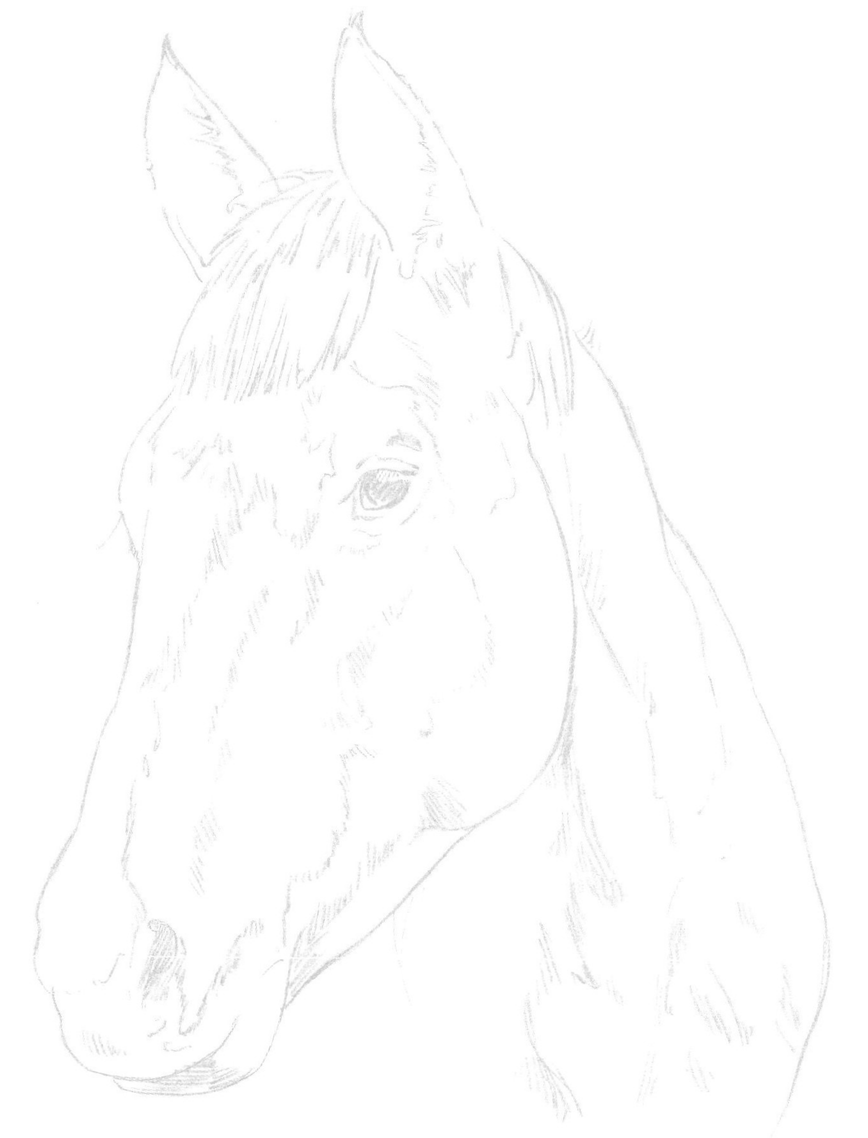

Pony

Ponies are a distinct species of animal, but they are drawn in a manner similar to horses. Work to establish the correct proportions of the body before working out any of the details.

1 Using an HB pencil, outline the basic body shape. Use ovals for the chest, shoulders, hindquarters, muzzle, and jaw. Draw lines for the neck, and use short, straight lines for the head. Draw the legs, paying attention to the hooves and joints. Use quick lines to suggest a mane and tail.

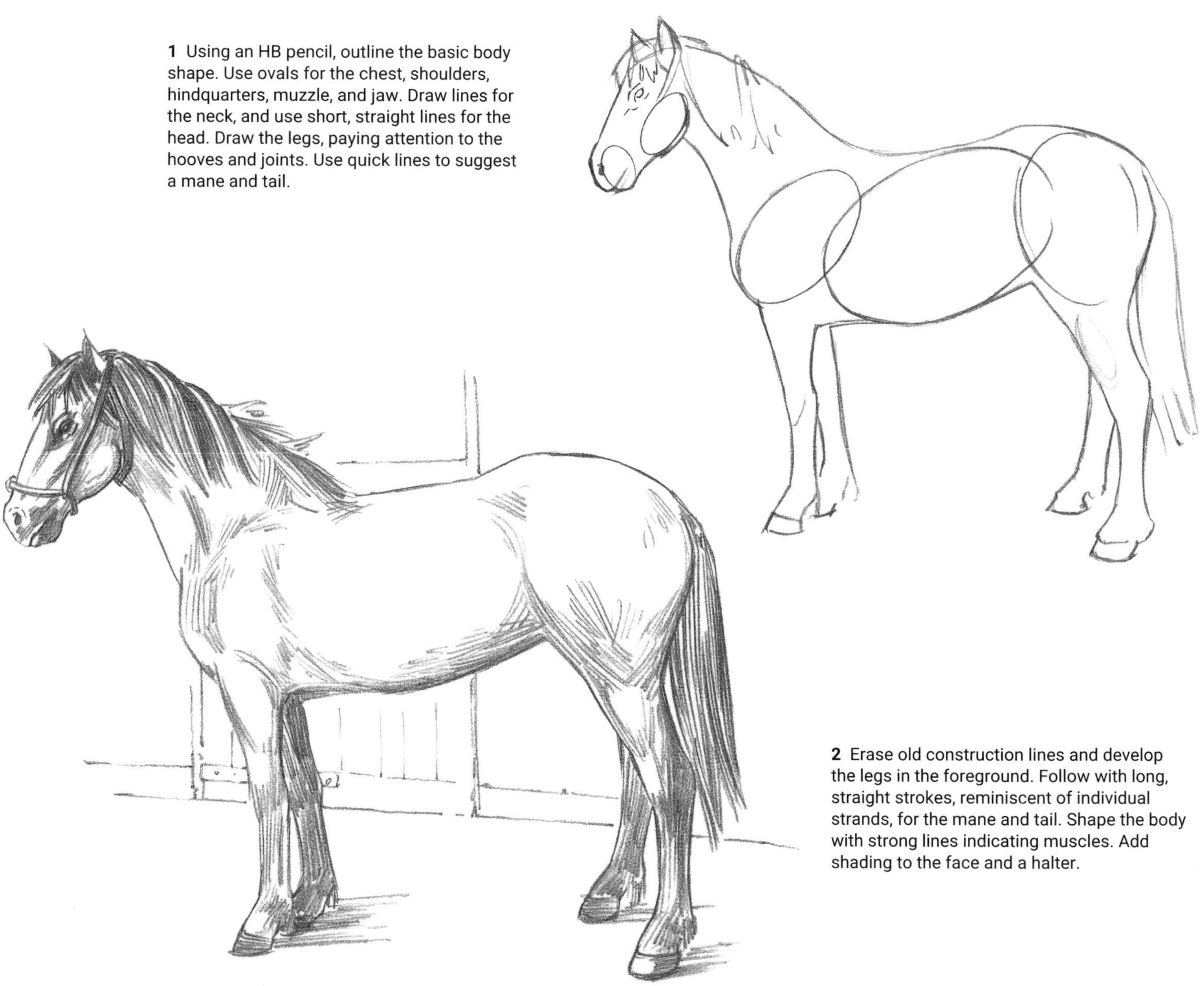

2 Erase old construction lines and develop the legs in the foreground. Follow with long, straight strokes, reminiscent of individual strands, for the mane and tail. Shape the body with strong lines indicating muscles. Add shading to the face and a halter.

Use the outline below to draw a pony in a side view.
Use simple hatching to create shading and shadow.

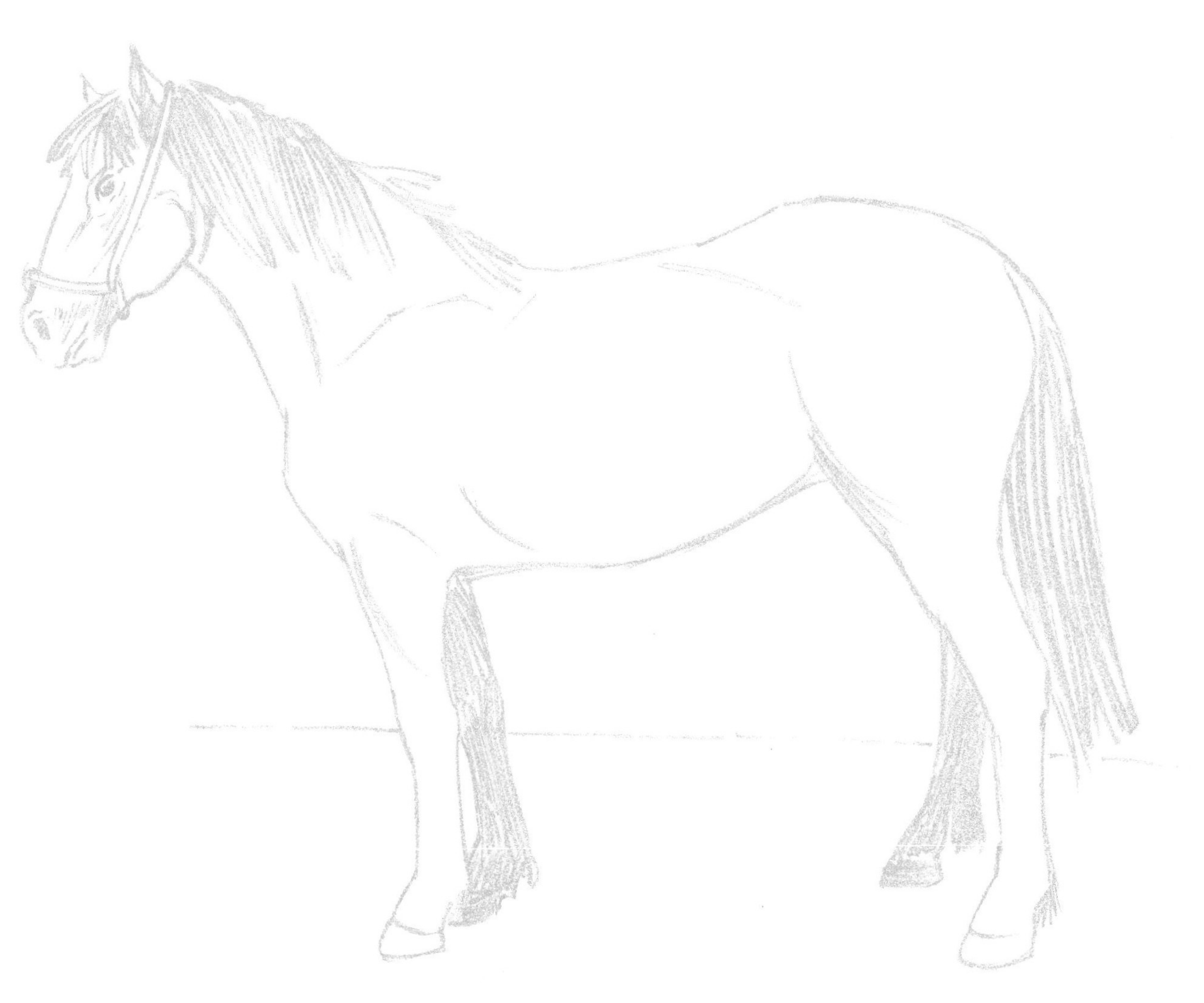

American Quarter Horse

The American Quarter Horse is a powerfully built, muscular breed, known for its agility and superior cattle-cutting abilities. The name "Quarter Horse" is derived from the breed's capacity to run at high speed for distances up to a quarter of a mile. Emphasize the strong hindquarters and muscular neck when you draw this horse.

Sketch the basic shape of the body. Notice how the angle of the horse makes its hindquarters appear larger to the viewer. This is called foreshortening.

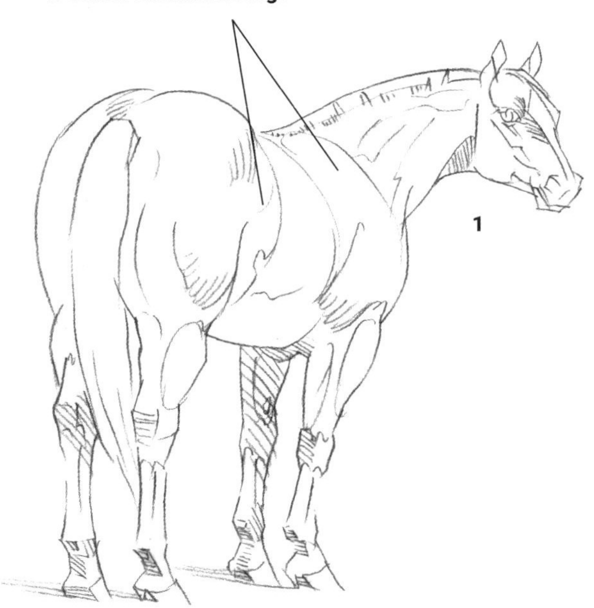

1

Use a blending stump to soften some of your shading to produce middle values; then build the form by applying darker values over this layer. As you lay in the dark and middle values, vary the angle of the hatching to follow the planes of the muscles, face, and legs.

2

3

Use a soft 2B pencil and blending stump to smooth out the strokes, leaving strong highlights to bring out the sheen of the horse's coat. Take care not to overwork the legs in your final shading.

Maintain the contrast between the light and dark values to emphasize the well-developed muscles of this majestic horse.

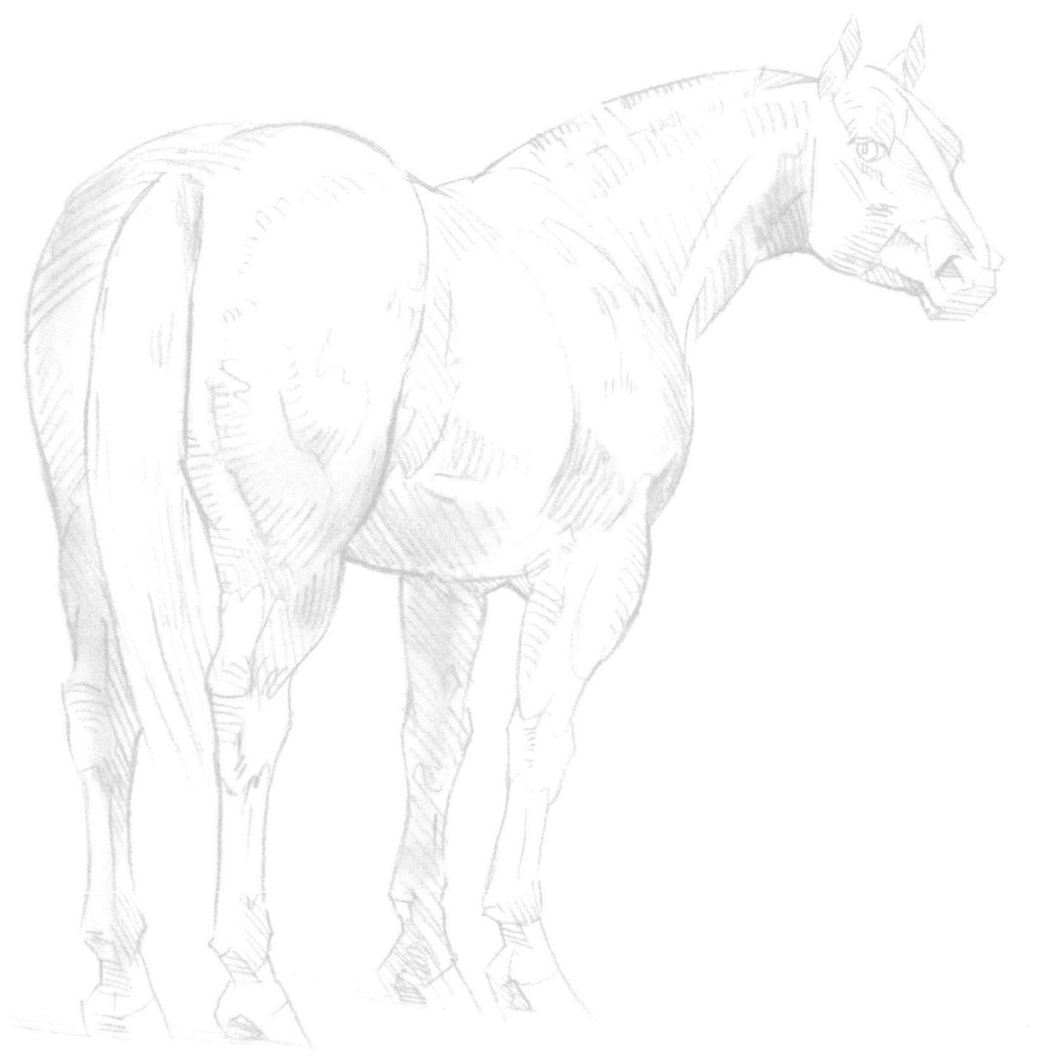

Grid Method

Although freehand sketching is a good way to learn to draw animals, there are also faster methods to block in a subject, including by tracing and using the grid method. Both methods have been used by artists for centuries, but finishing the subject still requires skill and technical ability.

How to Use the Grid Method
On a photocopy of your subject matter or a template, draw a grid of lines spaced one-inch by one-inch apart, like the illustration shown at right. On a piece of sketch paper, draw the same grid exactly. Both grids must have the same number of fields to maintain correct proportions.

Next, square by square, copy to your drawing paper the lines that you see inside each box of the grid featuring your subject. When you are finished, erase the grid lines or transfer the drawing to a clean sheet of paper and complete the portrait.

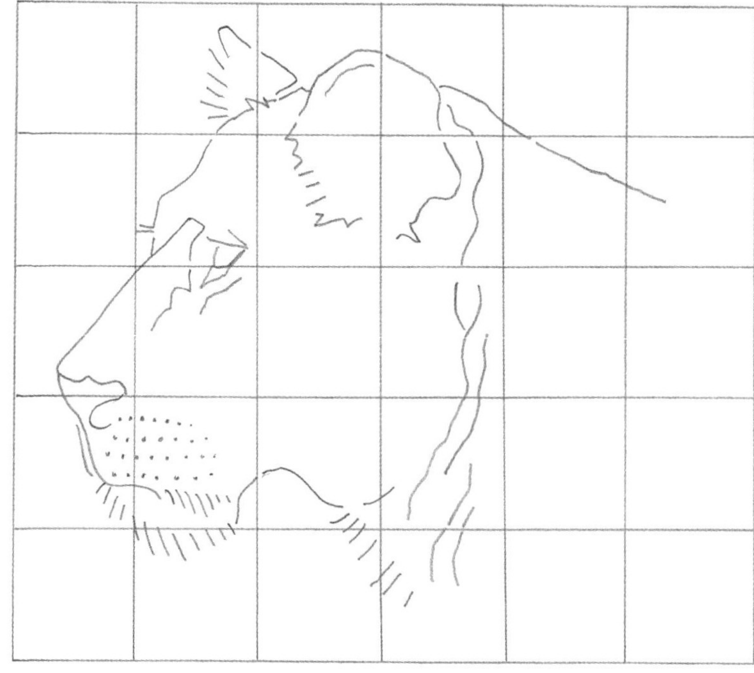

Use the grid lines below to draw the lion by copying what you see in each box. You can use this technique to transfer the drawing to a separate piece of paper.

Flamingo

With its long legs and gracefully curved S-shaped neck, the flamingo is an interesting animal to draw. Block out its basic shape before filling in the details. Just a few strokes are enough to indicate its distinctive beak and feathers.

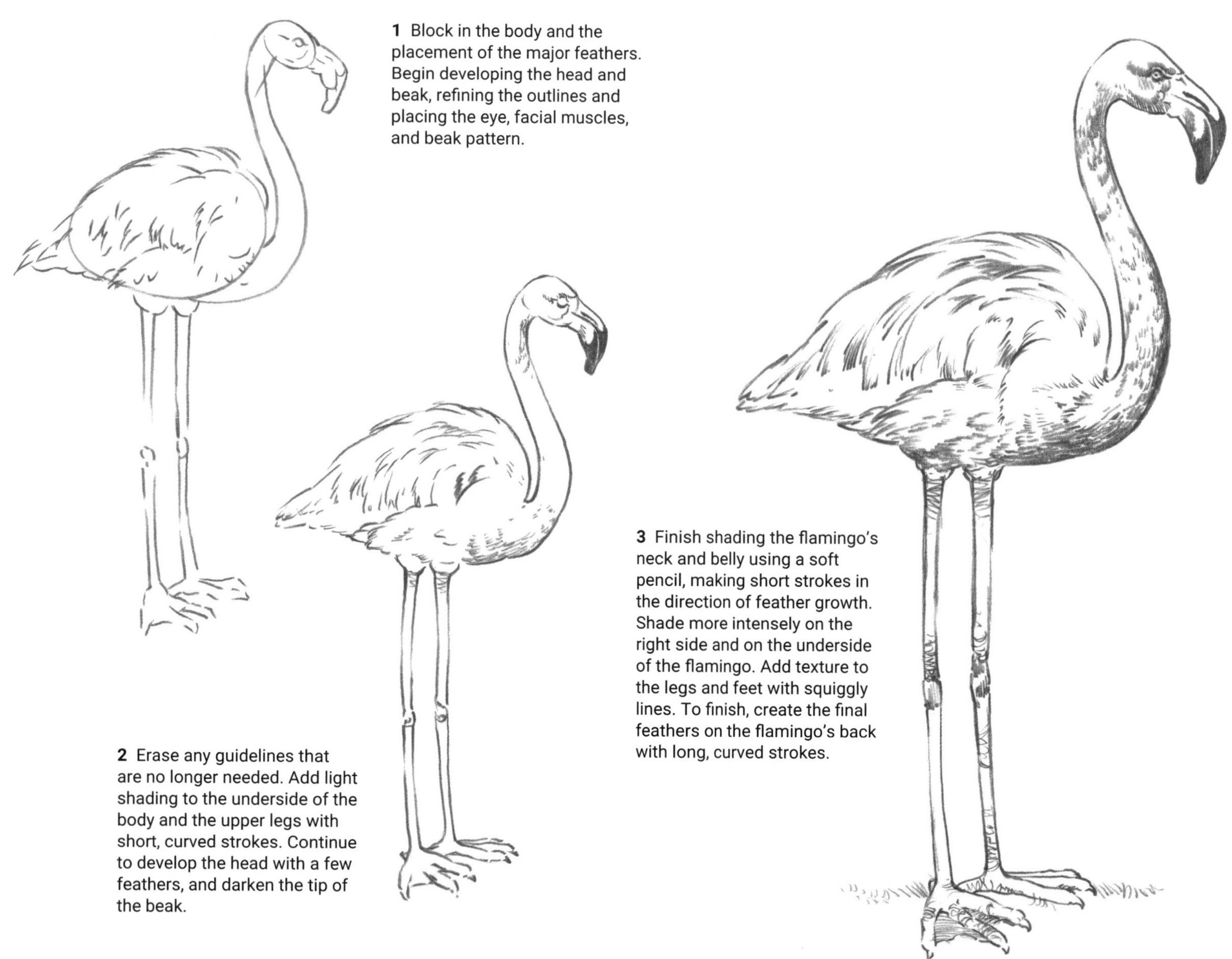

1 Block in the body and the placement of the major feathers. Begin developing the head and beak, refining the outlines and placing the eye, facial muscles, and beak pattern.

2 Erase any guidelines that are no longer needed. Add light shading to the underside of the body and the upper legs with short, curved strokes. Continue to develop the head with a few feathers, and darken the tip of the beak.

3 Finish shading the flamingo's neck and belly using a soft pencil, making short strokes in the direction of feather growth. Shade more intensely on the right side and on the underside of the flamingo. Add texture to the legs and feet with squiggly lines. To finish, create the final feathers on the flamingo's back with long, curved strokes.

Master your drawing techniques using the outline of the flamingo below.
Add a background to complete the scene, if you like.

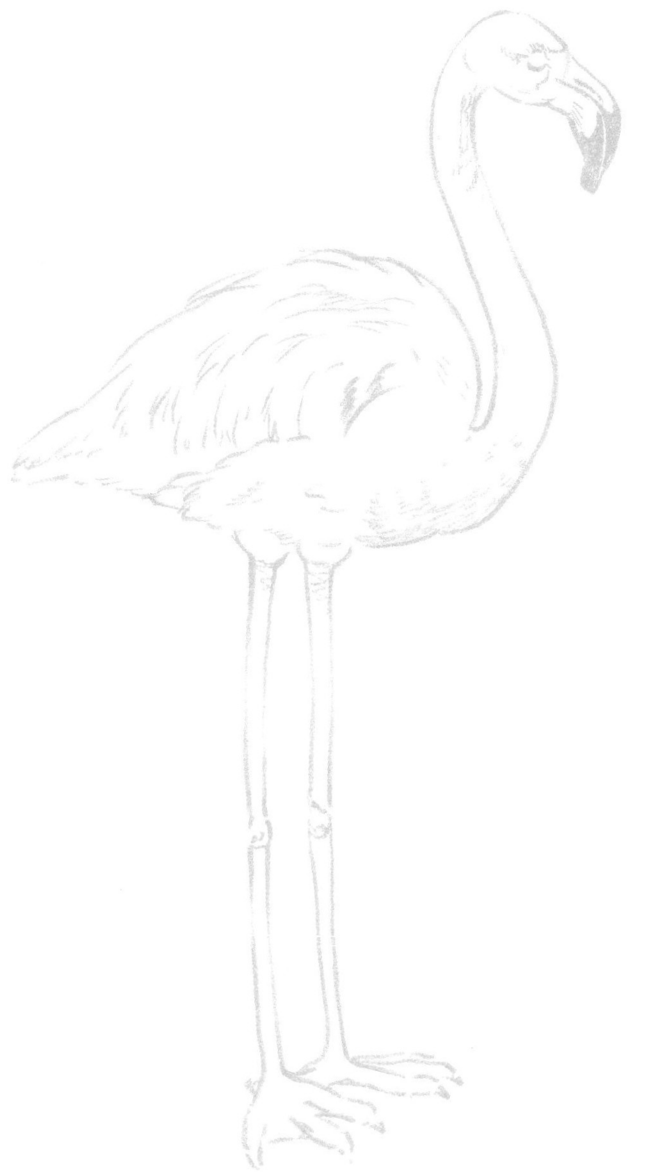

Toucan

Birds come in all shapes, sizes, and textures. This toucan's long, smooth feathers require soft strokes. Soft shading is also used to indicate the smooth texture of this bird's beak.

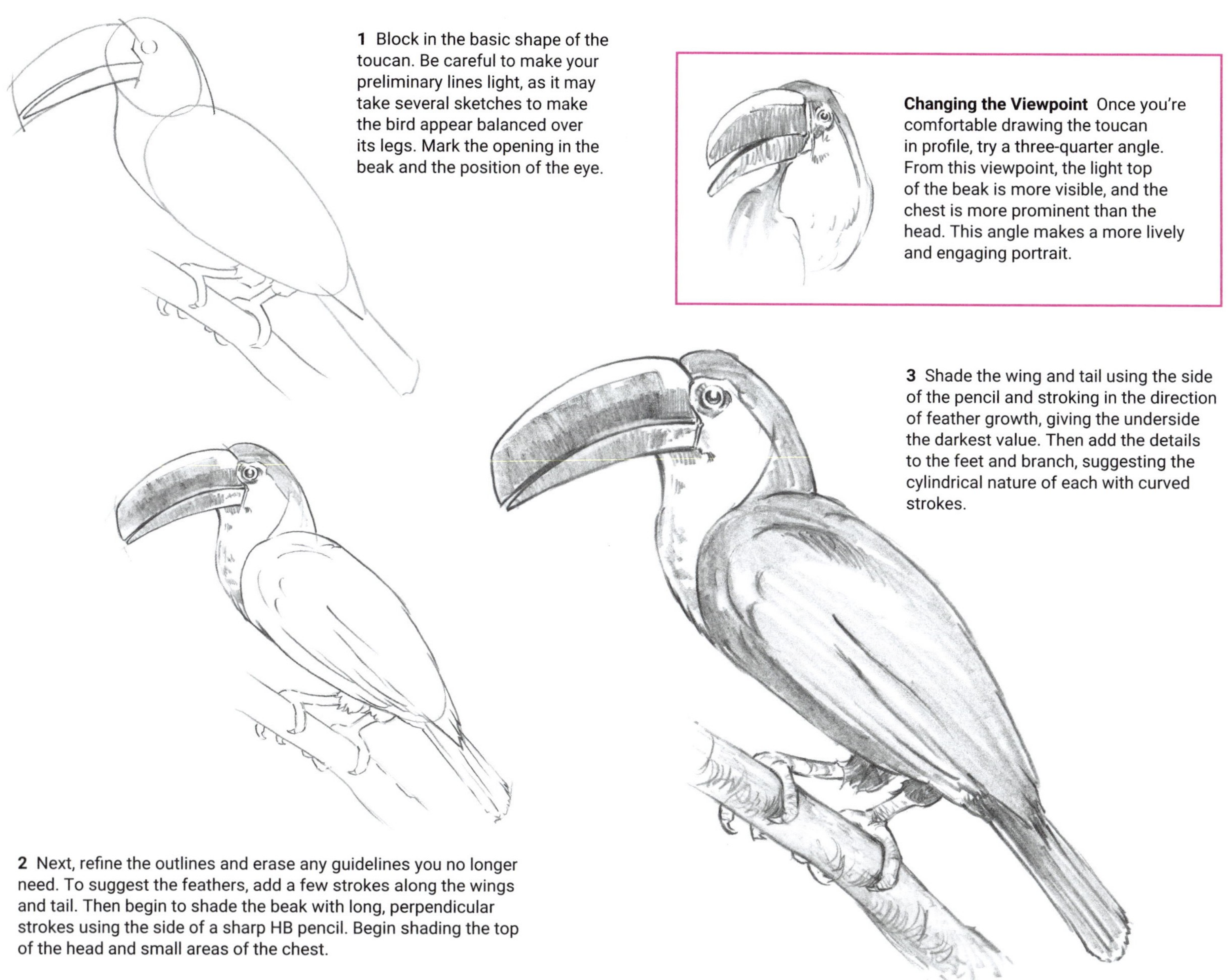

1 Block in the basic shape of the toucan. Be careful to make your preliminary lines light, as it may take several sketches to make the bird appear balanced over its legs. Mark the opening in the beak and the position of the eye.

Changing the Viewpoint Once you're comfortable drawing the toucan in profile, try a three-quarter angle. From this viewpoint, the light top of the beak is more visible, and the chest is more prominent than the head. This angle makes a more lively and engaging portrait.

3 Shade the wing and tail using the side of the pencil and stroking in the direction of feather growth, giving the underside the darkest value. Then add the details to the feet and branch, suggesting the cylindrical nature of each with curved strokes.

2 Next, refine the outlines and erase any guidelines you no longer need. To suggest the feathers, add a few strokes along the wings and tail. Then begin to shade the beak with long, perpendicular strokes using the side of a sharp HB pencil. Begin shading the top of the head and small areas of the chest.

Develop the feathers of this toucan with shading and lines.
Add details to the branch to make it look realistic.

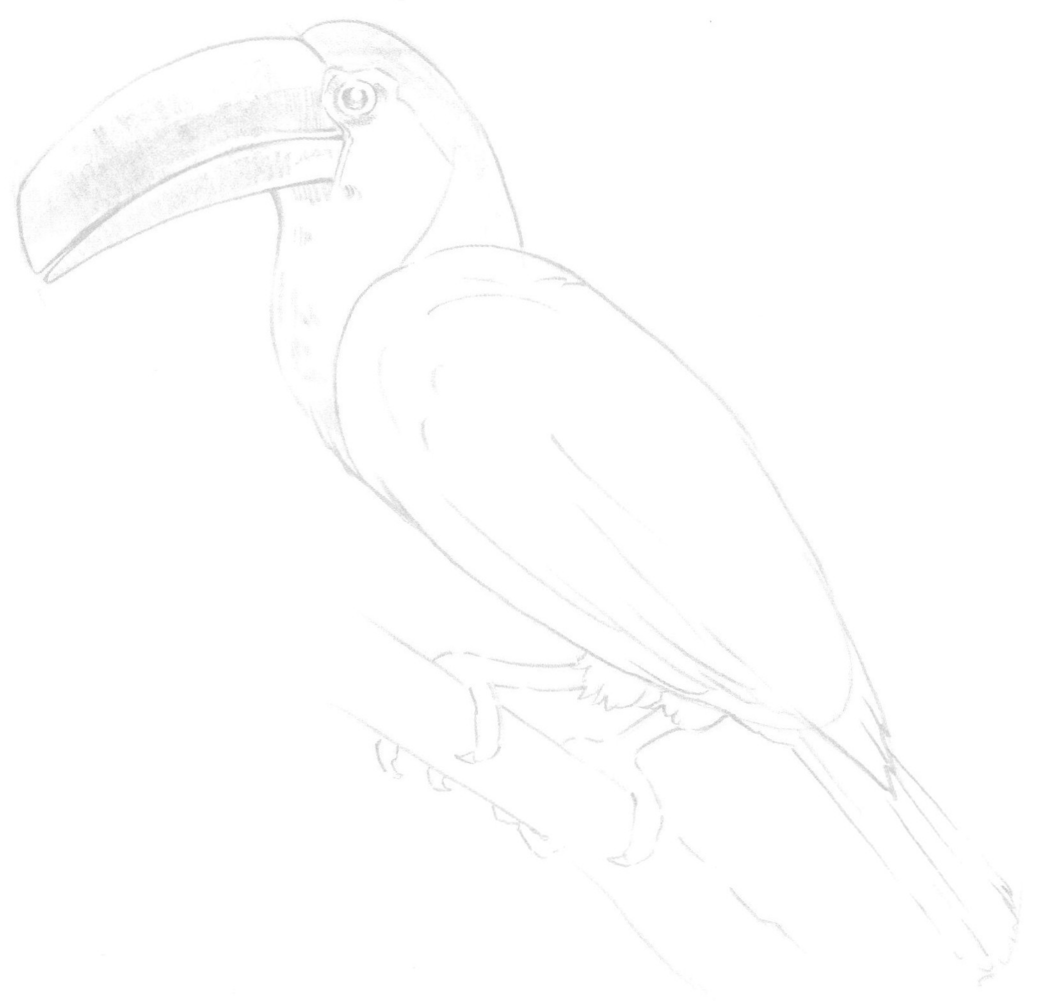

Composing a Scene

When drawing animals in a scene, it is helpful to plan your composition before putting pencil to paper. A successful composition directs the viewer's eye through the drawing, emphasizing the center of interest, or the focal point. The way you arrange the elements is the key to its success. There are many techniques you can use to create a dynamic composition, but the two shown below are the easiest for beginners to learn.

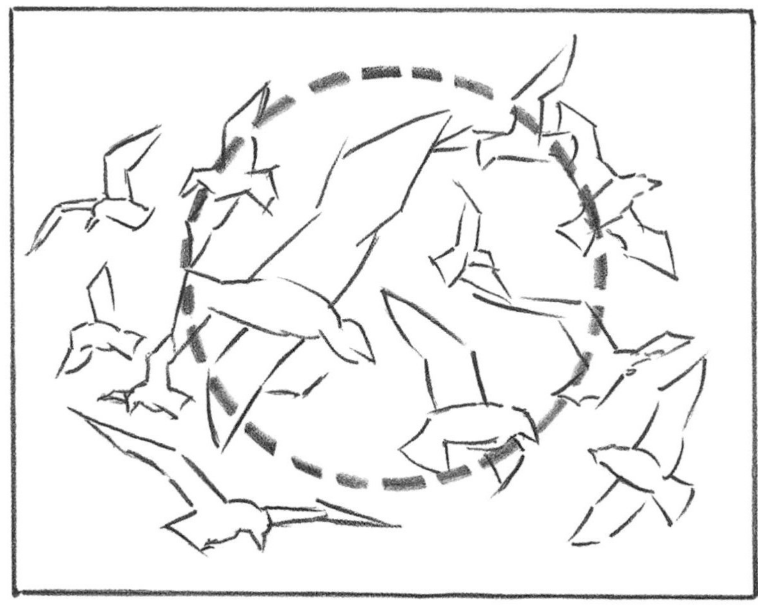

O Shape To draw the viewer's eye to the center of a composition, place elements of the scene around the shape of an O.

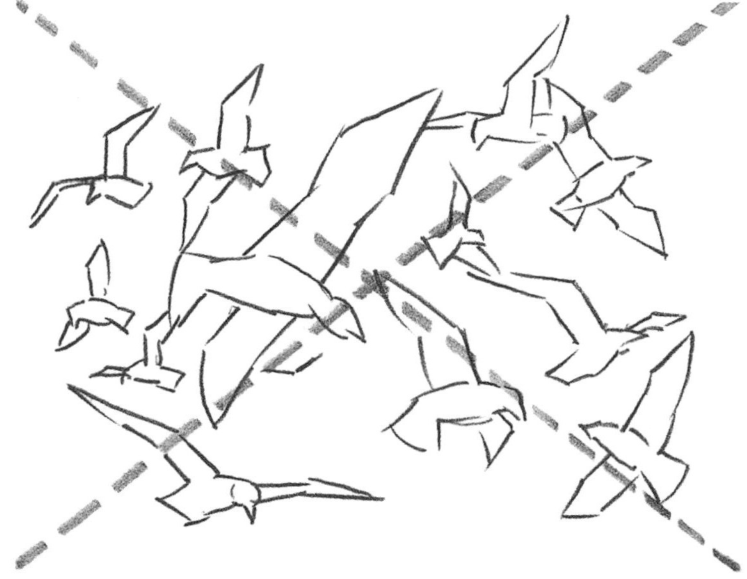

X Shape Use an X as a composition guide when you want to draw attention to a specific focal point in a scene. In this case, the eye is drawn to the largest seagull, which appears to be in the foreground and the dominant bird in the flock.

Complete the details of the birds in the outline below.

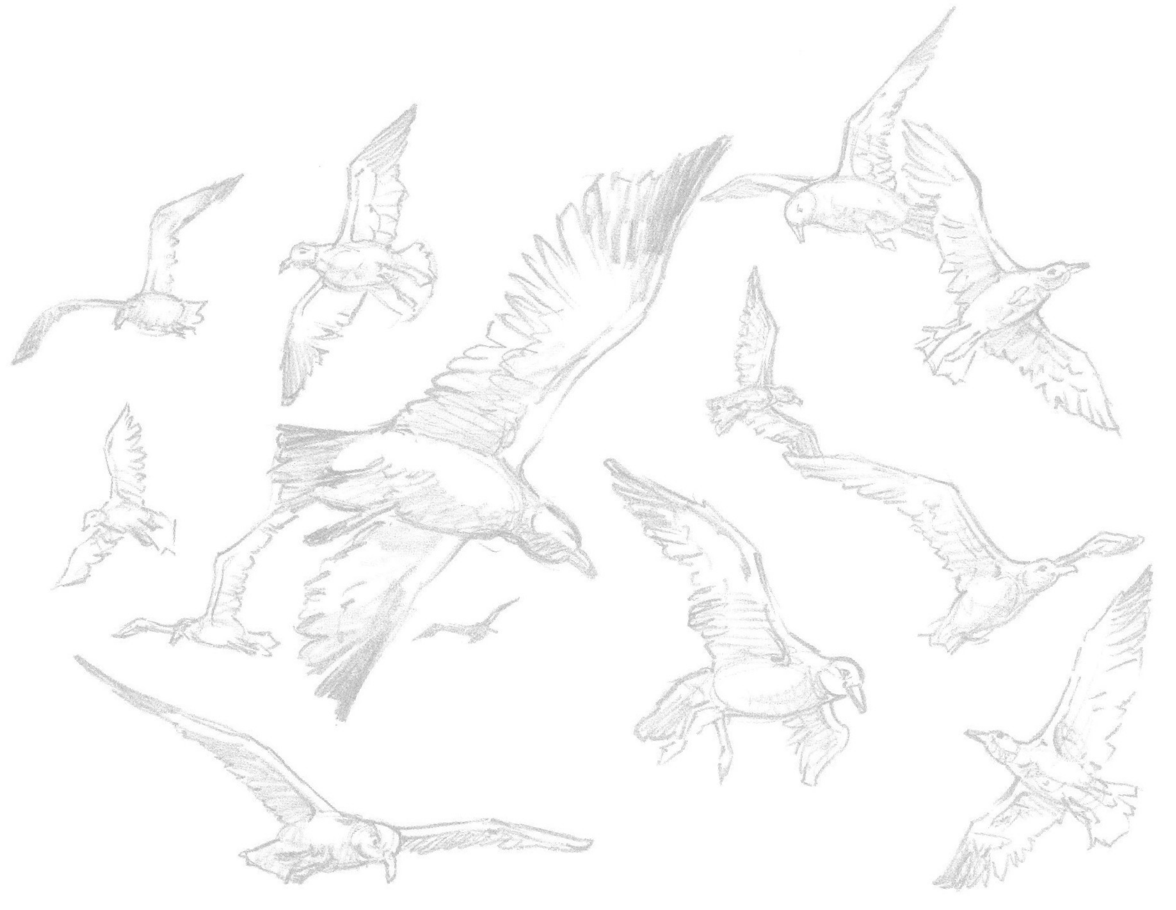

One-Point Perspective

Understanding the rules of perspective is necessary if you're to convey distance and spatial depth realistically. The first (and most important) of these rules is that objects appear larger closer to the viewer and appear smaller, or recede, as they move away.

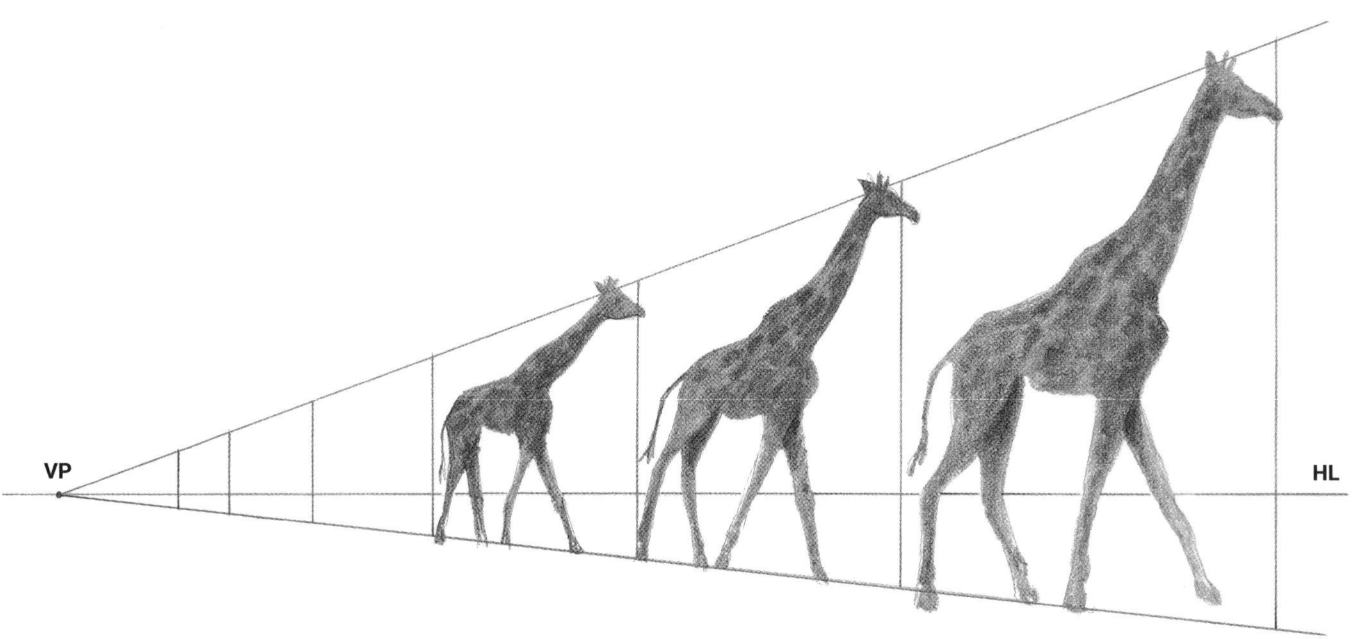

One-Point Perspective In one-point perspective, there is only one vanishing point (VP), or the point at which all perspective lines converge and seem to vanish. First, draw a horizontal line on your paper to represent the horizon line (HL), which is considered to be eye level. Then place a dot to the far left on the HL for the VP. Next, draw a vertical line to the far right that intersects the HL at a 90-degree angle. About three-quarters of this line should be above the HL, and about one-quarter should be below it. Imagine that this vertical line is a fence post (or your subject, like this standing giraffe). Now draw a line from the top of this post to the VP, and another from the bottom of the post to the VP. This V-shaped guide allows you to see exactly where the top and bottom of each successive post (or giraffe) is located.

Use the outline below to practice drawing giraffes,
or any animal of your choosing, in proper perspective.

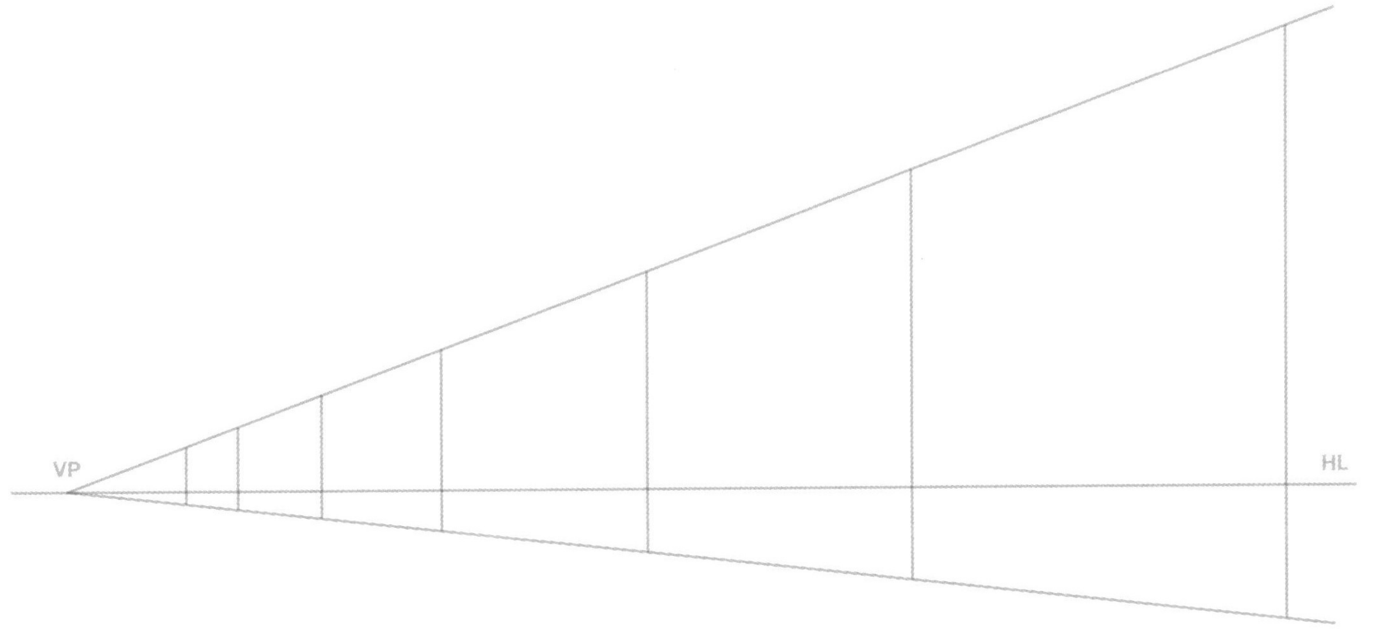

Foreshortening

Foreshortening is an important method of creating the illusion of depth in a drawing, and it works hand in hand with perspective. In foreshortening, the part of the subject that is closest to the viewer appears larger than the parts that are farther away. To draw this effect, enlarge the front part and shorten the lines that represent the areas receding into the distance.

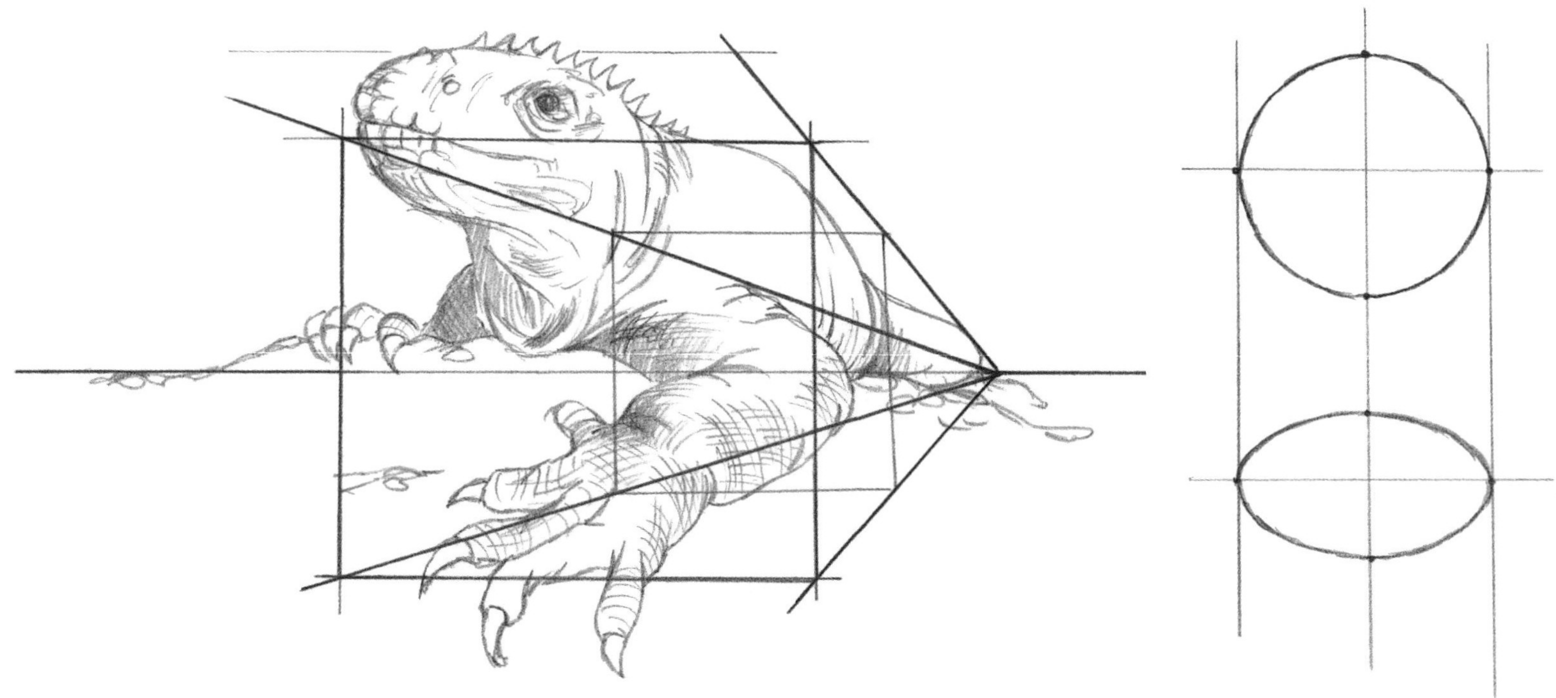

Recognizing Foreshortening This sketch of an iguana is a good example of foreshortening. Notice the difference in the size of the iguana's right foot compared to its left foot. The left foot was drawn much larger because it's closer to the viewer.

Visual Example To see foreshortening in action, hold a dinner plate straight out in front of you. It appears as a circle. Now tilt the plate slowly away from you. The plate now appears much shorter. This shape is called an "ellipse."

Use the diagram below to practice drawing an animal in a foreshortened position.

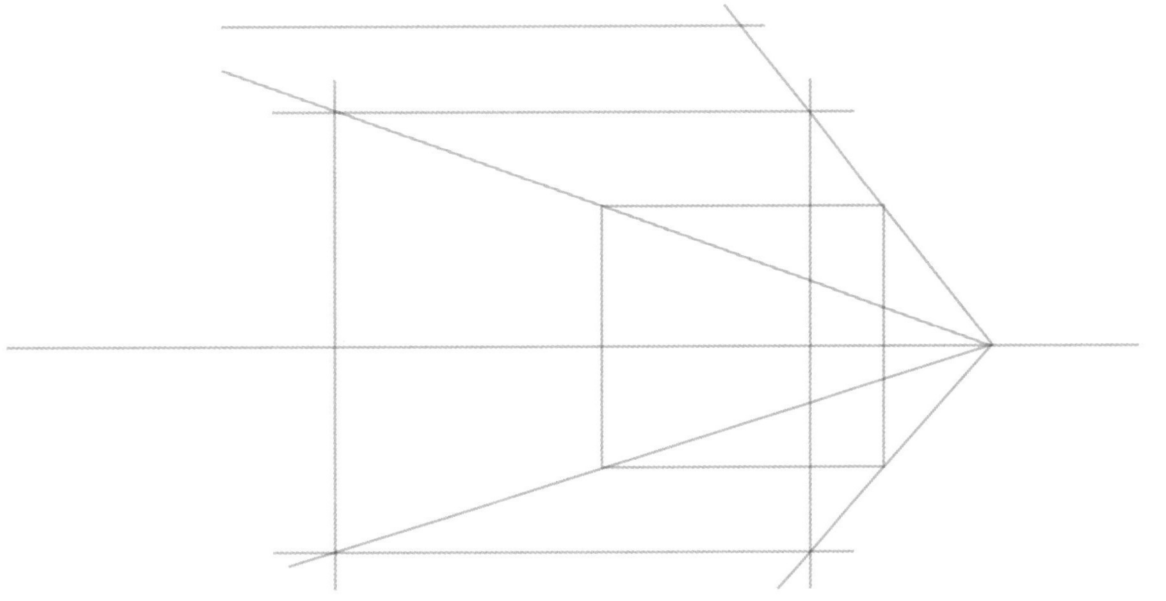

Quarto.com
WalterFoster.com

First published in 2026 by Walter Foster Publishing, an imprint of The Quarto Group,
100 Cummings Center, Suite 265-D, Beverly, MA 01915, USA.
T (978) 282-9590 F (978) 283-2742

EEA Representation, WTS Tax d.o.o.,
Žanova ulica 3, 4000 Kranj, Slovenia.
www.wts-tax.si

Walter Foster Publishing titles are also available at discount for retail, wholesale, promotional, and bulk purchase. For details, contact the Special Sales Manager by email at specialsales@quarto.com or by mail at The Quarto Group, Attn: Special Sales Manager, 100 Cummings Center, Suite 265-D, Beverly, MA 01915, USA.

30 29 28 27 26 1 2 3 4 5

ISBN: 978-1-57715-739-7

Digital edition published in 2026
eISBN: 978-1-57715-740-3

Produced by Coffee Cup Creative LLC
Layout by Debbie Aiken
Proofread by Aster Andraschko
and Stephanie Carbajal

Printed in Guangdong, China
TT042026

Featured Artists

Michael Butkus • Diane Cardaci • Walter T. Foster
Patricia Getha • Michele Maltseff • William F. Powell
Nolon Stacey • Mia Tavonatti • Linda Weil